EDITH PARGETER

Edith Pargeter was born in the si   ..iage of Horsehay, in the English county of Shropshire, on September 28, 1913. She attended Coalbrookdale Country High School for Girls in Ironbridge Gorge, and after leaving school in 1930 worked for seven years as an assistant in a chemist's shop in Dawley. She published her first novel, *Hortensius, Friend of Nero*, in 1936; five others (two of them pseudonymous) followed in the years prior to the Second World War.

Throughout the war Ms. Pargeter served in the Women's Royal Naval Service and continued to write. Among the novels she published during this period, *She Goes to War* appeared in 1942, and the three volumes of her wartime trilogy (*The Eighth Champion of Christendom, Reluctant Odyssey*, and *Warfare Accomplished*) in 1945-47.

In 1951, *Fallen into the Pit*, the first of her mystery novels featuring Detective Sergeant George Felse, was published. It appeared under her own name; ten years later, the second Felse mystery was published under the name "Ellis Peters," as would be the eleven further installments in the series.

Ms. Pargeter's best-known creation, Brother Cadfael, made his first appearance in Ellis Peters's *A Morbid Taste for Bones: A Medieval Whodunnit*, which was published in 1977. Nineteen other volumes of The Chronicles of Brother Cadfael, as well as short stories, were issued during the next seventeen years; they have been translated into twenty-three languages. Sales of the Cadfael Chronicles are in the millions worldwide, and they have been adapted for a popular series of television programs starring Derek Jacobi.

In all, Ms. Pargeter published more than eighty books, including many translations into English of Czech novels and stories. Among the numerous honors and awards bestowed on her, she received the British Empire Medal, the British Crime Writers' Association's Silver Dagger and its Diamond Dagger, the Mystery Writers of America's "Edgar," the Gold Medal and Ribbon from the Czechoslovak Society for International Relations, and in 1994 she was awarded an OBE by Queen Elizabeth II.

Edith Pargeter died in 1995, in Shropshire.

Also by Edith Pargeter in A COMMON READER EDITION:

The Marriage of Meggotta

The Coast of Bohemia

by

EDITH PARGETER

"Thou art perfect, then, our ship hath touched upon
The deserts of Bohemia?"

A WINTER'S TALE: Act III, Scene 3.

A COMMON READER EDITION
THE AKADINE PRESS
2001

The Coast of Bohemia

A COMMON READER EDITION published 2001
by The Akadine Press, Inc., by arrangement with the Estate of Edith Pargeter.

First Published in 1950 by William Heinemann Ltd.

Cover design by Jerry Kelly; woodcut illustration by Albrecht Dürer, from THE BOOK OF
THE *Ritter von Turn*, Basel, 1493.

A COMMON READER EDITION and fountain colophon are trademarks
of The Akadine Press, Inc.

ISBN 1-58579-027-3

10 9 8 7 6 5 4 3 2 1

"THE flight was beautifully easy until half an hour before we touched down at Ruzyne . . ."

Beginning in midair and quickly plunging its readers into the swirl of the journey it recounts, *The Coast of Bohemia* demonstrates the existence of what Margaret Lewis, Edith Pargeter's biographer, has called the writer's "Czech Connection." But this detailed and affectionate travel chronicle offers only glancing explanations of how the connection had been established and is understandably silent on how it influenced in later years the writer's life and work. Readers may thus welcome a brief attempt to place *The Coast of Bohemia* in context.

*

When Britain declared war on Germany in 1939, Edith Pargeter was twenty-six and had six novels (two of them pseudonymous) to her credit. She enlisted in the Women's Royal Naval Service (the WRNS, or "Wrens"), and was posted to Plymouth—leaving her native Shropshire for the first time. While serving in the Wrens till war's end, Pargeter became acquainted with several Czech and Polish servicemen, and on the strength of these friendships she decided to venture even farther from Shropshire, resolving to visit Czechoslovakia whenever circumstances finally allowed. Which they did in 1947: the writer and her brother took part in an international summer school near Prague. The experience, according to her biographer, was one "which obviously changed her life." It resulted immediately in a novel (*The Fair Young Phoenix*, published in 1948), and prompted a return visit the following year; that visit, in turn, resulted in *The Coast of Bohemia*, which was published in England in 1950 and is now finally made available, in this Common Reader Edition, for the first time in America.

When Edith Pargeter made her first visit to Czechoslovakia, the country was only just emerging from its long wartime troubles. Back in 1938, the country's borderlands had been ceded to Hitler, in keeping with the "appeasement" policies which were then believed by some to offer the chance of stopping the dictator's aggression without occasioning war. Six months later, however, Hitler seized the rest of Czechoslovakia, and it wasn't until 1945 that an autonomous government was reestablished, though as an integral part of the newly formed "Soviet bloc." During the February between Pargeter's first and second visits, the Soviet Union's influence over the country was formalized when a Communist coup swept aside the governing six-party coalition, and by June, as Margaret Lewis describes it, "a Soviet style constitution was in place and all opposition was being eliminated. This, then, was the atmosphere that [Pargeter] found herself in, a puppet state on the brink of being totally subsumed by the USSR."

Having thus witnessed the early days of Communist rule in Czechoslovakia, Pargeter happily lived long enough to see its ultimate overthrow. As Communism collapsed and political independence was restored to the Czech people, Pargeter wrote in 1989: "They and we have waited . . . for what we knew must happen, since no empire lasts for ever. None of us expected it so soon or so suddenly and totally, the delayed Spring in full flower at last. I doubted if I should live to see it, but I have! Nunc dimittis!"

"The delayed Spring" is a reference to the "Prague Spring" of 1968, when Czechoslovakia enjoyed a period of liberalization under Alexander Dubcek. Hopes for westernization, for democratization, were high. (In August 1968, however, those hopes were crushed, when the Russians invaded and reimposed strict Communist rule.) And it was during this hopeful period that Edith Pargeter was awarded the Gold Medal and Ribbon of the Czechoslovak Society for International Relations at a celebration in her honor at the Prague Writer's Club. She later described her reaction to the Prague Spring this way: "I have never, in any place at any time, known a people so absolutely united . . .; never known an atmosphere of such purpose and radiant joy. For me that was literally something new under the sun."

Between 1947 and 1989 Edith Pargeter visited Czechoslovakia many times; but even while in Shropshire she remained in touch with the spirit of the country throughout the years by becoming perhaps the leading translator into English of some of the masterpieces of its literature. She began her translations without intending to publish them: "I was just curious about the classics all my friends had on their shelves, and for most no translation existed, so with gramophone records and a grammar book I set out to make my own." Eventually they were indeed published, however, and to excellent reviews as well. Two of these translations seem particularly worth bringing to her readers' attention: Josef Bor's *The Terezin Requiem,* and Bohumil Hrabal's *Closely Watched Trains.*

In sum, the land and people of Czechoslovakia, their political struggles and their literature, had special significance for Edith Pargeter. A Gold Medal and Ribbon, a series of landmark translations, and the lovely narrative which now follows, affirm this much-loved writer's surprising and significant "Czech Connection."

—Thomas Meagher
Editorial Director
THE AKADINE PRESS

The Coast of Bohemia

AUTHOR'S NOTE

In printing this book certain accents necessary to the correct writing of the Czech language have been omitted as too distracting to the English reader, for whom the book is intended.

For their convenience the pronunciation of the more difficult names involved is given here. The author hopes that Czech readers will forgive the mutilation of their language.

The main emphasis in all Czech words comes on the first syllable.

PLACES

Brevnov	B-rzhev-nov	Spilberk	Shpilberk
Hradcany	H-rad-chan-y	Dobris	Dob-rzheesh
Domazlice	Dom-azh-li-tse	Vsenory	V-shen-ory
Petrin	Pet-rzheen	Roztez	Roz-tyezh
Cernin	Cher-nyeen	Melnik	M-yel-n-yeek
Opocno	Opoch-no	Kokorin	Ko-ko-rzheen
Podebrady	Pod-ye-brad-y	Cadca	Chad-tsa
Tyniste	Tyn-yish-tye	Zilina	Zhil-ina
Vysehrad	Vy-she-hrad	Ruzomberok	Ru-zhom-berok
Ratiborice	Ratibo-rzhi-tse	Lucanka	Lu-chanka
Karlstejn	Karl-shteyn	Dobsina	Dob-sheena
Olsany	Ol-shany	Zdiar	Zh-d-yar
Zizkov	Zhizh-kov	Kromeriz	Krom-yer-zhizh
Liben	Lee-ben (final n	Sumava	Shumava
	as gn in Avignon)	Stechovice	Sh-tyek-ovitse
Vysocany	Vyso-chany	Teplice Sanov	Teplitse Shanov
Holesovice	Hol-e-shov-i-tse	Marianske Lazne	Mari-ahnskeh
Prerov	P-rzhe-rov		Lahz-nyeh
Uherske Hrad-	Oo-her-skeh H-		
iste	rad-yish-tye		

PEOPLE

Sarka	Shar-ka	Tomas Bat'a	To-mahsh Bat-ya
Jenicek	Yen-yi-chek	Stefanik	Shtef-an-yik
Bozena Nem-	Bo-zhen-a N-	Venousek	Ven-oh-shek
cova	yem-tso-vah	Svabinsky	Shvab-in-skee
Havlicek	Hav-li-chek	Slavickova	Slav-ich-kovah
Zdenek	Zden-yek	Janacek	Yan-ah-chek

J is pronounced as the English y.
C is pronounced as ts, except in the instances given above, where it lacks the accent which turns it into a different consonant.
Ch is pronounced as in the Scottish loch.

CONTENTS

To the City of Prague,
for the Fifth of May:

In the month of flowers you come again to flower!
On the tree of faith new buds of hope are grown
From magical seed, from seed that never was sown.
And did they think you would not know your hour?
Azure and white and scarlet from every tower,
The opening sheaths spring out to the wind full-blown,
And blood-red blossoms burst forth out of the stone,
Making the grave a garland, the body a bower.

Rise up, my love, my fair one, and come away!
For lo, the seven-years winter is over and past,
The frosts are broken, the birds remember to sing,
Whose songs were hushed through many and many a May!
O Praha, put on your bridal beauty at last
For the month of flowers, for the miracle of the Spring!

LANDING AND BEACHHEAD

THE flight was beautifully easy until half an hour before we touched down at Ruzyne, when we ran into a very bumpy hailstorm, and lost our garrulity with startling suddenness. My companion, the Hungarian Jewess, and I had talked our way across Europe from our misty take-off at Northolt, through the brightening morning over Germany, to this moment almost within sight of Prague, but we both became very quiet after the first few switchback lurches and recoveries, and forgot our confidences in order to concentrate on not being airsick. She says that I turned pale green; I know that she did. It had been a short acquaintance, but a well-tuned one; since sharing an almost empty bus to the airport we had done everything with the unanimity of identical twins. Affinities still, we now felt remarkably queer as one woman.

The hail rattled along the plane, streaking diagonally across our window for a few spectacular minutes as if someone was trying to slash a way through. But in ten minutes it was all over. We heaved ourselves out of the last trough, the sun came out like a flash of lightning along the wing, and there below us the patterned land turned slowly, rising to us gently and as gently falling away. The greenness and the heat which accompanied it subsided as abruptly as they had arisen, which is one of the most reassuring things about airsickness; and by mutual consent we fished out mirrors and began to repair the ravages. A quarter of an hour later we were dropping in slow circles over Ruzyne, and because neither taking off nor landing affected us in the same way as hailstorms, we were able to glue our noses to the window and watch the rigid knots of runway growing wider at every circle, and the minute flat crosses which were aircraft revealing their markings first perceptibly, but too small for reading, then clearly and intelligibly. The knots appeared to be tied with steel ribbons, highly-polished and brightly dry, for here there had been no storm. We grounded at last so lightly that I could not distinguish the moment when we touched down. One minute the green fringes of the runway and the white distant buildings were still flickering alongside us like flames in a draught, the next they were steady, and we were running smoothly between planes of grass, turning a blunt corner, and pulling in opposite a long white range of buildings, a frame of flower-beds, and a railing draped with people, all staring intently at us.

They were too far away for me to be able to distinguish any special person among them, even when the aircraft door was opened, and we descended the ladder and stood on the tarmac, answering to our names and surrendering our passports to a brisk young traffic clerk, who spoke English of a distinctly transatlantic flavour. Honza's height would have singled him out easily, but I had no time to look for it. We were led away at once across the wide, glossy grey spaces of tarmac, and up a slope of concrete into the pass-port control office, where I soon discovered that I was the only one among us who couldn't speak Czech. The Americans who had changed planes at Northolt were all Czechs, it seemed, coming home for the Sokol Slet, and at the first question from the Customs officers they dived back into their ancestral language with an aplomb which I could only envy. At the time I knew perhaps as many as fifty words of Czech, and quite a number of grammatical rules, but they were never the words I needed, and the rules never by any chance covered the construction of what I wanted to say. There was no difficulty, however, for they soon found me an officer who spoke reasonably good English; he came along to me in the Customs hall, already armed with my passport, filled out a currency certificate for me, removed most of my five hundred crowns as duty payable on my gramophone records, which had travelled without a scratch, and turned my bags over to the porter, and me to my friend the Hungarian lady, for a hurried farewell before I went out to find Honza in the waiting-hall.

I never knew her name. She had come to England just before the war, and its outbreak in 1939 had kept her there ever since, separating her utterly from all her relatives. Of a large family exactly one other human soul had survived, a girl cousin in Budapest; and my friend was going to her now for a visit, after long misgivings and with mixed feelings. She longed to return to the one country which could ever be home to her, but she dreaded the emotional ordeal of seeing the wreckage of her own childhood, and being reminded at every turn of the loss of all her family and friends. But I saw, before we had spent an hour together, that her heart was already in full flight ahead of her, eager not only to pick up the pieces of the past, but also to examine and share some new young fervour for the future, the rumour of which had somehow reached and startled her even in London.

I parted from her with warm good wishes, and she went away to board her plane for Budapest. Perhaps by now she is already settled again for life in her native city; but even if it has not happened yet I am as sure of its ultimate certainty as I am of tomorrow morning.

After she had left me I went out through the swing doors into the waiting-hall, and looked round for Honza, but no one was there except a girl clerk behind the bookstall, and a big, plump man who sat with his back towards me, gazing out from the window. I knew the shape of the head, and the wide, sloping shoulders, even before he turned at the swing of the door, and showed me the beaming face of Dr. Novák. At the same moment Honza, who had been walking about outside while he waited for me to emerge from the Customs, looked in through the glass panels of the door, and came bounding in upon us, bringing with him a young, fair lady half his size. He said she was his mother; it didn't seem possible, but I accepted his word for it.

We stood shaking hands, and talking together two and three at a time, with all the usual first questions and answers about the comfort and speed of the journey. And in a few seconds of their company I lost all the queer feeling of unreality and dizziness which had lingered in my mind until this minute. Now I had really arrived; the nearness of friends was reassurance, welcome, background and peace of mind to me, as in the least familiar places it always is.

I had not seen Honza or the doctor since the previous summer, and in the interval Czechoslovakia had achieved what amounted to a major revolution, and by some mental trick had been expelled by most English people to a limbo many thousands of miles removed from civilisation—which is, of course, confined to the areas occupied by those who think as we want them to think, and do as we consider they ought to do. It was delightful to find that, after all, it had not moved, but was still as firmly situated in the middle of Europe as when I left it the previous year, that planes could reach it and deposit passengers there, and that, so far from wearing horns and tails, the inhabitants appeared as normal, as kind, and as independent as ever. I knew there must be considerable changes, of course; but that absolute change from white to black takes place only in the limited imagination, never in reality. Humanity remains obstinately human in spite of political distorting mirrors, whether they be coloured red, pink or true blue; and all things considered, I *do* like its face.

They were not changed at all, except that the doctor had lost a great deal of weight during his cure at Marianske Lazne, and Honza had surely lengthened by another quite unnecessary inch. They both looked well, Honza perhaps rather pale and attenuated from much studying; but the summer would take care of that.

I asked how Dr. Novák came to be there; it was pleasant to be met by three friends when one had expected only one, or perhaps two. He was in town upon some business, and had called on the Veselys to ask when I was arriving; and on hearing that they were meeting me that very afternoon he had elected to come along, too. It was arranged that since I had lost my lunch hour somewhere in mid-air, he and Honza and I should go right into town, where I could have a late meal before we collected the luggage from the air terminal, while Mrs. Vesela dropped off at the nearest stop for the flat in Holesovice, since the bus took a route conveniently close.

We talked hard all the way into town, and it was as if the bus were driving backward through the year in which I had not seen them, for before we were far from the green-stained roadway outside the airport, not yet washed clean of its war-time camouflage, we seemed to have lost the gap altogether, and to have picked up conversations we had left only yesterday.

The drive into town lasted nearly half an hour. At first we were running along a plateau of wide fields, with new housing estates just rising on either side; then we reached the outlying parts of town where old, self-contained villages are in process of being assimilated into the white villas and chromium shops of expanding suburbs. It sounds like an attempt at mixing oil and water, but architecturally Prague seems to me the home of reconciliation, both here and in the centre of the city, and somehow an unpretending synthesis has been achieved in which the mellow small baroque of the Brevnov monastery, and the sudden square white blocks of new flats, and the colour-washed houses of the villages, all settle happily together into the green frame of landscape, and nothing offends the eye even where there is much to startle it.

We left the battlefield of the White Mountain on our right hand, and the deep rocky cleft of Sarka's valley on our left, with one glimpse of the ravine like a sabre-slash in the flesh of Bohemia; and began to run downhill gently all the way into the city, overhauling as we went trams linked in twos and threes, those methodical, friendly Prague trams which will take you anywhere and guarantee you satisfaction, provided, of course, that you are not in a hurry. We passed through Dejvice, that pleasant residential suburb just in process of graduation from wealthy villas to mass flats, and began the level run along the ridge of Letna; and there on our right, beyond a curtain of trees, were the Gothic towers of St. Vitus' cathedral and the long roof of Hradcany, for once on a level with us instead of poised wonderfully on the skyline, as always one sees them from the city.

On Strossmayer Square Mrs. Vesela left us, and we swung right-handed on to the embankment; and there was the view I had been waiting for. Not quite the picture-postcard tour-de-force one sees from the end of Charles Bridge, but the foreshortened first taste of it, all the pinnacles of St. Vitus assaulting the sky, and the city above the city girdling them, the long, level roofs of the royal castle of Prague set like a crown on the green hair of the Hradcany hill. I have many great things still to see, but so far I know of no prospect which lifts up my heart and stops my breath as this does. Gothic towers have always a quality of tugging one towards heaven as in a rising whirlwind, and here the towers are themselves the culmination

of an upward rushing of roofs, palaces, gardens and
orchards, all climbing with an equal impetus of flight from
the level silver calm of the river, and the counter-balance
of bridges. I can see it twenty times a day, and never without an answering leap of the heart; at the end of a close
daily acquaintance with it for three months it is as new as
at the beginning, yet coming back to it has every time
something of coming home.

Now indeed I could relax, for certainly I was in Prague.
We crossed the Vltava, and came to the end of our journey,
where the air terminal building sits under the shadow of
the Powder Tower. We abandoned my luggage for the
moment to concentrate on my late lunch, and by this time
I was more than ready for it. In Czechoslovakia it is
necessary to give up food coupons even for restaurant meals,
and as yet I had no food coupons; on this occasion the
doctor supplied what I needed, but I said guiltily that I
must see about the necessary formalities at once.

"Tomorrow will do for that," said Honza cheerfully.
"I shall go with you to the police office, where we have to
fill in some papers, and then we can take them to the food
office and get your tickets for the first month."

It sounded simple enough. "And my visa is only good
until the end of this month," I said, "so I must get that
extended."

"Time enough!" he said airily.

After lunch we collected my bags, and for the time being
took leave of the doctor, arranging to meet him in the
evening at some quiet spot where we could sit and talk to
our hearts' content. Honza had already telephoned Karel
and Helena and added them to the party, so it was evident
that we should see the evening out among us in last year's
timeless style. In the meantime we took a tram at the
station in front of the Powder Tower, and made for home.

I had no time, in this first glimpse of the city, to make any but the most obvious comparisons with last year; but I saw that the shops were much emptier of goods, the result of the export drive necessary to pay for the enormous imports of food which 1947's lost harvest had made inevitable. If ever the weather hit a country below the belt, that drought had certainly hit CSR; in the first year of her cherished Two-Year Plan it had smashed all the nice calculations, forced the living standard down when by all the rules it should have been rising, and drained away all the textiles and household goods which the Czech housewife needed and desired, into the fund to pay for essential grain. No wonder so little was left in the windows! But at least the country was solvent.

The streets had a tendency to bunting and posters, I thought; balconies of party premises were rather heavily draped with flags and hung with red, and on some of the street-corners loudspeakers were hurling out national and Russian songs as if life depended on the range of the music. In the trams we rubbed shoulders with many country people in the rainbow-coloured national costumes in which I had never quite believed. One resists with difficulty the thought that those short umbrella skirts stiff with embroidery, the accordion-pleated, balloon-shaped white muslin sleeves, the quivering head-dresses of poppies and cornflowers and showering gilt-thread ribbons, the stiffened lace ruffs, the knee-high leather boots, are all museum pieces, kept now expressly for the edification of foreign photographers, and to decorate the Geographical Magazine. Instead, one finds them coming out freshly laundered for most Sundays and all festival days, the boots glossy, the bewildering sleeves and ruffs crisp from the gophering-iron. The men are no less gorgeous, with their cream-coloured felt trousers slashed at the ankles and embroidered down the thighs, their bishop sleeves, their belts and ribbons and flower-trimmed black hats.

Sophisticated young Praguers like Honza, equally elegant but in a very different style, view them with no less interest and curiosity than the foreign visitor, sometimes even with the same hint of condescension. Most of these, he said, were Slovaks. Your expert could tell you from what precise district every variation came, but Honza did not claim to be an expert.

"They are in town to see the Slav Agricultural Exhibition," he said. "There are specially cheap fares for them to come, and of course, even if they don't want to see the exhibition, it's a fine opportunity to visit Prague. Wait until we get into our part of town! You see them there in thousands, because we are quite near to the exhibition ground."

We saw them, indeed, at every tram-stop, and peering in every shop window; but we could not linger, for Honza had the luggage to carry the length of two blessedly short streets, and for my own sake I was anxious to settle in. We went first to his parents' flat, where we ran Mr. Vesely to earth in the labyrinth of warehouse, store and office which had once been the cellars of an inn. He was an older, darker, more substantial Honza, with a thoroughly Czech twinkle in his eye. I was more than ever sorry that my fragments of the language were too theoretical to be of much practical use. He was always kind enough and patient enough to speak what Honza called export Czech for my benefit, and sometimes we understood each other well, but generally speaking we were dependent on Honza as interpreter.

When we had drunk tea and eaten cakes, and I had unpacked my precious gramophone records, Honza took me round to the flat in the next house, where he had taken a room for me. He introduced me to Mrs. Burianova, and three Burian children, dwindling from a girl of eight to a bouncing and most cheerful baby, accepted me without introduction; and having seen me comfortably installed with everything I needed, even to a complete set of keys to house and flat, Honza left me to unpack.

We ate supper with the family after the shop was closed, and afterwards spent my first evening in CSR in the ideal way, sitting with friends in a quiet coffee-house, talking until a late hour. Helena and Karel came prompt to their time, and if we did not quite recover the moonlit nights of last year at Jevany, and the unrestrained discussions which went with them, at least we were together again. A pity that it had to be in a world broken in two halves, in which only a handclasp always convulsive and sometimes desperate held us together. On this first evening I think we felt the fever of that clinging; afterwards it relaxed, and I was able to enjoy their company and forget that a currency curtain, if not an iron one, threatened our future separation.

However, the main thing was that I was here now, and let the future wait. Tomorrow to consolidate, I thought, as I parted from Honza at my door, and crawled half-asleep into the couch-bed which Mrs. Burianova had made up for me.

And on the morrow we did consolidate. It took us all morning, and then the job was not completed, but as I enjoyed the process I could not complain. The sun was brilliantly hot that May morning as we went along Bubny Embankment to the police office, which proved to contain no police, but only two girl clerks imprisoned behind glass windows, and a small queue of people waiting their turn to ask for permits for things they needed. I was willing to wait, too, but Honza saw no reason to do so, since we had only to collect the forms, take them away, and fill them up at home. In any case we needed not only Mr. Burian's signature, but also that of the owner of the house; so back we went in the still hotter sun of mid-morning, and conferred over our four identical cards at leisure in the office.

Honza went round the corner and collected what we needed from Mr. Burian and the landlord, and we made the same journey again, surrendered three of the copies, and brought back the fourth in triumph, duly stamped.

By this time lunch was ready, and food being sacred, we deferred all further activities for the time being. Honza insisted that there was no great haste about completing the formalities, and we were a little bored with offices, so we played some of our English records, and then went off to a Czech film at the nearest cinema because the afternoon turned cloudy, and threatened us with showers.

"Tomorrow the doctor wants to take you to see the Agricultural Exhibition," said Honza, "so you can leave me your passport, and with that and the certificate we have got this morning I can go to the food office and get your tickets. As for your extension—time enough!" he said comfortably. "Now you are an adopted Praguer, that is enough for one day. And look, it is going to be a fine evening!"

It was a beautiful evening, and I walked on Letna with the whole family. We followed the path which clung most nearly to the edge of the escarpment above the Vltava, the steel-blue river and its bridges close beneath us, and beyond it the whole of the Old Town and the New Town spread out wonderfully before us, and the further hills already growing a little misty and silvered with dusk. Tower beyond tower, at the railed viewpoints I told them over, naming them to show how much I knew, and how much of last year's learning I had remembered. I had no sense of direction as yet, but I knew them by their outlines, the Powder Tower, the articulated twin towers of the Tyn church, the bridge towers, the green copper dome and slender baroque tower of St. Nicholas of the Little Town, and St. Nicholas of the Old Town with its rose-red turrets growing Indian red in the twilight.

Lights began to come out here and there, and above the invisible length of Wenceslas Square there was soon a coloured glow from many electric signs. The white swan which swims above the department store which bears its name lit up in illogical scarlet, and began to revolve steadily above the town.

My feet were firmly on Prague earth, and for three months all this was mine.

2

FARMERS' GLORY

DOCTOR NOVÁK collected me at nine o'clock next morning, and we walked to the exhibition ground in beautiful, blazing sunshine. I do not know what went wrong with me that day. The family always put it down to the heat, and from that time frowned upon my hatless state as often as the sun shone on me, and bore with my obstinate refusal to cover my head only with disapproving patience. As for me, I attributed it rather to the aftermath of a recent illness, and my journey by air following closely on its heels. All that is sure is that this proved a disastrous day, and caused a great deal of trouble to my kind hosts.

However, the morning was marred only by a slight unease as we paid our way through one of the many entrances into the grounds, in company with floods of decorative country people, young army men, excited schoolchildren, and sophisticated Praguers, and passed down a broad paved way between many pavilions into the central hall, a cool vast cave of a place, decorated with enormous figures and murals glorifying that overpraised human necessity, work.

The staging was certainly impressive. There were exhibits from Russia, Yugoslavia, Bulgaria and Poland, besides CSR herself, each country having its own section grouped separately, with fruits, sweets, preserves, every kind of foodstuff the expert housewife can concoct from every kind of produce the expert farmer can raise; and in addition to these many examples of ceramics, embroideries, hand-woven linens, carved woods, glass, jewellery, dolls, national costumes of every district from Domazlice to Dalmatia. We wedged ourselves into the slow-moving crowd in order to pass along the cord barriers and inspect the lovely hand-painted pottery at short range; but the doctor did not take kindly to this modest rate of progress, and I soon began to feel rather hemmed-in, so we drew out of the procession, and made a series of raids to whichever stands were least frequented.

The Russians were showing some beautiful carved ivory boxes, paper-knives and plaques, carpets from the eastern Soviets, gorgeously coloured lacquers from Palekh, in a convoluted folk-tale style between the Byzantine of ikons and the oriental rococo of Persian miniature painting; but besides these they had cases of preserved fruits, crystalline sweets sugared in all imaginable colours, chocolate, ginger in pottery jars, which fascinated the Czech young as honey draws the bear. Small boys pressed their noses to the glass, and gazed with an earnest, concentrated desire which in an ideal world would have called the sweetmeats out of their prison. Their fathers stared as reverently at the fantastic bottles of sweet liqueurs, but no miracle happened for them, either.

More people came thronging in, and it grew noticeably warmer, so we went out into the grounds beyond these main buildings, where were laid out, in the natural frame of park trees and shrubs, whole villages of little houses from all the Slav countries, and petrified plantations of tractors and combines, not to mention booths selling Yugoslavia's wines, and stalls dispensing hot sausages, ice-cream, and sugared cakes. The little houses, so perfect from the out-side, with their low eaves, colour-washed walls and blossoming window-boxes, were hollow shells within, showing diagrams and photographs of the use and abuse of the land. In the Polish cottages there were plans of the redistribution, from a panic of uneconomic strip holdings to a compact mass of planned small farms, each one capable of maintaining itself free from the debts and mortgaged harvests which have tied the peasant of Europe down to the land and his own poverty for centuries. There were charts showing how new electrification schemes were being brought to the isolated villages, and even models of whole tracts of country. Some of the diagrams explained themselves adequately even for me, but where translation was needed the doctor supplied it.

The exhibition ground lies on the edge of the Royal Deer Park, the Stromovka, and when enlarged, as for this show it had had to be, recedes coyly into it in all directions but one, luring you away into charming tamed forests full of strange trees conveniently labelled with their names. I had heard some grumbles that there had been wasteful felling of trees to make room for extra stands, and the murder of trees always seems to me a very serious crime; but there was only one large open space where the doctor confirmed that felling for this purpose had really taken place, and it did not seem so terrible. Elsewhere the standing trees had been carefully incorporated into the lay-out, making the groups of little pavilions look like real villages.

We moved on, and came to a sort of miniature Eiffel Tower of wood, with a staircase winding upward through its middle, and a gallery of grinning spectators round it. From the top the adventurous might hurl themselves into space in parachute harness, and be dropped, not too heavily, into soft sand below. It wasn't surprising to see young soldiers and enterprising Boy Scouts taking advantage of the opportunity, but what fascinated me was the spectacle of elderly countrywomen, brown and ripe and sweet as wrinkled apples, and probably grandmothers every one, plodding doggedly up all those stairs for the pleasure of making imaginary parachute jumps more appropriate to their hefty young grandsons, and arriving undaunted in the sand with a bump and a shout of laughter, so appreciative sometimes that they unstrapped themselves only to bolt back to the stairway and repeat the process. But by this time I was in no state to follow their example.

The doctor saw I was feeling off-colour, and suggested that we should walk on slowly out of the crowds, and make our way from the enclosure into the quiet part of Stromovka. But we lingered by the way to look at the livestock, and the little fenced-off plots of various grasses and fodders, and the poultry farm, and the spinners and weavers of woollen thread and cloth, whose wheels and looms had drawn a circle of great-eyed children. And beyond these again we were among the bees. I had never seen such bee-hives. They were like luxury bungalows, big enough for men. There was even a polished wood trailer-hive which could be hitched on behind a car, as big as a small caravan, and its sides pierced with a series of brightly-coloured plastic slots like letter-boxes, in and out of which the bees were posting themselves merrily. If it is possible to flatter bees into producing a record honey yield, I should think this community ought to leave all competitors standing.

We came into a narrowing walk here, and all the noise was left behind us; and soon the path terminated in a small gate.

"And here," said the doctor as we emerged, "this road goes to Troja Island, and from there we can go across the Vltava and see the Zoo. Shall we go?"

It was probably unwise, for by this time the signs were ominous; I think the sugared cakes on the exhibition ground had hastened the demoralisation within me. But we went.

The Vltava, which flows through the main part of Prague due north, emerges from the city to make a great sweep eastward round the promontory of our suburb, and westward again north of it, and thereupon leaves Prague once again in a northerly direction. Beyond this westward bend of the river lies Troja, with its rising fields, and its villas soon fading gently into villages, and its castle in symmetrical baroque flaunting a swirl of grand external staircase before it, populous with stone Titans in alarming and anguished action, as is the way of baroque everywhere. And there is the Zoo, just as the doctor had said, sprawling over a large area of ground, and sporting outside its gates a flurry of vociferous buses, which seem more irritable than other buses, I suspect because they have had to come a great way round by the Barricades Bridge, far away to the east. But on foot you can get there easily by crossing a foot-bridge to Troja Island, walking across the width of it between the fun-fair merry-go-rounds, fortune-tellers and sausage stalls which live there all the summer, and leaving it again by the bridge of moored boats for the use of which you must pay one crown per person, and which, incident-ally, has a startling habit of disentangling itself between visits, and manifesting itself on your next trip as a series of moored fishing boats and a ferry. The price, however, is the same, whether you walk or are drawn across by a chain: adults one crown, children fifty hellers.

By the time we reached the Zoo it had become clear that I was no longer fit company for anyone; and I ought to have had the sense to acknowledge it and go home, but I did not want to spoil the day, and I cherished the hope that all would yet be well. However, it was anything but well. I soon began to be repeatedly and direly sick; and all I remember of the Zoo is a charming little polar bear cub who was sitting on a slope of grass playing with his keeper and making love to the passers-by for buns, and a night-mare interlude when we sat on a bench facing the enormous wire cage of the birds of prey, arched high against broken cliffs, and watched a vulture leisurely doing dreadful

things to a ragged splash of raw meat. After which my
condition deteriorated rapidly; but I was rather faint just
then, and there was no other seat near-by. I never want
to see another vulture, especially feeding.

It ended, of course, in our having to call off the unsuc-
cessful day and go home by car. I was only too glad to get
back to the Vesely flat, where everyone made an unnecessary, undeserved but very comforting fuss of me, and
hounded me to bed to sleep for about eighteen hours, and
arise at last wobbly but quite recovered.

Later I visited the exhibition again, and found it intriguing that it should change so much in the course of its two-
month span. Exhibits were always disappearing, and new
ones materialising from nowhere. There was a pavilion
full of miniatures of formal gardens, in which Honza was
particularly interested, for his father was busy building a
house, and his head was already humming with schemes
for the garden, though as yet it consisted entirely of hard-
trodden earth, sand-piles, mortar-smears, and all the debris
of building. He liked to see shrubs and trees spaced not too
formally in vistas of lawn, in the English fashion, and we
pored together over plans which showed the nice placing
of every tree. Sometimes there were queues for fruit from
the exhibits which were continually renewing themselves.
Always there were queues at the Yugoslav wineshop, which
sold at quite low prices; and here I saw the most completely
drunken man I ever saw in CSR. They are not, to my mind,
frequent there, though the Czechs themselves will tell you
quite seriously that they have a drink problem on their
hands. Turning-out time in most small English towns, in
my experience, will show you more drunks in ten minutes
than I saw in a month in Czechoslovakia; but the authorities do not regard that as any reason for being complacent.

This first week-end happened to be Whitsuntide, so
everyone was on holiday. Mrs. Burianova's Vera, aged

eight, had a new long white dress for the occasion, made by
her mother, in which she went awed and happy to church,
carrying her little basket of flowers. We, less devout, went
off early to find good places on the route of the great procession of the Agricultural Exhibition. Mr. Vesely was
already away at the new house, for he had very little
labour employed on it, and could not afford to lose a full
week-end's work. But the rest of us went out to join the
crowds, Mrs. Vesela, Honza, Aunt Eva and myself. As
far as streets were concerned I had still no sense of direction, though I could find my way by glimpses of the river
or the Hradcany well enough; and still I don't really know
exactly where it happened that we were called into a first-
floor flat, and installed resplendently in the windows along
with the family, luckier by far than the people who were
massing below along the pavements.

The Czechs love processions, marathon processions which
go on for hours and are punctuated, as often as distance
makes it appropriate, by brass bands rich and cavernous
with bass, or gypsy string orchestras with their 'cellos and
double-basses slung from their shoulders by broad leather
straps. On the days of such shows as this all meals are
movable feasts. If you fear you will be hungry you simply
stow some sandwiches—Czech vintage, none of your tissue-
paper English sizes—in your pockets, and eat them when
and where you feel inclined; and when the show is over
you go home and get dinner, whether it is then noon or four
o'clock in the afternoon. They do not lack a time-sense,
but they have not the exaggerated sense of time's dictator-
ship and custom's sacredness which ties us down to fixed
hours, even when we have no one to please but ourselves.

I was naturally curious to see as much as possible of
Prague's country visitors, and in the pursuit of that end
time was no object to me, either. All the cushions from the
rooms of the flat were piled up on the window-sills, above

the gay flower-boxes, and we leaned comfortably upon these and enjoyed a grandstand view; all of us, that is, except Honza, who was bent on making pictures, and spent most of his time down in the street, dancing complicated measures between tableaux with his camera at his eye, and several times almost getting swept away among the marching detachments.

There was a pleasing lack of rigid discipline about the whole thing. As often as the nearest policeman turned his back the crowd stole another yard of the street, and as often as he returned to clear sufficient space for crawling traffic to reach a turning and get off the route, they gave back before him just the necessary number of inches to avoid the wheels, and no more. As for such minor embarrassments as Honza and the other amateur cameramen, they were considered to be adults, capable of taking care of themselves and avoiding being a nuisance to others, and the police stood back and watched their antics with tolerant grins. Nor were the marchers, as we found when they came into sight at last, any more severely regimented. They held what I have always considered to be the Royal Navy's views on marching, that what matters is to get to where you are going, not to look like automata in the process.

We heard fanfares first; the sound of trumpets goes excellently with so golden and clear a morning. A troop of cavalry led the way, on exquisite horses such as every army keeps for ceremonial occasions; and their trumpet-calls seemed to blow the way clear before them, so instantly did the crowds settle into stillness. Then came the country people, each group bearing the name of its town, and wearing the local costume, many of them bearing banners, or pictures of President Benes or Premier Gottwald, or busts of the President-Liberator, or carrying garlands and baskets of flowers soon to fade in the noon heat. There were many decorated lorries and carts, carrying scenes from history, symbolic angels, bivouacs of Boy Scouts, tableaux from the Chlumec Farmers' Rising, from the Austrian days, from the dark time of the German occupation and the concentration camps; and others demonstrating the challenge of the present and the promise of the future. Co-operatives of farmers marched together, and the Unions of Czech and Slovak Youth, and the "blue army" of railwaymen, and the gorgeous black and gilt groups of the uniformed miners, sporting their full regalia, with high round caps, shining badges and tossing plumes like hussars. I saw one brougham-load of imperious Austrian ladies sweeping along nose-in-air, playing to the crowd for all they were worth, and ragged Czech youths running alongside, attempting to beg from them, and being beaten off by their footman. And a full wagon of harvesters driving home tired but triumphant at the end of a celebration, pretending to be resplendently drunk, even down to a large doll which did duty for the baby.

And for hideous contrast, a lorry festooned with barbed wire, and a great plastic hand gripping it from within as if in agonised determination to tear a way through; this for all the lost years and wasted men of Terezín. It startled me that they should see fit to remember such things on such an occasion, but it struck no wrong note with the crowd. It is not practical to pretend, even for the purposes of holiday, that one of the realities of the past, out of which the future has to be constructed, can be ignored without loss; and to be practical is, as I have discovered, a cardinal Czech virtue.

But best were the district groups, marching to their traditional songs, displaying their traditional dresses, often performing their own special dances as they came, with a precision which suggested long practice in covering miles of road after this picturesque but exhausting fashion. Brass bands led them, and often one could distinguish who was

B

coming by the tune, before the name of the village was readable. So many of these villages have their local song, an anchorage for the mind in exile, and a cry of pride in peace. It makes no difference whether they are gay or sad, whether they go with a boast and a wink, like the one from Kutna Hora, or a remembering sigh, like: "O Velvary", they are the small national anthems of home, and there are no other songs like them. Moreover, they give to brass bands the dignity and simplicity of grand music, and I would trade you all the virtuoso tone poems specially written for brass band by so-and-so for one verse of "Sly Panenky Silnici", played Czech fashion, with the rolling bass of the last four lines booming its heart out, and blowing the dust off the road in clouds.

The bands came in their dozens this day; some of them were very good, some were just enjoying themselves without either inhibitions or scruples. Guild bands, town bands, village bands, Sokol bands, orchestras of Slovak gypsies fiddling away for dear life, half-obscured by their unwieldy instruments. I refused at first to believe that anyone could march about a city actually playing on a double-bass, whereupon Honza shot away downstairs again to capture permanent evidence; and I still have the print he made of a beaming gypsy striding out gaily and sawing away at his instrument, with the triumphant legend on the back: "*Can* a gypsy play while marching?"

The geography of Czechoslovakia began to take much more shape in my mind during that morning, making use of living pictures as schools teach by still ones. We listened for the songs, we watched the dazzling colours, and I learned.

" 'Koline, Koline!' they are playing. These are people from Kolin. You were there last year, do you remember, on the way to Kutna Hora. We bought fruit in the square, and put it in the wooden rack of that very bad bus, and it became jam, and dripped through on to the people underneath."

"Look, these coming now are from Chodsko, from the frontiers round Domazlice. You see the axes they carry? They are a special people, the keepers of our south-western frontier, who used to have their own privileges in return for that service. They make there characteristic pottery, like that vase and plate we sent you at Christmas, with the black ground, and those brilliant flower patterns, very often red poppies, and dog daisies."

"Those beautiful dresses are from Hana, in Moravia. It is very rich farm land there, I think the best in our whole country. Hana farmers are wealthy, and independent, and set in their ways. Perhaps someone from there would tell you they are also a bit slow in the uptake, but no one else is allowed to say that."

"And oh! look now! Here are the real show-pieces, from Moravian Slovakia. That's a district for you—one whole piece of folklore."

They were certainly very gorgeous, the young men long and slim as wands in tight dark knee-breeches embroidered down the thighs to accentuate their length and slimness still more, polished boots up to the knee, white shirts with loose sleeves of elaborate needlework, short zouave jackets, merely two armholes joined together by a frame of stiff multi-coloured embroidery, wide rainbow ribbons falling from neck to ankle, and narrow-brimmed black felt hats ringed with flowers and crested with two slender white plumes a yard long, which swept gracefully curving down behind. The girls were designed to give a different silhouette, like spinning tops, with brilliant skirts pleated and puffed out over many petticoats, and aprons like flower-gardens or Victorian greeting-cards; wide-sleeved blouses showering lacy flounces round the elbows, bodices and collars blazing with gold and silver and peacock threads, and on their heads lace caps lying snug to their round cheeks, and gay scarves softly draped over them. They were like humming-birds, quivering with jewel-like colour.

We leaned out of the windows and waved handkerchiefs at them, and shouted: "Nazdar!" which is a beautifully plastic greeting, and can mean anything from "All hail!" to "Cheerio!" And they waved and shouted back as they passed, part of an animated map of CSR walking under our windows.

We stayed until Honza had used all his films, and Mrs. Vesela was growing restive on account of the dinner, for it was already afternoon. Then we took leave of our hosts with many thanks, and went home to eat a late lunch, and play more English gramophone records. Afterwards Honza and I walked in the Old Town until supper, poking our noses into several churches, all of which proved to be in the middle of services, and full of people.

We finished our Whit-Sunday entertainment, late that evening, on the embankment near Palacky Bridge, wedged in crowds so solid that they stopped the tram lines, and had to be pushed in bodily, like compressing a sponge, in order to let the groaning, clanking cars pass by. Across the river from us was the ground where the great firework display was laid out, but all we saw of the set pieces was a pulsating glow of sulphur yellow and rose and electric green, lighting the tree trunks in upward-flowing streams of colour, and making a small lurid day in the darkness. The sky pieces, however, were fine, and we applauded them warmly with the rest, though I think by this time we were half-asleep on our feet after the long, hot day. Mrs. Vesela and Aunt Eva were with us, but we disgraced ourselves by losing them on the way home.

Honza had suggested moving off as soon as the display seemed to be nearing its conclusion, in order to be one jump ahead of the crowds in the late scramble for trams; and we slipped away, all four of us, to the tram route we needed, and stood waiting for a car, but our number did not come until the show was over, and great streams of people were appearing from the embankment. Hurriedly we decided to walk back one stop, and so still be one jump ahead; and as invariably happens when one does this, the car we needed came into sight when we were midway between stops.

"Can you run?" yelled Honza, and set the example. We tore along the street and arrived at the earlier station just as the tram had loaded, and was again gathering way. I looked back, for Honza had fallen behind to encourage the stragglers; but Mrs. Vesela and Aunt Eva were well behind, and on seeing me hesitate the undutiful son and nephew shouted: "Get in!" and hurled himself aboard after me. We left them standing, and sailed by at speed. After us, the deluge! All the crowds from the fireworks were now milling along the road hungrily after transport, and I am afraid that the other two walked home.

3

PRAGUE SPRING

ON Whit-Monday morning we wandered over Letna, and down on to Kampa Island under the shadow of Charles Bridge, where a painter had set up his easel in the sound of the white weirs, and was sketching the secret channel of the Devil's River, which separates Kampa from the Little Town. Everyone paints on Kampa. Even the inns say: "Rooms for Artists". In particular everyone paints the Devil's River, with its rich shadowy bracken-brown and olive-green and cobalt water drawing the warmth of willows and sky and old mellow walls into its darkness, and the wheels of mills still turning here and there to break its silence with a rounded, rhythmic plashing.

They say that to see Prague at her best it is necessary to be there in blossom-time, when all the hills are foaming with flowering cherry and apple and plum. I had missed that delectable season, but the green was still young, fresh and radiant, with latent sunlight in the leaves even when the sun did not shine. I am never sure whether it is better to stand on the top of Letna, or at a window of Hradcany, and look down on the spires of Prague, or to go down into the snug recesses of the Old Town or the Little Town, as we did now, and look up at the leaping roofs above. You cannot do either without finding yourself awed by beauty, for Prague is royally dressed as becomes a capital city, one of the oldest in Europe.

But something of this you can buy on a picture postcard;

it is there for even the one-day caller to see as he hustles through the continent. Less accessible charms come to light if you stay long in the town, and learn to take short cuts by all the mouseholes you can find. For Prague is an intimate town, as hospitable and yet as retired as some of the old provincial capitals in England, offering her subtler serenities only to those who have time to appreciate them. They do not call, but wait and hope to be visited. The Little Town is full of them, narrow shadowed streets under the leaning step-gables of old houses, deep doorways into islands of trees and gardens and gracious wandering palaces, all shut behind an innocent stone wall and a façade of small shops. I soon learned to peer into every such doorway for the sunlight and space beyond, for the black and white chipped sgraffito walls patterning the cool shade, and the shimmer of lime leaves making the sunbeams green, and the receding long arcades, gateway beyond gateway, withdrawing the last mysteries still from sight. There were sudden holes in walls, where stone stairways climbed precipitously uphill or fell away alarmingly down, dipped under low archways, and slithered out of sight. There were little pathways along backwaters of the Vltava, green with willows, quiet from the world, and obscure climbing streets which brought us to squat Gothic inns, weathered to dull gold by the centuries, beetle-browed, drowsing with their many-gabled hats pulled down over their eyes. There were other insignificant streets where suddenly between plate-glass windows writhed out tumultuous baroque Titans, holding up the lintels of tremendous doorways, and the lifted gaze found above the shop-fronts a great symmetrical sweep of palace-wall, lit with iron-latticed casements.

Between the pearls which are hidden, and those which lie upon doorsteps pretending to be grains of sand, one has to be a little clairvoyant or a little in love to reach a just appreciation of the beauty of Prague.

In the afternoon we all went out together. As we rattled back towards the Little Town along the Embankment of Captain Jaros I remarked, in extremely lame Czech, that I hoped this time we should all manage to come back together. Mrs. Vesela laughed, and hoped so, too. Neither she nor Aunt Eva bore any malice over being left behind last night.

We went up the tree-covered slope of Petrin by the rope railway, gazing down through a framing double curve of green branches upon an expanding view of the roofs and towers of Prague, golden in the full drowning sunlight. On the top of the hill pleasure-gardens are laid out, and a small observatory sits under the lee of a great stone wall. It runs, this wall, right from the beginning of the park-like rise of Petrin, only a short street away from the Legions' Bridge, up and over the hill, and down the long slope on the other side, to end close to Strahov monastery, about fifteen hundred metres distant.

"Do you know what that is?" asked Honza.

I knew it was called the Hunger Wall, but didn't know why.

"It is your old friend Charles the Fourth, again," said Honza. "It seems not only under Austria or in the First Republic did we have slumps and mass unemployment. In his reign there was a time when many poor people had no work, and no food, and he had to feed them. But he didn't want to take away their self-respect by making them live on charity—or perhaps better to say he didn't want them to learn to expect free meals and forget how to work —so he employed them on building this wall, and paid them wages for it, so that they all earned their bread."

"Although he didn't really want a wall at all?"

"I suppose not, because you see it doesn't divide anything from anything, it is just a wall. But he did want it as the right way to fill their stomachs. But don't you think he was rather an advanced psychologist for the fourteenth century?"

And I suppose he was, though it does seem that there must have been a field for more useful building than the Hunger Wall, in the fourteenth century or the twentieth. However, there it is, snaking its crenellated dragon spine all across Petrin, and diving steeply down the slope among the fruit trees; and there it has been for six hundred years, and I doubt if the next six hundred, given fair wear and tear, will make much impression on it. Beside it, incongruously, stands the prospect tower, a small copy of the Eiffel Tower; but its lift was out of action, and today we did not feel like climbing the spiral staircase on foot, so we left it behind, and walked out to where the great Sokol stadium stands on the Strahov side of the hill, looking out over miles of softly rolling country.

We approached it at one corner, its great white side stretching away to the right, and so out of sight. There were still six weeks to run before it would be needed for the opening of the Eleventh Sokol Festival, and encamped under its enormous shadow was a whole small town of huts, offices, half-assembled columns, piles of wood and sand and soil, like the maintenance town which thrived under the protecting shadow of Hadrian's Wall. No one was working there on this holiday; we went through into the arena, which was littered with materials, and stood small and lonely in that colossal emptiness, looking round at the half-finished tribunes.

Usually the rest of the world thinks of Sokol purely as a national organisation for physical culture, practising a particular kind of mass callisthenics which gets its effect by quite simple movements, possible to almost anyone who is prepared to give time, concentration and practice to them. What matters is the assembly of numbers to their performance, the picture of the whole, not the consideration

B*

of the individual. Sokol produces star gymnasts, but cares nothing for what might be called, in gymnastics as in any other field, the star system. The importance of the individual—and he is important—is his contribution to the perfection of the team; a team of perhaps a few dozens at regular meetings, of a few hundreds at district assemblies, of thirty thousand or so at the great festivals. But Sokol is much more than this, for it interests itself in music, art, and every kind of instruction which can contribute to the mental and moral development of Czech youth. Teamwork, and the need of the individual member not merely to subject himself to, but to perfect himself for, the team, is the keynote of all that it does. When you have observed such excellences as the choral verse-speaking of boy and girl Sokols at the Radio Exhibition, or the victory of the women's team at the Olympiad, however, you have observed only the first few ripples of an ever-widening outward motion which engulfs circle beyond circle the whole of life.

I do not suggest that every Sokol member realises it, but I do say that it is implicit in the movement. It began in 1862, with the falcon in captivity, as a magnetic force helping, with the resurgence of the language, and the personal devotion of great men, to hold the nation together. The art in which the individual then had to perfect himself was that of being a good citizen of the beloved but submerged state, and the team was the state itself, which if he did not live to see, his children should. But beyond this again the dedicated idea cast another ripple, and now the citizen must enlarge his ambition to become a complete person, and the team became humanity.

No Czech ever put it to me in such terms. Mr. Vesely spoke proudly of the voluntary spirit which moves all who give their time and energy to Sokol, and the motto: "Not for glory, not for gain!" I already knew. But the Czechs do not grow lyrical about their achievements, nor about the means by which they achieve. And as I have said, the full implications of membership may dawn on only a minority of members; I have not the least doubt, however, that they were perfectly clear in the minds of Miroslav Tyrs and his compeers, who first forged this weapon of the spirit; and the history of the movement, through difficulties, persecutions, and the last extreme test of the occupation, justifies the largeness of the vision.

We returned to the Hunger Wall, and the green slope of hillside planted with fruit trees; and Mr. Vesely asked Honza to take us down by the shortest way, which he did rather too literally, for soon his chosen path became a steep series of earthen steps, dropping heavily.

We came out into Carmelite Street in the Little Town, and turning left towards Charles Bridge, arrived in a few minutes at a flight of steps retiring briskly upward on our left, and at their head the church of the Virgin Mary Victorious. Here Mrs. Vesela remembered the presence of the miraculous image of the Child Jesus of Prague, and drew me in to see it.

Above a lit altar in its own particular chapel we found it, a small wax doll, so smothered in jewelled garments that it looked only like a silk tea-cosy studded all over with gems, and decorated rather surprisingly with a head and hands, set in the centre of a radiating blaze of gilt and light, like the pearl in the concavity of the shell. The head was the conventional cluster of curls, and the face must, when new, have been the conventional pink-and-white blank baby-doll face; but the sliding centuries have worn away the pink and white to a plaintive pearly gloss, and softened the features into a pale pathos which is strangely touching in the stiff magnificence of the setting, as if the child was some poor little overbred Infante of the Spanish court, propped up in a sarcophagus of royal robes to pose for

Velazquez, and staring at the world for ever from his canvas with a fading face of misused childish bewilderment, dedicated to a few sickly years and an early death.

But the few years of the Child Jesus of Prague number already three hundred and fifty, and as far away as Spanish America they know the small, worn, translucent face. I am unable to feel the reverence of the devout for these poor little manikin mounds of clothes; for me it is incomprehensible. But another kind of delight and awe clings about the Jezulatko, the patina of its history, polished with the thoughts and hopes of all those people through whose hands it has passed, as if the invisible caresses of faith, justified or unjustified, of prayers answered or ignored, have been the means of paling and wearing away its substance. A lady of the de Lara family came all the way from Spain to marry a nobleman of the Pernstein family, back in the close of the sixteenth century, and brought the Jezulatko with her; and a daughter of the marriage gave it at last, in the national twilight of the White Mountain, into the care of the Carmelite monks, and they made for it this chapel in the house of Our Lady Victorious.

Further along Carmelite Street there is one of the hidden pearls which the stranger might easily pass by. All you see from the street is a broad double door in the wall, but beyond it are the gardens of the Vrtba Palace, climbing the hill by giant's strides in dwindling terraces, each decorated with stone balustrades and figures and vases, from an enclosed court of apricot trees at the bottom to a minute railed platform at the top. For the last stage, after mounting by several staircases, you let yourself in by a small door to the interior of the stone arbour, and climb a last spiral stairway to emerge high in air, looking down upon the Little Town. We were lucky, and were given the key to take with us, for the custodian wanted his Whit-Monday in idleness like the rest of us, and was glad to find us willing to make the trip unescorted.

We climbed the steel staircase, and came into the evening sun on the topmost terrace. Behind us the hill-slope continued to ascend, but more gently, merging into the orchards of Petrin. Immediately below us were the falling concentric semicircles of the garden, and the lovely low roofs of the palace running in long, complex lines, mellow below the eaves with creeper; and outward beyond these went all the mazy roofs of the Little Town, parted here and there by invisible streets, from which traffic noises reached us only as a murmur like a distant stream in a pebbly bed. Beyond, again, was the blue sickle of river, and on the other side of it all the climbing towers of the Old Town rose sharply outlined into the light. On our left, above the gabled palace roofs lifted tier on tier, we could follow the long rise of Hradcany hill, and the castle and cathedral on its crest lay outspread so near and clear and level with us that it seemed as if we could reach out and touch the walls, or stroke the great green dome of St. Nicholas, where it lay just below.

Our Whit-Monday wanderings ended here. I saw much of Prague again next day, when we spent the morning pursuing my visa extension from the Ministry of Foreign Affairs in the Cernin Palace, to National Street, from there to Smichov, and from Smichov back to National Street, where we finally ran it to earth. A large part of this tour was unnecessary, and arose from a mistake; it was Honza who asked for the department we needed at National Street, and he was so plainly Czech that the policeman sent us off to Smichov under the impression that our business was over a Czech passport instead of a foreign one. When we had trammed doggedly back again and found the right office everything proved to be very simple. I filled in one form, stuck on a twelve-crown revenue stamp, and received in exchange a paper which authorised me to be still in CSR on June 3rd, when I had to come back and have my three-month extension logged in my passport.

Honza had an examination hanging over his head in these days, and had no time to play, but Helena was generous in devoting herself to me, and very happily I wandered about Prague in her company, in the continuing paradisal weather of spring. With her I walked all through Sarka's valley, that rocky and wooded cleft which dives deeply into the body of Bohemia from the terminus of the Nr. 11 tram. There are two restaurants and a swimming-pool in the heart of it now, but when these are out of sight —and the valley winds so tortuously among its rocks that you see the evidences of civilisation for only a short time— you can almost believe that you are many miles and many centuries from modern Prague, back in the wild days when Sarka and her Amazons chose this place for their campaign against men, and enriched Bohemian folk-tales with the bloodthirsty episodes of the *Women's War*.

You hear the whole story in the third tone-poem of Smetana's "Ma Vlast". The only thing the music does not make clear is why Sarka, reputedly as beautiful as fierce, hated men so much that she plotted the deaths of any who came within her reach. I ought to have found out by now, but I have never done so. All I know is what the vivid music tells: how she ambushed the warrior Ctirad and his men by having herself bound naked to a tree in this valley, as if left exposed to die by casual bandits, her women soldiers in the meantime lying hidden among the rocks and forests within call. You hear the brisk, gay march of Ctirad's approach, the sudden pause of wonder, the enthusiastic rescue, and the high gallantry of the night's camp, with its many healths drunk in celebration of her beauty; the stilling hush as man after man the soldiers roll away into a bemused sleep, and then on the quietness the sudden steady call of Sarka's vengeful horn, and the swoop of the women on their helpless enemies, the brief bloodshed. I do not know which is more terrifying, the turmoil and expectancy of Sarka's mind at the beginning, or her wild peals of triumph at the end. I feel that someone must have behaved extremely badly to Sarka in her days of innocence; but even so her retort was unnecessarily wholesale.

It was after this trip through the valley that I first made my own way home by tram, alone and in the dark. It was not much of a feat, but beginnings are necessarily small. We had talked and talked until nearly eleven o'clock, our invariable habit when I visited the flat in Dejvice. Karel came to the tram-stop with me, and already I had found out what numbers were of use to me, and knew how many stops there were to Strossmayer Square. I even knew that after half-past ten my ticket would cost me five crowns instead of the usual two crowns fifty; and the language difficulty counts for nothing on these trips if you know the route, since you have not to name your destination. A ticket on a Prague tram is a ticket to anywhere that Prague trams go, two crowns fifty from one end of town to the other if you wish; you can even change twice with it, at the correct places where the routes cross. The citizens usually carry season tickets, which bear their photographs, receive a fresh stamp for each renewing, and must be shown when required. Honza's amused me because he had had it for years, and the photograph it carried was that of a wistful-looking child of fourteen or fifteen; I doubt if he could really be identified as the same person, if some more than usually officious inspector cared to question the likeness.

Later I often travelled on the trams at about half-past ten, and was almost invariably entertained by some thrifty traveller who objected to paying the night fare. It was wonderful with what ingenuity and energy they would erect arguments against parting with that extra two crowns fifty. The usual one was: "I got on this tram at twenty-eight minutes past ten. I know it's after half-past now, but is it my fault if you don't come round for the fares in time?" And the usual reply, from a good-humoured but equally determined conductor: "I go on taking fares as fast as I can, and all the time. At half-past ten prompt I start charging five crowns. It's past that time now, and I want five crowns from you." Usually he got it, but for love they would spin out the argument as long as the journey lasted, enlisting witnesses, comparing watches, and dissecting regulations until every soul in the tram had signed up on one side or the other. It was the most sacred rule of this game that the fight was never private; anybody could join in, and everybody did.

But the trams of Prague are a dangerous subject, being inexhaustible.

It was Helena who showed me the Jewish town, too, one morning when we had an appointment at the office of the Syndicate of Czech Authors, and were whiling away the time between shops and sightseeing until twelve o'clock. We left our tram at the Old Town end of Stefanik Bridge, and dived hopefully into the rabbit-warren of the Cloister of Saint Anezka, into which all alleys for a furlong round inevitably lead. A wilderness of early Gothic run insanitarily to seed, this picturesque slum contains the most bewildering conglomeration of closes, passages, archways, ruined churches, sudden green naves open to the sky, and assorted portable rubbish you need wish to see; decrepit little houses, themselves centuries old, have been built on to the standing parts of monastic ruins centuries older, and used the fallen stones for their own substance. Once you are in you wonder how on earth you are to get out again, for every small court, showing you a hopeful tunnel in the opposite wall, merely brings you into yet another court tottering away in another direction, and every alley curls round into another alley, or deposits you on a private doorstep. I suppose everyone in Prague would agree that Saint Anezka ought to come down; to look at it is fascinating, but to live in it must be appalling. But no one likes to take the responsibility for bringing history to a full stop. To destroy it, as Honza says of the Prague trams, would be like demolishing the Hradcany itself; the city just wouldn't be the same. The Hussite wars and the fire of 1689 both attempted to level the cloister, and had no success; a city council moved by modern ideas of sanitation may be more effective in the end, but for that undeniable gain something will be lost, as it always is.

The Jewish town is quite close, and suffered from the same fire in the French-Austrian wars, though the famous Old-New synagogue survived when all eight others were destroyed. What remained of the old Josefov quarter was demolished in the nineteenth century, for the same reasons which will ultimately see the end of St. Anezka's Cloister, but this is still the centre of what Jewish life remains in Prague, and I saw here several conventionally long-coated and black-hatted orthodox Jews, some even with the ear-curls of tradition, and long beards. The synagogue and the Jewish Town Hall stand close together, opposite to the approach to the cemetery. The synagogue is small, plain, with a steep roof, and a tympanum like a praying hand, and has the dignity of the occasional English tithe-barn in its simplicity and completeness. A middle-aged guide showed us round, and the interior did not disappoint me, for it has the same quality of pride in what it is, and not what the visitor in search of superlatives would like it to be. They show you there the chair of Rabbi Löw, who made the Golem, and started a whole train of metaphysical literature ending, or perhaps only pausing for breath, in Mary Shelley's *Frankenstein*.

Somewhere in this dim, proud, gracious and pathetic place the clay figure of the Golem is supposed to be hidden. Rabbi Löw's exploits in this esoteric field of learning, which the Christian churches would almost certainly have regarded as implying compact with the devil, do not seem to have dimmed his holiness in the slightest, but only to have given a new gloss to his halo of wisdom; as if the Hebrew church enjoyed an altogether wider and more scientific outlook than its newer rivals in the matter of human knowledge and its limitations. I dare say less apocryphal activities than the animation of the Golem would have sufficed to get him burned under Rome; to be a mathematician was often quite enough.

Everyone who ever went to Prague, I suppose, has written about the Jewish cemetery. Few things come up to the guide book in this life; the cemetery surpasses it, but I still do not quite know how or why. Nobody knows how old it is; the newest tombstones are two hundred years old, the oldest probably a thousand. They say there are more than twelve thousand people buried here, in five deep layers. But what one feels here has nothing to do with these minor facts. I resented being shown round it; I wished not to meet anyone else there, and felt that they had got into my private garden when we did meet them. It is the most secret, intimate and suggestive place I know, and once you are in it the world recedes far beyond the mere confines of the wall, which is high, and shuts out sound. The necessity for measuring time goes away with the sensation of place, and to be in a hurry, as we were, is here an offence, for which I apologise. Some cemeteries are attractive because they lie open to the sun and the air; this one is attractive in spite of the fact that it crouches, hides itself, shuts out the light with a thickset roof of white elder trees, themselves very old. It was too late for me to see them in flower, but they were in the fullest and tenderest green of leaf; and obscurely about their roots the tomb-stones sprang out of the soil as if they, too, had grown there, so thickly in many places that a mouse could hardly have passed between them; old, jagged, black stones like sets of broken teeth, all the more mysterious and pathetic because the strange characters on them could tell me nothing about the sojourners underneath.

Rabbi Löw is here, for all his alchemies. They show you his tomb, and at all times you will find massed in its ledges and crannies many small stones and pebbles, for here you can drop a stone and make a wish with the guarantee—how valuable I do not know—that it will be fulfilled. Mine was, but it so happened that its fulfilment depended on the intelligence of someone else, and I fear the credit belongs to him rather than to Rabbi Löw.

When we left the cemetery Helena said: "Where one has to make wishes I always wish the same thing."

I asked her, naturally, what it was.

"I wish to be happy," she said. "After all, everything else is contained in that. Happiness depends on so many conditions that its existence must mean all those conditions are reasonably fulfilled. So for me to be happy, my country must have some good hope in life, and all the people dear to me must be fairly happy, too. I could not get the whole of that into any other wish.

But she did not say, and I did not ask her, if all the visits to all the wish-granting shrines had had the desired effect. If beauty is in the eye, I suppose happiness is somewhere in the mind, busily adapting itself to circumstances where it cannot adapt circumstances to itself; and to know that one has it is as rare, as to know that one has had and lost it is common and pitiful.

4

Opocno Week-end

I spent the week-end with Dr. Novák and his family in north-eastern Bohemia, at the town of Opocno.

Honza saw me off on Friday morning, at the unconscionable hour of ten minutes past seven. We went early to Wilson station, but the train was already in, and rapidly filling; we sought out the one coach which ran straight through to Opocno, and found a place in it. It was a saloon coach, and the seats boasted some firm and sparse padding, instead of being merely shaped wood; but I am not sure that this was quite the luxury Honza seemed to think. I have travelled in both types since, and found the wooden seats much more comfortable than might be expected, while this padding proved in an hour or so to be in all the wrong places. Czech railway accommodation does not claim the sybaritic standards of British, nor the speed, though I found it pleasant enough, and its timing remarkably accurate. So far as my experience goes, you can meet a Czech train, short distance or long, with the conviction that it will arrive at the time promised, almost to the minute.

Honza left me a little time before the train was due out, and I was interested to see, a few minutes later, that he was still standing on the platform, though well aside from where I sat at the window. The reason was made plain when I chanced to look out again, and caught him in the act of pointing me out cautiously to the guard. I was divided between gratitude for his care of me and indignation at his assumption of my helplessness, but I think the indignation must have been the more clearly visible from where he stood, for he quickly grinned, raised his hat, and departed. I must say that the guard did his part faithfully. Whenever he had a few minutes to spare during the three-hour journey he came and told me how many more stations there were to Opocno, and at the end he appeared in the doorway of the coach and beckoned me silently, in the manner of an angelic or ghostly visitant indicating that my hour had come.

We puffed rather deliberately eastward from Prague, through Podebrady, Chlumec, Hradec Kralove, and on to Tyniste, where some complicated version of the universal railway game occupied about ten minutes, and finally shot our coach out backwards on the northward run to Opocno. The lovely weather of Whitsuntide was gone for the moment, and it was a day of cold occasional rain.

Dr. Novák met me at the station with a small, battered but gallant Tatra car, and we drove up to his flat in a big old house in the town. His family was numerous and cheerful, I found. Besides Mrs. Novakova there were two boys, Jenik and Jirka, aged seventeen and fourteen, an aunt, and a small nephew of five years, Jenicek, who was visiting them from Moravia. Jenik was absent for the moment, taking an English examination which would qualify him to visit England with a schools party in July if he negotiated it safely. He was the pianist of the family, though Jirka played a little, too, and everyone sang. Jenicek and I sang together beautifully, or so we two thought. Our version of: "Ach, Synku, Synku" managed to stay in the same key throughout, but by the second verse had already developed into a race, and the third was an all-out, down-the-straight affair with heads down and ears laid back; but I had difficulty with the consonants, and he invariably won. He was a charming little boy, at the gap-toothed stage between first set and second, which perhaps made the consonants even easier.

Opocno is a small provincial town just within sight of the Eagle Mountains which border what used to be Germany but is now Poland. It has, like all Bohemian towns, a square big enough for a city, with trees and a garden, and most of the main municipal buildings grouped around it in a sensible and convenient manner. Across the narrowing end of the square an ancient small monastery and a modern community house face each other. Take the road out of town in this direction, and you pass closely by the end of a large lake—I call it a lake, but the word they use is fishpond, so I conclude that it is artificially made or stocked—and then along a high, tree-shaded road towards the mountains. Leave the square by the uphill corner, and along a small winding street you come into the quiet close where the church stands, and beside it the gate which leads to the castle.

It is national property now, together with the deer park which falls away precipitously from its terrace into a deep ravine, and climbs out again on the other side by rocks and stairways of earth and stone. The castle itself is a hollow square, arcaded about its court, and facing outward into air across this forested gulf, with a squat round hunger tower set a little aside from it, overhanging the precipice. From the crest of the slope opposite, or from the floor of the valley, it looks magnificent, and its position makes it plain that it began life as a fortress; but it has all the comfort of the gentler castles which were meant to be lived in. It belonged to the Colloredo-Mansfeld family, and still contains their belongings; furniture, portraits, chandeliers, are all in position, the accumulated trophies of the late Count's travels in all parts of the world turn the hall and the armoury into museums, even the books are still in their shelves. The custodian keeps such a high polish on the floors that the arrival of a school party to inspect this piece of history is nothing short of a disaster on a wet day; and the day of our visit was wet, and the children came. We sympathised with both sides, but that solved nothing. In some such showplaces felt overshoes are the order of the day, and to judge by our friend's lamentations this will be true of Opocno just as soon as he can get delivery of enough felt overshoes.

This must be a most popular school visit. Once admit any normal boy to the armoury at Opocno, and all the wiles of Merlin will be needed to get him out again. It is an enormous room high up in one wing, with shelves and benches all round, and the larger pieces, such as armour, and the gigantic early guns, arranged in the centre, to give free access everywhere. Everything is here, from cannon to cross-bows, many and various military caps, every kind of fearsome firearm, not to mention modern rifles and sporting guns, and trifling by-products of the armourer's art such as thumbscrews, locks and keys as big as window-grilles, grapples and chastity belts. Until then I confess that I had never believed that these last really existed; I thought some historian with a misguided sense of humour had made them up. I am wiser now.

What interests me about armour is its almost invariable smallness; few suits I have ever seen would go on an average-sized man of today. Physically mankind seems to have advanced by many inches in not so very many centuries. I have hopes of its mental and moral growth, too, in spite of all the religious and political red-herrings being dragged across the path of our judgment to make us think otherwise.

The children clattered in as we were leaving, and distributed themselves about the trophied hall like shot scattering, among the African tomtoms and Egyptian

basalts, the skulls of crocodiles and masks of lions. I would
not have cared for the job of collecting them together when
the time came to leave, in a place so full of fascinating
corners.

It was too wet to walk in the deer park that day, though
we lingered to admire the view from the terrace; we went
home and enjoyed a musical evening, instead, with
national songs, and Dvorak's Moravian duets, and when
everyone was hoarse with singing, we deputed our musical
entertainment to Jirka and the gramophone, and listened
to the whole of "Ma Vlast" again. It is a pity that these six
tone poems should ever be separated, though it is certainly
better to be familiar with only "Vltava" and "From Bohemia's
Woods and Meadows" than with none of them. From the
first chords of Lumir's harp on Vysehrad to the final ride
of the saviours from Blanik, "Ma Vlast" is a unity; to extract "Vltava", lovely though it is even alone, is nevertheless a mutilation.

Strange how these legends of the saviours repeat themselves in many lands alike, without any apparent contact
or common origin! In Britain it is King Arthur and his
knights who sleep under a hill waiting until the hour of
national peril when they shall be needed; we have even
our own Shropshire version, where in time of crisis Wild
Edric and his fairy wife and his army ride out from the
Longmynd to join battle again as in their lifetime. In
Czechoslovakia it is the holy armies of St. Vaclav who wait
in the hill Blanik until the country needs them. People
have claimed to see Edric's ride occasionally in the crises of
Shropshire; I have never yet found a Czech who is prepared to say he has seen the banners of St. Vaclav issuing
gloriously from Blanik, not even in the days of the Prague
rising. Nevertheless, I think the deliverers were abroad,
making use of the minds and hands of ordinary men. Other
times, other methods.

Jirka had some school business to attend to next day, although it was Saturday; but the doctor, the aunt, Jenicek and myself made a trip into the mountains in the afternoon, right to the borders of Poland. It was a beautiful drive, and the sun came out again in full strength, but as we began to climb among the wooded foothills of the Eagle Mountains it soon grew colder. The road was shut in between wooded slopes, and wound through long villages strung along both sides of it. For some time we followed a stream, increasingly stony and turbulent, like all mountain brooks. The forests shed their few deciduous trees, and became mountain forests. The villages showed fewer and fewer brick and plaster houses, more and more wooden ones, and each one we passed was more certainly a mountain village than the one before it. The road wound arduously, making great sweeping bends to lift itself out of the valley, and more clearly now we could see the peaks of the hills, rounded, grassy and wooded to the crest, except for the highest, on which the trees shunned the fullest exposure, and bent modestly into shelter in crevices and small valleys. In the slopes and on the heights we saw several outcrops of concrete forts and emplacements breaking the green of the turf.

"These are the fortifications which the Germans gained at Munich," said the doctor. "We were not even given a chance to remove anything or destroy anything."

Well, it is not Germany which meets Czechoslovakia now about fifty yards from the tourist hut known as Masarykova Chata, on top of one crest of the Eagle Mountains; it is Poland.

We drove past the hut to the car park, and left the car; there is still one slight rise to climb, among the stunted bushes, and then you are on the frontier. I crossed it, and did not know my offence, for there is absolutely nothing to show where the line of demarcation lies, except in one spot a small stone like a milestone, with CS on one side, and D on the other—D for Deutschland, since the stone has not yet been renewed. Nothing else of any kind shows that two countries meet in this place.

"I suppose this," I said, "is a part of the deeply-guarded frontier."

"Oh, you could be interned if you went down into one of the villages, there," said the doctor. "You would perhaps be imprisoned for three days, and then put back over the border. Just like anywhere else."

The north-eastward descent into Poland was somewhat more gradual than the way by which we had climbed, softly rolling country going downhill in woodland and pasture, and distant villages outspread below. North-westward the sun picked out vividly another of the bastions of Bohemia, the long-lying snowfields of the Giant Mountains.

"I should have thought, though," I suggested, "that there would be some frontier and Customs men about, smuggling being the profitable job it is—at any rate on most borders."

"Oh, they will be somewhere not far off, I expect," he said comfortably. "but they don't seem to be here."

On the way back we did meet one of the service, about three miles from the frontier. His head was bare, his green tunic was open, and he was pushing a bicycle up one of the steep stretches of the road, and whistling as he went. I never saw a man more determinedly off-duty, and we met no more of his kind.

We visited the borders of Poland again next morning, but in another direction, due north from Opocno. The doctor had to go to Nachod to attend a conference of intellectual workers which was to be addressed by the Minister of Education, Dr. Nejedly, and he proposed that I should go along at the same time to see the town and the castle. Jenik, back in triumph from his English examination, came with us.

Nachod is a modern textile town now, sitting innocently in the wide valley which slants down into Bohemia from what used to be Germany, between the Giant Mountains and the Eagle Mountains. The narrowest part of the gap is here, where hills draw protectively in on both sides, and on one of them the castle of Nachod stands, a watch-tower over the Sedan of Czechoslovakia. Once through here, and there opens to an advancing army the whole great plain of Hradec Kralove. How many times that tragedy has been repeated in history I do not know; but the occasion best remembered was in June, 1866, when the Prussians broke into Austrian ground by this pass, emptied themselves into the plain, and fought out there the battle of Sadova. It is counted as a Prussian victory. I wonder! For several miles along the road before you enter the town you see among the fields and woodlands scattered stone obelisks and little stone crosses, and if you ask what they are, or go to examine them, you find always the same thing. Prussian graves. I suspect the unfortunate conscripts underneath found Sadova a poor victory.

Jenik and I left Dr. Novák at the hotel where the conference was being held, and climbed by steep pathways and many steps up the castle hill. The whole slope is covered with lilacs, but we came just too late to see it in flower, and only a few late and falling spires of purple remained. There is a terraced courtyard commanding fine views on one side, but to see the whole sweep of country, right from Poland into the plain, you must climb the great spiral stairway up the tower, the only part of the building which we found open on this particular Sunday morning. Half-way up, a small doorway to one side gives on a railed opening, where you may look down into the bottle-shaped interior of the hunger tower. An electric bulb is slung low in the grisly place to show its depth, and the way the walls draw in at the neck to make escape impossible. It would seem that there was not much to choose between the habits of the nobility and gentry in the Middle Ages, whether in eastern, central or western Europe, for this is precisely the French oubliette by a different name, somewhere to put what is better forgotten.

On top of the tower the wind meets you even when there is no wind at ground level. You have the whole valley spread out for you below, another hill as sudden as your own fronting you opposite, north-eastwards the widening pass cradling Polish villages, south-westward the road into Bohemia, and at your feet, almost forgotten, the town, its factories tucked away into the deepest fold of the valley. You could drop a pebble into the middle of the square, among the parked cars.

When we had wandered round every part of the ramparts, and explored the view with field-glasses, we went down and drank coffee in the hotel until the doctor joined us. The meeting was still in full swing, and Professor Nejedly was just then speaking; for a while we went quietly up the stairs to the conference-hall to watch him in action. But we had to get back to Opocno, and had plans for visiting the Grandmother's Valley at Ratiborice on the way, so we fortified ourselves with coffee and left, defaulters from the cause of the cultural workers for the rest of the day.

Finding Ratiborice was not so simple an operation, as we soon discovered. The best-known way was closed because of road repairs; a second ingenious detour brought us up sharply against a similar obstacle; but we became even more determined to get there by fair means or foul, and managed it at last by a narrow and difficult road, but intact. On the way I learned who the grandmother was, and why her valley is famous.

Bozena Nemcova was a Czech writer of last century, one of the compeers of Havlicek and Neruda and Palacky, who revived through the Czech language a sense of history and nationality in their fellow-countrymen, and laid the foundations of the first republic just as surely as Masaryk built on them later. Young pictures of her show that it was no mere conventional tribute to say that she was very beautiful. I say young pictures, but indeed she did not live beyond early middle age. She was married at sixteen, to a man much older than herself, and though it was a love match, it fared no better for that. She found the fulfilment she needed in the cause of her country, and was the friend of all the great men of the spiritual revolution. She it was who, when the Austrian authorities prohibited demonstrations of national grief at the funeral of Havlicek, met the cortège and laid on the coffin a crown of thorns.

In her later years, and in the time of her unhappiness, when little was left of the personal promise of her life, Bozena Nemcova wrote a novel about her childhood, *The Grandmother*. It is about a family of children, the eldest of whom, Barunka, is the author herself, and about their life here in the valley of Ratiborice with their grandmother, through all the seasons of the country year. No one suggests that all of it is to be taken literally; it is truth, but truth beautified, memory, but memory coloured by longing. Everyone is in it, the countess at the castle, the girl at the inn, the Austrian conscripts and the small country tradesmen. And everyone knows it by heart; the children read it in schools, and their parents have copies at home. So famous is the grandmother that a relief of a scene from her story adorns Bozena Nemcova's gravestone in the Slavin on Vysehrad, where the Czech great ones are buried, and here at the entrance to the green valley where she lived there is a statue of the whole family, grandmother, the children and the dogs.

The nicest thing about this valley is that cars are not allowed in it; they must be left in a parking place just at the entrance, almost opposite the inn, and close to the grounds of the castle. The second type of castle, this, not a fortress, but a gracious mansion. From this place you walk down a short descending road, and there before you opens out a great water-meadow, oval and quiet in an enclosure of wooded hills, its grass rich and full of flowers. Along the road and the stream, edged with pollard willows, the cottages are threaded like beads on a string, among them the grandmother's wooden house in the old bleaching-ground, steep-roofed and snugly low in the eaves. Just beyond is the mill, and the weir where poor mad Viktorka in the story used to sit and sing to herself. Trees shade the houses, and the lush grass of the stream-side is alive with butterflies; there is no noise there but the very slight stirring of the wind in the leaves, and the small water-noise of the stream, and in summer, as I saw it, these are almost silent, for the enclosing hills keep off winds, and the brook is full, level and still. This is the tranquillity which she remembered with longing in her later life, among struggle and storm, and out of which she made a classic.

On the way home to dinner we passed through the village of Val, and the doctor remarked that in the afternoon the district rally of Sokol was to be held here. This would be a rehearsal for the Slet, and an excellent opportunity to see what local stresses lie behind the finished product one witnesses at Strahov.

It was quite a local fête, with a brass band to supply the music, and at the side of the exercise ground stalls were busily selling buns and beer and ice-cream. The district president directed proceedings from a high rostrum at one side of the field, by means of a few coloured flags and even fewer words; and all the population of Val, and many people from the surrounding district, were watching criti-

cally from the cord barriers, and pulling to pieces the performances of all their friends. Great numbers of the audience were in Sokol uniform. It was the first time I had seen
it at close quarters or in any numbers, and I studied the
effect with interest.

Here, as among other flights of the bird kingdom, the
male is the more gorgeous. The women's full-dress uniform
is a well-cut costume in light brown cloth, worn with a
white shirt and a dark-brown beret; but the fitted waist of
the coat is, to me regrettably, spanned by a leather belt
which reduces the long lines of the young and slender, and
makes the middle-aged look more dumpy than they need.
With the men's looks no one, surely, could quarrel, though
I doubt if those knee-high boots, excellent for riding, are
quite as comfortable as they might be for marching about
the city of Prague. The dress has hardly changed at all since
the movement was founded, and its most striking property
is its adaptability to any face, figure or age. It consists
of deep, dove-grey breeches and hussar coat, which can be
slung on one shoulder by its neck-cord in warm weather,
a red shirt, and a round black cap with a hawk's feather.
To this is added in cold or wet weather a black frieze cloak
with a hood. The effect is good on the young, where it
achieves an innocent Robin Hood swagger; but magnificent
on the old, giving them a hidalgo's dignity. At Val I
saw old countrymen, with faces burned to Indian bronze
by years of outdoor living, and hands like the roots of trees,
wear it with a kingliness which is seldom the endowment of
kings.

The children—for you may begin your Sokol career at
six years old—wear sensible adaptations of the same colour
scheme, shorts and red shirts for the little boys, red and
fawn frocks for the little girls.

We arrived just too late to see the women's display, but
in time for the young girls of fourteen to eighteen years, who

exercised in trunks and sleeveless blouses of cornflower
blue. They massed outside the arena, and on the director's
signal marched in and disposed themselves by means of
complex doublings and countermarchings which are a
particular feature of the great stadium shows. There is a
real art in getting thirty thousand people arranged accurately about an enormous space like the body of the Strahov
stadium, and by means of movement, and the use of the
colours worn, keeping every spectator not merely interested,
but fascinated, every moment of the time. Compared
with this the actual exercises look easy. And the entrance
has to be varied for each group, and for every appearance of
each group, which means that for each of the main displays
the directors must have ready at least half a dozen different ways of getting their performers into position, and
as many of getting them neatly out again at the end of their
show. A few markers with flags guide the more elaborate
movements, but even so the best of these entrances look like
minor miracles when seen from high up in the tribunes.
Here the effect was quite different, for we were near enough
to see the personal side, the look of fierce concentration
on the young faces, the bitten lip and quick flush which
followed some minor mistake, and the agonised snatch
with which some anxious girl recovered her white exercise
ring after too strong a throw. All those white plastic rings
rising and falling, the white belts, and the white whirling
arms against the supple blue bodies, made dazzling
patterns.

Then we saw the boys of the same age, in red brief shorts
and white singlets, exercising without apparatus; and after
them the men, full Sokols, in close-fitting navy-blue
trousers of jersey, fastened under the instep, and the same
white singlets. Their music was a waltz reminiscent of the
slow movement of Dvorak's Fourth Symphony; it has
stayed in my mind ever since. Specially written music for

such occasions is seldom great music, but I thought the standard of this original Sokol music pleasantly high. In view of the generally accepted statement that "every Czech is a musician" this might be expected; but this is one of those national half-truths which most of the natives will repeat to you only with a wink.

These local displays were going on then all over the country, from Cheb to Kosice, and everywhere the same critical conversations were going on along the sidelines, as friends conferred over the performance and assessed the prospects for the real thing.

The fête continued even after the show was over, since there is no point in closing down early when you have a fine day, a brass band, a clear space of turf, buns and beer. The band was beginning to play for dancing when we left, and from what I have seen of Czechoslovak bands they would be still playing at midnight if the beer held out. But we went home and had some more music; there was always music in the Novák house.

The next day I had to return to Prague, but the best train of the day was in the late afternoon, so I had time for a long walk during the morning, out by one of the level main roads from Opocno, setting out purposefully between great flat fields towards the village of Sebechnice. One of the main changes I had noticed in the country districts since the previous year was that more cattle were being raised in the open, instead of in the byres. In the mountain pastures, which were useless for crops, cattle at graze were naturally a common sight enough, but in 1947 I remember the cows were almost invariably indoors in the softer lowland country. This year they were often to be seen, even here in the plain.

At Sebechnice I turned off the road towards the lake, and at first was taking a blind alley, but an old woman met me, and spotting me for a foreigner, as invariably everyone

c

did, paused to ask where I wished to go. I said, to the water, adding unnecessarily that I was English and spoke very little Czech. This was my one perfect sentence, being the one I used most. She pointed me on to a further turning, assuring me that it would bring me to the lake; which it did, and I made a complete circuit of Opocno's fish-pond, this last stretch in the open fields.

The lake is long, and tapers at this distant end into reeds and shallows; all about it are trees, close enough to veil but not to obscure it. As I drew near to these reedy shallows, the width of a field intervening, I saw a wild activity of birds about it, and heard a continuous pandemonium of screams and calls which could belong only to gulls. Honza had sent me photographs showing black-headed gulls about the bridges of Prague, and assured me that they arrived as regularly and punctually as spring itself for the breeding season. Here at Opocno they swirled about the end of the lake in their thousands, and though I was too far from them to be quite sure, I believe there were herring gulls as well. They kept low between the trees for the most part, sending up occasional high flurries to spin for a while like feathers tossed up by the wind, and gradually settle again. Their din—I love to hear it, but a din is exactly what it was in this concentration—seemed to assault the ears with a strident ambition to prove that Shakespeare was right. Here in the heart of Europe, in the sealess centre, I heard one of the most challenging sounds of the sea.

This ocean music was one of the strangest and pleasantest memories I carried away from Opocno when I left by the six o'clock train, seen off by Dr. Novák, Jenik and Jenicek to whom I waved good-bye with much regret, though I hoped to see them all again before I had to leave CSR.

I always enjoyed train journeys alone, though involved conversation was beyond me; much could be done with my few words, some goodwill on the part of my neighbours, and a few signs. In this case I found a seat opposite to a middle-aged man travelling alone, and had been sitting only ten minutes or so when he leaned over and asked me how I liked the country. He could have been perhaps a skilled worker or a small tradesman; and he had realised at once, of course, that I was English, and though he had no English of his own, was prepared to use pidgin-Czech in a good cause. Within a few minutes more he had confided to me, in no subdued voice, that CSR was now finished, no more good. I assured him that I did not agree, lest he should labour under the delusion that I was politically calculable merely by virtue of being English; but he was entitled to his opinion, and I was glad he did not hurriedly close the conversation upon my disagreeing with him.

It is obvious to me that to be the neighbour of Germany, and to have learned once, by the most appalling experience, that western friendships either cannot or will not protect you from her, is a circumstance which will largely control your policy independently of other considerations, since self-preservation is the first instinct of countries as of men. We at least have a ditch round us, and its worth was proved again, if it needed proof, in 1940; yes, even in these days of air power we have seen the sea save us. But in spite of all the gulls breeding upon the lake of Opocno, CSR has no sea-coast; only upon the east the whole Slav world, one family no matter what bitter quarrels have torn them in the past, and upon the west Germany, the immemorial common enemy. In one world there could be safety without any need to choose; unhappily we none of us enjoy one world, and once the break is acknowledged— and we are adjured daily to be realists—the choice of Czechoslovakia is, in fact, Hobson's choice. To scream indignation is merely silly.

We could not quite argue the case in these terms, but

we got as near as we could with our limited vocabulary, before he got out at Tyniste, where we played the railway game for a further ten minutes, and then ambled out backwards, tacked on to the long-distance train from Moravska Ostrava and Olomouc.

5

CIRCULAR TOUR TO KARLSTEJN

ANY trip arranged by Helena was generally acknowledged to be an adventure. Karel alleged that whoever allowed himself to be beguiled into travelling with her, especially if she had looked up the trains, was taking his life in his hand, or at the very least risking his night's rest. The Helena-proof time-table, according to him, had not yet been invented. However, she made a special journey to the station to make sure of the trains to Karlstejn, and when questioned by Karel, asserted positively that she had looked back three times to make sure she had the right times, and each re-check had only confirmed it. Therefore he despatched us with his blessing, in the assurance that this time the hoodoo would not work.

Everyone goes to Karlstejn. It is only an hour from Prague by train, and one of the show castles of Bohemia; and the Karel of its name is again the great Emperor Charles the Fourth, of Charles Bridge, and Charles University, and the Hunger Wall. There is no escape from Charles, for he was one of the chief builders of the city, and take him by and large, a very fine specimen of a ruler for his time, too. It is true he had four wives, but the matches were dissolved only by death, and a natural death at that. You can see them all in the triforium of St. Vitus, in portrait busts; the king bearded, with eyebrows which turn slightly upward at the outer ends, and give him a faint appearance of a satirical smile, though the equally characteristic smiling look of his mouth has no satire about it; and the four ladies, two Annas, Eliska and Blanche, all of them reasonably good-looking, two of them almost beauties. Three of the patrician noses have been chipped and flattened by the accidents of the centuries, for they have been there since about 1360; only Anna Svidnicka survives entire, but for a negligible piece chipped out of her round cap. She has flowing hair, a pensive face, and a slight Mona Lisa smile. She is the third wife, and the only one of whom they say that he married her for love; and a very popular play, *Night in Karlstejn*, connects her name with Charles' favourite castle.

It seems that the place was built as a retreat from the world, a kind of royal hermitage shrewdly combined with an extremely safe royal treasury. Here he used to withdraw to commune with his soul, or his God, or both, an exercise in which women, even Anna, had no part; and therefore women were forbidden to enter, lest they should distract the royal contemplative and his suite, who were expected to be as devout as their master, or at least to give the impression that they were. According to the play, Anna resented this, and in order to see what went on behind her back, made her way into the castle disguised as a page. She was found out eventually, but Charles, though he would not relax the rule that she must not spend the night there, sent her away to another lodging with the promise that he would follow and join her; thus tactfully making it a victory for both sides. I do not know whether there is supposed to be any historical foundation for the story, but Czechs are fond of the play, and perform it regularly. It was to be done this year in a special production in the courtyard of the castle, in celebration of the sixth centenary of its completion.

We left from Smichov station, immediately after lunch. As frequently seemed to happen at Prague railway stations, there was reconstruction going on, and having booked our tickets at the normal office, we had to walk the length of the street to a siding to find the train. This was my first trip in the usual short-distance coaches, with their wooden seats, but I found them comfortable enough. The line ran out of Prague in a south-westerly direction, through the industrial suburbs, past quarries, and under the cliff of Barrandov, soon to leave the Vltava for the Berounka, a clean, sunny, broad, peaceable river alongside which we ran all the way to Karlstejn. Rounded, forested hills rose to enclose the valley sometimes, and the familiar villas which decorate the environs of every capital city began to be a feature of the landscape, ranging from the minute hut-bungalow to the sumptuous white pavilions of the wealthy, for all these lovely districts for twenty miles around are the playgrounds of Prague, especially in any spot where the bathing is good.

Helena warned me when the first view of the castle was approaching, for it is not to be missed, being also possibly the best. The villas are almost left behind here, the valley is wilder, and on our right hand the river flowed bright in sunlight, with folded hills, dark with trees, beyond it. We stood watching these, and suddenly two green cones, superimposed one upon the other, moved apart like curtains to show the castle on its own hill beyond, to display it for a moment slowly revolving before our sight, and as gradually close over it again, so that by the time we came into the station it was quite lost.

Karlstejn is much restored, and bears little resemblance to the original castle, as seen in prints; but I guarantee that when the hills unclose and show it to you as you pass in the train, you will not care if it has been restored a hundred times. Above the widening V of the hills the third hill soars in green of trees and sheer grey of rock, and out of it towards the summit the outer buildings begin to grow as if the wind had rooted some stone seeds there long ago. Flanking towers buttress the walls from below, thrusting up strong, blunt steeple roofs to punctuate the sturdy crenellated fortifications, which run up and down the sheer rocks and recede into the trees. Higher again the main buildings climb within this frame, three great masses of masonry moving upward like irregular steps, with steep dark Gothic roofs above the light stone, and many windows looking down upon the valley. And above these again, on the highest point of the hill, stands the tower, rearing the same peaked roof against a pale-blue early summer sky. It is as if the rock had flowered.

At close quarters it is possible to be superior about Karlstejn, but I defy any but the most impervious of mortals to find fault with its placing in the scene.

Leaving the station, we walked back a little way on the same side of the river, and came to the bridge. On the castle side the road runs, glossy and dark, under sheer hillsides, which encroach so closely upon the waterside that in some places the way has had to be cut through the rock itself. A little further back still on this side, and there opens on the left the sudden valley which conceals the village, winding away into the folds of the hills. Accordingly the village is long and thin, rising slowly along road and brook which thread it together; and once well into it you see the castle again, overhanging the little colour-washed houses and modest red roofs with the splendour and inappropriateness of a vision. As you walk through the village the road grows steeper, passes close about the foot of the rock, and winds round it in a rising spiral, to reach the pathway which again rises left-handed to the gates. By then you have made a complete circuit of the castle hill, and on the last stretch of the climb have reached the walls, and are walking within them, looking out over the valley as from a terrace.

We entered the courtyard by an archway under a guard

tower, and walked into the auditorium of the sixth-centen-
ary theatre, where several workmen were busy filling the
level cobbled space with wooden benches, ready for the
play. The stage was a watch-platform raised to look out
over the wall, and the small space about it; it looked very
modest, but the castle itself was used as a containing setting,
and the king's suite galloped up through the archway and
dismounted there just as they did six hundred years ago.
I regret I missed the performance.

Another archway on the left leads into the inner court,
and here we arrived with a bump at the commercial side
of antiquity, complete with cloakroom, admission tickets
and picture postcards. We were the only people there at the
moment, so while we waited for a party Helena led me
down many steps to the well-house, a big, barn-like room
where the great stone-rimmed mouth gaped at us six feet
wide, and behind it, reaching high into the shadows, the
enormous wheel which worked it, wide enough for two
men to tread it abreast. The shaft was sunk by the miners
of Kutna Hora, and a tremendous undertaking it must have
been, when you consider the elevation of the castle on its
rock. The timbers which sustain the wheel are the original
ones; you may believe this, for they are punctilious in
pointing out everything which is not original, instead of
leaving you to suspect as much. An old man dipped a
ladleful of water from the bucket on the rim, and dropped
it into the well, slowly counting off eight seconds before the
faint chime of its arrival came up to us clearly. He is even
willing to drop the bucket when he has volunteers to fetch
it up again, which happens more often than you might
think. Once, he says, two young soldiers set out to break
the record, and did it on the run in about three minutes;
but today no one felt like reducing their time, and there
were no offers for the job.

Castles may be as individual as they please, but the

c*

process of being shown round them is much the same everywhere. When there were enough of us to make the effort worth while, we were marshalled in the inner court by a young girl, and led away briskly up a staircase and into the first rooms.

Our guide had a demure face and dark, gay eyes; and on beginning her official recital in each room she would fold her hands, drop the pitch of her voice several notes, and put on a lecture manner quite different from her everyday one. But her lively eyes remained throughout sharply aware of her own absurdity and ours.

The first room is full of drawings, paintings and prints, dating back several centuries. Here you can see how the castle looked before the final restoration of the late nineteenth century, with its shallower Renaissance roofs from about 1590, which some critics prefer to the present romantic Gothic ones, pierced with small eyelets and overhanging in deep eaves. But to me the high tower looks, in these older prints, like a very large man wearing a hat many sizes too small for him; for once I am on the side of the nineteenth century.

From the windows there were irresistible views of the valley and the village, and the wooded hills rising to front us on our own level. In the Hussite wars the castle was besieged from these neighbour hills, and so badly battered that for long afterwards it was left to go to ruin. The range was not too great for mangonels as well as cannon, and by lobbing into the castle rubbish and carrion, in addition to stones, the investing armies showed an almost twentieth-century appreciation of the possibilities of bacteriological warfare, and started an effective epidemic. But the stormy days of Karlstejn, I hope, are long over.

The tour is nicely calculated to work through a crescendo, from the outer halls of the knights, and the museum rooms full of relics from the past, through the austere royal apart-

ments with the king's private altar and incomparably
uncomfortable-looking prie-Dieu, through the loftier building which holds the chapels of the Virgin and Saint
Catherine, and the bare stone prison of the Cervenka, to end
with the high tower, and the Chapel of the Holy Cross.

The real treasury begins with the chapels of the Virgin
and Saint Catherine. The large chapel of the Virgin has
walls covered with contemporary paintings of the life of
Charles, and from the Apocalypse, faded and damaged a
little by the passage of time, but still very fresh and bright.
The ceiling is bright blue for heaven, full of gilt and silver
stars and small, surprised, half-length angels, and there
is a charming little figure of Saint Catherine, in the back-
ward-bent attitude of the Middle Ages, when the gait of
women was modelled on the frequent, slow-moving dignity
of pregnancy. The tiny chapel dedicated to her opens
from a corner of this room, and is built entirely into the
wall. To enter it you go through a small doorway, long
lost, turn left again after the few paces needed to carry you
the thickness of the wall, and you stand looking into a
narrow vaulted chamber, with heavy ceiling bosses knotting
the groins, and its walls encrusted all over with semi-
precious stones in the Czech fashion, great polished polygons of amethyst and jasper and agate and topaz. Low in
the wall on the left is a passage big enough to admit papers;
for here Charles used to immure himself sometimes in a more
than Lenten austerity, and even for state business he would
not leave the chapel until his retreat was completed. In the
meantime, the Empire could not be altogether neglected;
hence essential business was conducted through this hand-
slit in the wall.

The high tower is approached by a long enclosed bridge
of wood from this building, and before its doorway you see
the natural rock breaking through and welding itself into
the masonry of the ramparts. The walls of the tower are

enormously thick, for they had to guard the jewels of the
Holy Roman Empire and the charter of Bohemia. The
staircase winds about the interior of the tower, and its walls
are painted with the legends of St. Vaclav and his grandmother St. Ludmila, the patrons of the land. At the head
of the staircase you enter the king's treasure-casket.

The chapel is broad, and not very lofty, and the roof-
vaulting springs from rather low in the walls, dividing them
into six equal arched spaces, one in either end, and two in
either side wall. A gilded screen cuts the room accurately
in two. The lower part of the walls, to the articulation of the
vaulting, is formed of precious stones as in St. Catherine's
chapel, set in crosses, and the interstices between them
gilded and filled with smaller veined polygons of onyx,
agate and amethyst. The whole of the ceiling is gilded,
and covered entirely with starry bosses, and above the
chancel the sun shines golden on the right hand, and the
moon silver on the left. Originally all of these stars were of
gold; many still remain, but the lost ones cannot be
replaced by their peers in these days, and the new ones are
of gilt. But perhaps most precious of all, the six spaces
between gold ceiling and jewelled lower walls are filled
with a series of fourteenth-century paintings of all the
saints you can imagine, and some of whom I had never
heard, each in his own square gilded frame, and bearing
his particular insignia of martyrdom. The names of some
of the artists are known and respected, Dietrich of Prague,
Nicholas Wurmser, Thomas of Modena. The collection
must surely be unique, and is in wonderful preservation.

When we had gazed our fill we wandered down the
stairs again, past the grievous pictured story of St. Ludmila and her grandson, and made our way down from this
highest point by the walls, gazing out as we went from the
eyrie of kings to the cottages of common men in the valley.

I have found people who dismiss Karlstejn as phoney,

but I do not agree with them. It is much restored, but with love, and I think effectively, and every care is taken to indicate what is new, and what a genuine legacy from 1360; and if you add up the genuine you find that it is very much, and very beautiful, and if you regard the new without prejudice you must acknowledge that it is worthy and on the whole wise. Moreover, at the end of all your criticisms the odds are that you will suddenly catch that view of it again from the village or the train, and it will take your breath away just as it did the first time, and leave you content that anything so lovely should have survived six centuries to give you pleasure, whether changed or unchanged.

In a little restaurant at the crest of the village we drank coffee, and ate rolls which Helena had had the forethought to bring with her, since in the less frequented places it is sometimes difficult to buy food at tea-time. Then, convinced that we had almost three quarters of an hour before we need be at the station, we walked back very gently, and stood for a while on the bridge, admiring the smooth sweep of the Berounka, between its cliffs and meadows. While we lingered here a train went past in the direction of Prague, but secure in Helena's three re-checks we thought no evil. All the same, said Helena reflectively as we walked on, it was queer that she hadn't noticed one in the time-table at this precise time; but we would look again when we reached the station.

It was reassuring to find several people waiting on the station when we reached it, but since like all small Bohemian stations it was single-sided, and therefore both lines were approached from the same spot, our companions might well be waiting for a train in the opposite direction. So we looked up the train again, to make doubly sure.

"There you are!" said Helena in triumph. "Just as I said—it's due in a quarter of an hour, and——" Here she stopped with a gasp and a groan, and then began to laugh. Against the train was a small symbol which we traced below to its meaning: "Only on Sundays and holidays". Helena had done it again.

The next train to Prague was in about an hour and a half. We began to laugh so immoderately that two cheerful-looking workmen who were standing close by asked us, quite simply, to share the joke. They proved to be perfect examples of the regular traveller who in all countries knows the railway system a great deal better than the average railwayman does.

"There's a train due for Beroun in a few minutes," they said. "If you come along with us on that, you can get a train back to Prague from there without waiting so long."

A railwayman, on the other hand, joined in to assure us that we should not.

"Take no notice of him," said our friends blithely. "Go and book returns from here to Beroun. We haven't been travelling this line all these years for nothing."

"I'm catching it myself, anyhow," added the younger one.

So Helena ran, in a great hurry because the Beroun train was already coming in, and booked two returns to cover the remaining distance, and we all scrambled into the nearest coach together, and puffed away in the opposite direction to the one we wanted to go.

They spoke no English, but some of their conversation Helena translated for me, and some of it was plain to be read in their lively gestures and gay grins. I never saw two merrier men; the younger one especially was bubbling over with fun, and kept us entertained all the way to Beroun. Hearing that I was English, he wished to know what was my impression of CSR, and gave me his own views in one sentence, which Helena translated gravely: "He says: 'Everyone smiles, but has a sorrow in his heart.'"

I looked at him intently, and was, and still am, utterly at

a loss to decide how seriously I was meant to take this, for his eyes were still twinkling with fun, and when I said truthfully: "I don't believe it!" he burst into delighted laughter, and went on cracking jokes until the guard came along to examine our tickets. The situation became still funnier then, for it seemed that in his haste the booking clerk at Karlstejn had given Helena one adult ticket and one child's, and we had now to buy yet a fifth ticket to cover the deficiency.

At Beroun we left the train, and were in the act of referring the matter to a railwayman again, since our friends were somewhat behind us in leaving the coach, when the merry young man shot across towards a siding, waving us wildly with him.

"Take no notice of him, he knows nothing. That train goes to Prague by the other route, and it's due out at once."

He had been right up to now, and was obviously used to doing this, so we took his word for it, and shot aboard just in time, as the train pulled out. He travelled with us only one station, and then made his farewells, and withdrew in the direction of home, still laughing. As for us, we proceeded peacefully towards Prague, by a higher plateau route where the wind swept across wide fields, in contrast to the Berounka valley. In the end it proved to be a quicker way back, and we were as early at Smichov as if Helena's Sunday train had really been running.

"We shall have our work cut out to explain five tickets to the ticket-collector," I said, as we walked along the long platform towards the exit, "especially the child's."

"We shan't explain them," said Helena firmly, "we shall just hand him the lot, and go past quickly and get on a tram before he has time to work it out."

Which we did, and trammed home shakily in the twilight to reassure Karel that his wife's reputation as a travel agent was still unimpaired.

6

Prague from the Cab of a Lorry

Mr. Vesely wanted some lacquers for the house, and found that the factory which was perfectly willing to supply him could not do so for want of one of the raw materials; so he contrived to get hold of the required ingredient for himself, and one afternoon took it out to the works by lorry. It was not a matter of a great quantity, only one drum of white powder, but enough for his needs; and as I was at a loose end until Helena called for me at four o'clock, he suggested that I should ride with him.

Our way lay over Hlavka Bridge, which crosses the island of Stvanice, and through the outskirts of the New Town to the National Museum, where we turned left and drove up the Avenue of Marshal Stalin, for we were heading out of town due east, a way I remembered well from the previous year, when we were out at Jevany, and had always to enter Prague by this road. The extraordinary modern church in King George Square, dark grey and studded with whiter points, with a tower, if that is the word for it, very broad from the front and extremely narrow from the side, like an exaggerated tympanum, had been one of my land-marks on these drives. It rose now suddenly on our left hand, impressive and strange, and I knew where we were. We had one call to make, then we returned to the long, straight, wide avenue levelling itself purposefully eastward, and soon we were running between the cemetery walls of Olsany.

These cemeteries also I remembered; no one who has once driven the length of their walls could forget them. All I had seen yet was what one sees from the road, the long, high walls almost completely hidden by flower stalls, wreaths, lamps, stones, urns, all the bright accoutrements of death in Czechoslovakia; but in particular a shimmer of flowers in all colours, made into crosses, hearts, cushions, growing in pots, cut in blazing bunches, flowers in every imaginable shape. Above this dazzle of gold and flame and blue rose the trees which give shade everywhere within the walls. In and out of the main gates of the cemetery many people were moving; the Czechs tend graves with scrupulous care.

Not far beyond this place the tram-lines end, and the town becomes increasingly green with the encroaching fields of the country. We went on until the occasional groupings of houses close to the road had ceased to be particles of the town flung off in its energetic growth, and become clearly villages, with a life of their own. The road rose, and began to roll gently over wide fields, proceeding in long-sighted leaps in the direction of Kutna Hora. Presently we turned right from the road by a narrow lane, and there were the long, low white buildings of the little factory, and the usual scattering of interesting things in its yard, scrap and empty barrels, and sacks both fat and flat. We drove in, and turned about in the space before the sheds, to make departure easy.

I had supposed that I might be in the way, and was willing to stay in the cab for the few minutes we should be here, but Mr. Vesely drew me out with him, and we went into the sheds together, while two of the men rolled in the keg of powder. Mr. Vesely soon disappeared into the office, and I was left free to roam about and investigate the many interesting smells of gums and shellacs and spirits, and the bright colours which lurked in the bottoms of empty cans and glass vessels along the benches by the wall. It was a very personal sort of place, small and pleasantly casual. The benches carried small scales, tins of materials, unidentifiable bottles, and drums of turpentine and spirit. By the time Mr. Vesely came back I had had my fingers in several intriguing mixtures, and found a large notice saying: "No Smoking!" which I pointed out accusingly; for, as always, he had a cigarette going.

On the way back we had another call to make in the suburb of Strasnice, to the south of the Avenue of Marshal Stalin. Suburb is the right word, I suppose, for shops and houses of the city kind came with us downhill to the small workshop where we stopped; but just beyond, the cul-de-sac ended, blunting itself against a field, and the buildings in sight there suddenly disposed themselves country fashion among cultivation, and dwindled to the character and comfortable low shape of cottages. Another swallowed-up village, not yet quite digested.

Here we dived through a doorway and down a short flight of steps to a long, cool workshop below ground-level, where one man was cutting up a sheet of thick tin into rectangles, and another was converting these rapidly into large cans. A little office was shut off at the end, and a door at the back led off into interesting prospects of pipes and tins and assorted metalwork. It seemed to be another small family business, of the kind father and sons and sons-in-law might run between them.

We had come to collect various drain-pipes, collars and joints which were being made here for the house, but had to content ourselves with taking away a very small part of what was due. Getting delivery of any kind of building material was the same type of endurance test as in England, it seemed; one waited, and grumbled, and wondered what things were coming to, while the houses grew by painful inches. However, we took what we could get, and drove on philosophically towards home.

When we reached the main gates of the cemetery, where the custodian had a little office, Mr. Vesely stopped the lorry and asked if we had time to go in. I thought we had, for Helena was not coming until four; and I was very glad to have a glimpse behind the high, flower-hidden wall. The grave of Mrs. Vesela's family was here, and he wished to visit it and water the flowers which were planted on it. The custodian produced two large cans of water, and off we went, threading the long avenues of the most modern part of the Catholic cemetery. And when he had refreshed the flowers, which were mercifully shaded by trees, and plucked away one or two almost invisible hairs of grass which had ventured to root among them since the last visit, we returned the cans, and set off on a tour of the whole place.

Like the old Jewish graveyard, it is full of trees, though less thickly covered from sight than that secret spot. There are many wych elms, leaning protectively over some of the older stones. You see whole colonies of German names together, from the time under Austria, and many of these have now no one to care for them so exquisitely as the Czech graves are cared for, though all are kept neat. Many things interested me here, for the attitude to death of the living of a race is a very revealing window on the race itself. We have well-kept English graveyards, of course, but seldom do they reach the stage of being gardens in their own right. Here almost every plot had growing flowers, and there appeared to be no convention about mourning colours, for the rainbow itself could be no more brilliant. Yet the convention of family mourning in personal dress still holds good, and startles you daily in the street by the sight of young girls in dead black from head to foot, and older women in funeral veils into the bargain. The period prescribed for such challenging shows of grief is not long, at least for the young people, but it seems all the more remarkable that the custom should have survived the war, and the textile shortage, which between them effectively ended its dwindling existence in Britain.

Besides this blaze of flowers, every grave here has a lantern to hold a candle or small lamp. Often they are built into the head-stones, or sometimes stand separately before them. On All Saints and All Souls—perhaps on one or two other festivals also—all these lamps are lighted. I should like to see Olsany then.

Another thing strange to me was the idea of having the picture of the dead person somewhere on the grave. Usually it was a photograph, framed under glass and set into the stone, but sometimes it was reproduced by some curious process in the surface of the stone itself, a clear black and white photograph staring out from polished grey granite, with eerie effect. I did not care for this custom at all. Photographs are bad enough interpreters even in life; it seems to me that the imagination, unassisted, could do a better job of perpetuating after death what was memorable in a person. Yet it can happen that one's heart is caught sometimes by a face looking out so. Inside the court of the Clemtinum there is a solitary grave, one of the many which spring up under your feet in the streets, along Letna under the trees, everywhere, since Prague became a battlefield in May, 1945; a young boy, killed on that spot. His grave, youthful face compels you to stop and salute him with your attention for the moment he needs to make you remember him for life. There is another, even younger, in the cemetery outside the abominable little fortress at Terezin; he is about sixteen and he laughs. Neither is he lightly to be forgotten. Is that enough, I wonder, to justify all the unfortunate reproductions by which the dead, if they could be consulted, would scarcely choose to be remembered?

We crossed the road at length to visit the Russian cemetery, and the place where the men of the Resistance are buried. There is a little Russian church there for Orthodox funerals, and somewhat aside from it the sudden red-and-white flamelike enclosure of the Russian war graves, where lie the men of the Red Army who fell in the relief of Prague. This is an imposing sight. At one end is a memorial, tall and white, upon which all the graves face; and every stone is uniform in its slightly tapered shape and brightly white surface, and the red star which marks it; but here, too, there are sometimes photographs, and the faces which look out at you, proud and good-humoured in their uniform, are the faces of individual young men. In the gentle personal atmosphere of the family cemetery I had regretted the pictures; but here they seemed to me to do some real service for the men buried among strangers.

A little further on we came to another enclosure, with a flagstaff in the centre of a patch of thin turf, and a much smaller number of graves grouped round it. The ground here had an arid look, and many of the graves were marked only by wooden crosses still, though they were tidily kept. I saw that these were British dead, most of them R.A.F., some, surprisingly, from the army. There has been, I think, a great deal of difficulty in identifying some of them, and verifying the identification of others, which accounts for the fact that they have still only the original temporary crosses. How it will look eventually it is too early to say. At the moment it presents a very sad appearance by comparison with the rest of the cemetery.

By now we had used up all our spare time, and drove straight home, where Helena picked me up, and we went away to the Kinsky Gardens to visit the Museum of National Culture, and later to meet Karel for supper at the garden restaurant on Petrin, where we sat late over the lights of Prague.

The next day was Corpus Christi. Already I had seen little street altars, decorated with images and greenery, going up for the occasion on Hradcany Square and in many other places, and I found that our own Strossmayer Square had one, also, as well as two or three flower-sellers with their baskets, waiting to capture the custom of the devout, who must have flowers for the procession. Many little girls were scurrying about in their best long festival frocks, pale pink and white and flowered, clutching little baskets decorated with ribbons and early roses, great butter-fly bows standing proudly in their hair. But I spent the day out of town with Helena and Karel, an hour or so away from Prague, at the villa of a friend, so I saw no more of the celebrations.

We spent a lazy day in the garden of the villa, and in the late afternoon walked through the forest by lovely aromatic paths some five miles to the railway station at Vsenory, where we took a train for home. After this lotus-eating day I slept late. My alarm-clock in the mornings was the chorus of indefatigable housekeepers beating carpets in the interior court of the flats, which was under my window. It was divided, this court, into many little enclosures, one for each house, with a patch of grass and some little trees in the centre. Here on wooden frames they spread out their rugs every morning, and woke vociferous echoes from the high enclosing walls as they beat them. And in the process, as a rule, they also woke me; but after a day spent entirely in the open air I was more than usually difficult to wake, and disgraced myself by being still in bed when Mrs. Burianova brought in my breakfast. Coffee, "but not from coffee" as Honza used to say, and "buchty", yeast buns filled with a paste of poppy-seed, for which I had developed a very decided liking. But if, like certain foreign athletes of whom Helena told me, you are afraid of being drugged by this unfamiliar delicacy, you may fill them with jam, or fruit, or whatever mixture you like best.

This morning I went out with Mr. Vesely again, first to a factory in Zizkov, and then out to a large timber-yard for a load of wood for floor-boarding. Over Hlavka Bridge again to Zizkov, under the railway line, and round the westward end of the long, lofty ridge of Zizkov hill, where the Resistance Memorial rears itself high in air like a great white stone ship which never sails, the Czech lion for its figurehead. South of the ridge is the suburb of Zizkov itself, rising more gradually again southward to another hill; and north of it is Karlin, flattened between the ridge and the river, a slightly dingier quarter, full of factories, with a large barracks which was full of SS troops in 1945, and gave plenty of trouble before it was reduced.

We drove up a short, steep hill into a narrow yard, where turning the lorry proved none too easy, and Mr. Vesely went off in search of more pipes. Here we were shut in by high, old buildings put together at complicated angles, like any warehouse quarter of any city. I know back alleys in Liverpool which have exactly the same flavour. I sat in the cab, swopped a few laborious words with one of the workmen who paused to pass the time of day, and watched everything which went on within my vision. I liked these retired corners of the town, where time seemed no object, in spite of the fact that CSR had become a land of targets and two-year plans.

Here again the summing up of our success, it seemed, was: "Malo, malo!" "Little, very little!" But we took what we could get, and jolted down the narrow cobbled hill again and under the railway bridge, and turned east through Zizkov, with the pipes rolling gaily about in the back, and we two bounding off the cushions in the cab. The lorry behaved like a skittish pup when it was not loaded, and Honza, because of his height, had to take great care, when he drove it, to avoid cracking his head against the roof; but when loaded fairly heavily it was as sweetly reasonable as a tactful wife.

We bounded down a long hill, with the railway below us on the left, and a large white hospital towering over us on the right, crossed the line at the foot by the usual black-and-white-poled level crossing, turned into Queen's Avenue, and set off purposefully north-eastwards out of town, through the industrial suburbs of Liben and Vysocany. Liben and Holesovice hold hands across Liben Bridge, one encircled by the eastward detour of the Vltava, the other sitting outside it; they have harbours, and build river vessels here, and interesting things go on with dredgers, lighters, trains of barges, and all sorts of craft. Vysocany joins itself loosely to the eastern fringe of Liben, and sprawls away from town until it has almost detached itself altogether. The trams grow tired of the long, straight run along Queen's Avenue, and turn back into Prague again; and the road leaves the factory-lined suburban street, and winds away to the north into field country, climbing as it goes, to the wide upland plains where the military airfield lies, with a thick white water-tower making a landmark for miles around.

We skirted the rim of the airfield, and turned in through a gateway in a long wooden fence, past a little office where people were handing in their permits for buying wood, and parked the lorry near to the gate while Mr. Vesely went in search of the person he wanted to see. I was again allowed to wander about as I liked, and made good use of my time. Here we stood rather high, and had discovered a bleak little wind, sharp enough to remind us that after all it was still only May.

The timber-yard was level and large, and full of piles of wood in planks and beams. People were coming in and diving into the office with their permits every few minutes, a man with a van, two little boys with a hand-trolley, a woman with a basket, who presently bore away one modest beam of wood under her arm. A young husband and wife, also with a handcart, were trying to assemble on it a load of wood much too big for the accommodation, loading and unloading and beginning again with infinite patience. Further along, the buildings of the sawmill began, and a set of trolley rails made easy running for the wagons propelled by hand from one block to another. I like the scent and sound of sawmills; even some Czechoslovak paper has that smell of fresh-cut wood about it, a warm, light-brown smell. There were many women employed here; they brought the trolleys along, four or five of them pushing heftily together, and usually a good deal of laughter and noise came along with them. Some were mere girls, a few middle-aged women; to judge by their faces and their unending flow of back-chat, they were enjoying themselves.

We had to move the lorry up a little to draw it alongside the woodpile from which it was to be loaded. The planks were very long, much longer than the body of the lorry, and the longest protruded so far that their weight seemed precariously aswing on the tail, ready to shift an inch or two the wrong way and spill out when we drove off. When the tally was complete they were tied down, but even so the balance remained capricious, and from the time that we set off again westward along the edge of the airfield I was continually peering through the back window to make sure we hadn't yet shaken anything adrift. We became a sort of Sister Anne act, every few minutes asking and answering:

"Is it all right?"

"Yes, it's all right."

We had to crawl all the way to Troja, but even so our lively load clapped its hands for joy every time we went over a bump or round a corner. Early in the trip we attached a red rag to the end of the planks, where it waved gallantly as we went. The drive was an easy one, since we had not to return into the town; but under these conditions it was also a very slow one. When we finally crept along the unmade road to the house, Mr. Vesely set to work to unload his planks single-handed, for except at week-ends he had usually only perhaps one man working indoors, and sometimes no one at all. He declined help scornfully, and tore into the job as if his life depended on it, while I went up to the crest of the hill behind the house to look at Prague from a new angle.

There are some wonderful views to be had from the tops of the Troja hills, clean across the nearest stretch of the Vltava, across the promontory of Holesovice to the other bend of the river and the spires and towers of the Old and New Towns; and on the right hand, standing high and lovely as from every way, the crown of the Hradcany.

Behind you, as you stand there among the goats and allotments and week-end huts, there is no more of Prague. Troja is in it, but not of it, and beyond the villa fringe, and even within it, keeps all the characteristics of the village. For this reason, because it has a foot in both worlds, I find Troja particularly attractive; but it has its drawbacks as a dwelling place. To walk through Stromovka and across the boat bridge is delightful on a spring day, when you have all the afternoon at your disposal; but imagine doing it in bad weather with a heavy basket full of groceries! And the only alternative is that maddening jaunt by bus and tram, all the way round by the Barricades Bridge.

The new house, of which the outer building was already complete, stood on sloping ground; the soil had been cut away from the back, and one entered by walking a long plank across a gulf. Honza delighted in exaggerating the spring of his step in the middle of the passage, when his gait became a series of chamois bounds; but people less secure of their balance went more staidly. Half-way up the staircase there was a hollow in the brickwork of the wall, which was not yet plastered, and here a mother bird was raising four young ones in a cosily retired nest, quite undisturbed by the passing workmen. They were Mr. Vesely's pets; he was fond of birds. This time the nest appeared to me to be empty, and I was afraid some neighbour's cat had had a lucky find.

"Oh, they've gone!" I said, craning to look inside, the hole being slightly high for me.

"No, they haven't," said Mr. Vesely, and made a minute chirping noise, whereupon four enormous red mouths opened in the dim brownness of the nest. The house was already helping one mother to rear a family in comfort, at any rate. She raised them successfully, and much later they left, thus kindly allowing the electric wiring to be done, and the walls plastered, with inconvenience to nobody, except Mr. Vesely, who had to keep dipping his hand ever deeper into his pocket.

We were very late going back for lunch that day, and he remarked cheerfully that he would be beaten for it. The truth was that he went in and out exactly as he pleased, of course, and was never expected back until someone saw him coming; and Mrs. Vesela's peculiar magic was that there was always a meal ready for him when he did come in, no matter how unearthly the hour he chose for his return.

When we all came out here together only three of us could ride in the cab, so it was Honza's lot to ride behind; and when he did so, as sometimes happened, in clothes too precious to be risked by sitting on the side of the lorry, he would stand balancing himself like a trick rider round all the hairpin bends and over the bumps of Troja's roads, and one of us would be continually looking behind to reassure the others that he was still aboard. He would descend at the end of the ordeal as grave and debonair as he got up, and remark tranquilly that his father drove rather slowly!

7

The Deserted Spa

At the end of May, on Sunday, the 30th, came the election. Voting in CSR had always been on a system of proportional representation, and on an agreed party list; and on this occasion the agreement between all four parties on a joint list for each district had robbed the poll of its interest, since there was now obviously nothing to do but vote for or against one set list of candidates. To vote against was to vote for nothing, since in spite of the avowed right to stand as an independent with the backing of any group or groups representing over a thousand people, no one, so far as I know, had availed himself of this privilege. However, to permit at least the vote of dissent, a blank of the same size as the candidate list was issued to all voters. But at the same time there was a strong disposition to attach the stigma of treason to anyone who used it. Posters about the streets read: "White ticket—black intentions!" or hinted that the use of the white vote would be limited to those who planned another Munich. I should not like to give the impression, however, that this feeling was confined to enthusiastic Communists or the printers of propaganda posters. I know of at least one among the gentlest of my friends who told me that he was sincerely troubled in mind with regard to any deviation from absolute solidarity at such a time, for fear what seemed merely a statement of independence should prove a weapon in the hands of reaction.

A far worse error was the declaration that the vote need not be secret. The Czechs had always been used to voting behind a screen, as we do, by inserting the list of their choice in an envelope, which they then posted in the ballot box, and discarded the other ones in a basket. The procedure remained the same, and the furnishing of the polling booths also; the only change was that people were told they need not take advantage of the screen if they did not wish to do so. Whether the intention was sinister or not, the obvious result was to make some people afraid of using the screen, lest they should be different from their neighbours, and be marked down as men who had something to hide. Especially was this the case in small communities where everyone knew everyone else. I regretted the change deeply, for Czechoslovakia's own sake, but was eager to hear at least how the actual machinery of the booths worked, since a great deal depended on the local election commissions. On balance it was much as you might expect; where the first voters in the morning, whether from design or habit, walked behind the screen to vote, the whole procession throughout the day followed them solidly. Where the earliest comers were determined to make their vote as public as possible, or for exactly opposite reasons feared to make them private, others were inclined to resign themselves to the same procedure. I was interested to see, in the newsreels afterwards, that several of the ministers of the retiring government voted secretly.

The arrangement of the booth made a good deal of difference, too, since obviously where the screen was placed handily it could be used with less unease than when pushed aside into a corner. But it did not always work out as would have been expected. I heard of some polling stations where the screen was placed at a conspicuous distance from the tables, and yet where the whole procession of voters moved resolutely round it, and of others where it was readily available, and yet went almost unused. I also heard of at least one booth where the Communist member of the commission supervising sent everyone behind the screen, so that no differences could possibly be made between them.

Polling day began in slight drizzle, but later it cleared up, and the afternoon was cool but fine. I spent it up the river, with Jaroslav and his little boy, going by river steamer to Zbraslav, where part of the national collection of paintings is housed in the castle once used by Franck. The town is small and pretty, and over it hangs a beautiful wooded hill with the church poised like a small castle on top. But we left it fairly early, and chose to walk back part of the way to Prague beside the Vltava. Midway there is a village—I have forgotten its name—where Jaroslav used to lodge once, just before the end of the war, when the Praguers rose against the Germans, who thereupon tried to move in all available troops from the countryside around to suppress the insurrection in the city. Here at this village some small gesture of defiance displeased them, perhaps even held up their advance upon Prague for a time. They took from each house one man, and shot them all, sixty-five, including a few soldiers. Their mass grave is here beside the main road. This was the natural instinct of the German even when he knew his war was virtually over, for three days later even Prague had peace.

We know of so many such incidents that they cease to mean very much to us; but I was with Jaroslav, who could read down the list of the dead, and pause at every one to point out the house where he lived, to remember his parents, or his children, to describe some little personal way he had. He knew them all. For that reason it is right that we should not only read and remember the things which were done, but visit and talk with those who survived at close quarters, if we want to come anywhere near understanding.

Imagination is not enough. I knew about the other hostages taken out of Prague flats and offices at this same time, forced to remove their own barricades to let the tanks through, and afterwards to walk before those tanks for a screen, so that the defenders could not even use their pitiful small arms against them without killing their brothers. I knew, but believe me, I knew a good deal more about it when I had heard the story from Jaroslav, who had been one of them. I knew about the separation of husband and wife who fell victim to the anti-Semitic perversion of the German mind, and were swept away into distant concentration camps; but it came home like something quite new when I heard Zdenek say of his wife Jana: "I looked for her everywhere, and I found her at last in Belsen."

By the time we had got back into town some loudspeakers were already giving election results, and outside party headquarters and on Wenceslas Square large crowds were standing to listen; in some places they had already begun to dance in the streets. It was all over bar the shouting, and there was not much of that. But the monument to the sixty-five hostages murdered in that village on the way to Zbraslav linked up with peculiar significance with this election day, for me at least. That grave represents what is and must always be a strong and constant factor in Czech politics, so long as the world remains divided, perhaps the strongest of all, since it can reconcile the otherwise irreconcilable.

The following day I went to Karlovy Vary with Helena. We had booked our tickets with a little coach office which ran regular services, usually taking one batch of holiday-makers or patients and returning in the evening with a load of unfortunates whose holiday was over, but often carrying day-trippers like ourselves among its passengers, too. The journey took about three hours, with one stop on the way, and our tickets covered some sort of snack at the inn where we should make the halt. None the less, Mrs. Vesela would not let me go without ample provisions in case the snack was inadequate; and as the start was to be very early, and by this time I was trusted to get about unaided, I did not have to disturb the family in the morning, but got myself up by a borrowed alarm-clock, and made my way by tram to the National Theatre.

Several people were already waiting behind the theatre for our coach, most of them laden with luggage. We had planned to be early so that we could stake our claim to good places, but the bus waited until everybody was assembled, and then came in, with the result that everyone let go of his conversation instantly, grabbed his luggage, and made a bolt for the doorway. I freely admit I am not up to Czech standards at grabbing seats in buses. Helena did well, but not well enough, and the best we could do was two separate seats; it was not important, except that it was a defeat, and this game, like most other games in CSR, is played to win. Strictly within the rules, and good-temperedly but with all one's might.

Helena had asked her neighbour, even before I got into the coach at all, if he would be so kind as to change to the single seat opposite, and let us sit together; but he saw no reason why he should, and said so vigorously. As he was also nursing a large suitcase on the seat beside him, and so leaving her only half of her due space, Helena promptly retaliated by calling out to the driver to ask if all luggage should not be banished to the roof. The suitcase was removed in spite of its owner's grumbles, and honours were even. We proceeded to settle down and consolidate.

The road to Karlovy Vary heads out of Prague due west, and soon after the last traces of the capital are left behind, the first traces of the Kladno region of mines begin. The villages have hardly time to be characteristic Bohemian villages before they again become uncharacteristic, their clustering cottages darkening into the closer concentration of mining houses, their background of level green fields, beet and strip crops and occasional pasture, broken by the shafts and slag heaps of the pits. The road avoids Kladno itself, but passes near it, and a mere shadow of the grey appearance of English industrial areas dims the bright Bohemian colours of the countryside for a while. The road moved ahead of us in long leaps, only slightly undulating, and soon I saw away on the left a clump of trees and a small roof, and a light-coloured wall enclosing a plot of ground which by its size suggested a village cemetery. I knew it from photographs; this was Lany, where the Masaryks are buried, one of the most sacred spots in the country.

Once we were clear of the mining districts the hop-fields began, and among the crops on both sides of the road sprang up the familiar lace-work of poles and lines, with the green tendrils already climbing sturdily. Some of the gardens showed a flourishing growth, and were saluted with approving comment from the bus as we passed. The farmers had had a bad time with their beet, I heard, by reason of some disease, and whole fields of it had had to be ploughed in and treated before a new crop could be sown; which would mean, even if the second sowing did well, a late harvest and a smaller sugar content. And sugar is white gold in more than name to CSR. But at least we agreed the hops looked well, and though the grain was very short for the time of year it might yet be satisfactory, given a better supply of rain. There had been showers enough, at least, to allay the fears of another disastrous drought like last summer's.

Soon the ground began to rise, and distant hills heaved themselves out of the horizon, as we reached the soft inward edges of the border country. More upland pasture, more cattle out at graze, more richly scented pine-woods, and the villages shedding, little by little, their red Bohemian roofs

D

for mountain slates of grey. More ominous sign of the approach to the hills, the ditches of our road began to show us on either side a rotting harvest of scrap metal, some of it still recognisable as German transport, complete even to the shot marks, some of it fallen apart into rusted plates of steel and twisted tangles of engine mashed together into an inextricable mess, a mere mud of metal. All of these had been wrecked in that wild rush to escape from the country in 1945, when the war machine of the Reich finally fell apart, spirit and all; wrecked, and pushed madly from the road to clear the way for others in just as great a hurry behind.

"Surely," I said, "this stuff is worth collecting. Why don't they fetch it away for scrap?"

"They say it would cost as much to carry it as it would fetch," said Helena, "and probably more. So here it lies until we can gradually find time and labour to move it."

Well, it does not beautify the road to the mountains, but it does make it a stimulating exercise for the imagination. You can almost feel the last waves of that panic still quivering on the air.

Higher up in the hills another memento of old stresses makes itself seen. Gleams of whitish surfaces appear along the slopes, among the pine-forests, breaking ground only here and there, the concrete emplacements of the old second line fortifications. Here you are already well into the shadow-land of the border regions, where the name of Munich lingers like the refrain of an old song about an older wrong, already legend before it is even passed from immediate memory.

An abrupt hill of curiously regular shape, like an inverted basin, but fluffy with trees in full leaf, shot up skyward on the right. Angel's Hill, Helena called it. Soon afterwards the road topped the rim of a deep valley, and began to swoop downhill into it by great zigzag leaps, down from the fringes where the lovely forests lean over it on every side, into the elegant cosmopolitan whiteness of Karlovy Vary, where it lies along the floor of the bowl. By descending levels we skipped from forests to sanatoria, all compound of suntrap windows; again to vast white wedding-cakes of hotels in architectural styles roughly between palladian and pantomime; and finally to the town, the shops and the square, the tree-shaded streets and the colonnade of the mill, where promenading water-drinkers take gentle exercise, just as they do, I suppose, in almost any spa in almost any country.

But we found, as we walked along towards the main spring, that there was something very different indeed about Karlovy Vary on this particular day. It was less a spa than the ghost of a spa. The trappings were all there, the beautifully-dressed shop windows, emptier than usual, but still exceedingly elegant, the attendants ready to draw water at the springs, the expectant hotels and sudden little funiculars which shoot away uphill in surprising places; all that was missing was the people. Even spas have a permanent population, but without their visitors they look as bleak and startled as the north shore at Blackpool in mid-winter. Karlovy was rich, lovely, polyglot but empty.

We speculated on the reason as we walked along to the pavilions which surround the main spring, a thirty-foot fountain gushing with slightly fluctuating pressure in a wide mosaic basin, the wind catching at its plume sometimes and bending it to spray the floor for yards around, for it springs at normal ceiling height into the open air. Once, said Helena, there had been a dome over it, but it had been damaged during the war, and replaced by the present curious erection of ellipses of wood, an open framework, its white paint stained brown by constant spraying.

"One of the few things for which we have to thank the Germans," said Helena. "I like it better as it is now."

The water of Karlovy stains things in time by laying over them a fine brown deposit which sets into a stone coating. In the shops we saw small ornaments which had been treated to give them a souvenir value, and I found them as unpleasing as most local souvenirs, besides being ominously suggestive.

"If it can do that to a statuette," said Helena, uttering my thoughts for me, "what could it not do to one's inside?"

None the less, we tried it; it has only a faint taste, not unpleasant, and is hot, like many of the town's springs. You may take it or bathe in it for most internal troubles, diseases of the liver and kidneys, catarrhal stomach complaints, as well as such very different illnesses as gout and diabetes. You may also come here to lose your fat, if in these days of world austerity you are rich enough to afford fat. Through the centre of the spa, past the main spring, past the baths, steaming here and there from outflow pipes discharging into it the natural hot water, flows a stream in a straight artificial channel, crossed occasionally by a bridge, and flanked by the elegant colonnades where the patients take their prescribed gentle exercise.

We met only a handful of earnest-looking promenaders walking with their china cups, like exaggerated pipes, with a hollow stem branching from the handle, through which the waters can be siphoned with proper deliberation. The cure is a leisurely but exacting business, demanding the whole of one's time if the thing is to be done properly.

When the persevering patient progresses beyond the stage of pacing the colonnade he is ordered more strenuous walks in the forests. We took the easiest way to the same delectable pastures, by a funicular railway which climbs to one of the highest spots over the town, and deposits its passengers at the foot of another prospect tower, from which they may survey the whole rolling, forested countryside. The town terminal of the line, when we entered, was deserted except for the conductor, a long young man with whimsical eyebrows, who sat in the sunniest window doing a crossword in the daily paper. He said that the car would leave in a few minutes, and seemed rather pleased to have two people in need of it.

We asked if the beginning of the season here had been as bad as it looked now.

"Oh, no," he said, "you should have seen the place last week. Things were warming up nicely. No, this is a freak week-end. All those who were here went home for the polls, and only the first handful have had time to come in today. Give us three days, and we'll be filling up again."

So the election had been responsible for emptying the spas. That implied that the overwhelming majority of the visitors were Czech. Time had been when a general election could have been held without drawing away even a considerable fraction of the spa population; the change argued on one side that more ordinary Czech citizens were enjoying the amenities of their own country, which is good, but on the other side that very few foreign visitors were bringing in valuable currency, which is undoubtedly bad for CSR, and also that few were getting the desirable treatment for their ailments, which is obviously even worse for them.

The funicular man, seeing that I was English, began a thoughtful rehearsal of his vocabulary in that language.

"Everybody comes here, so I learn all—a little! All that matters! Yes, I learn enough English. Good morning, good evening, how are you? Very nice weather! I love you!——"

We agreed that it was enough. When we finally crept up the forest hillside and parted from him at the crest he said: "Good-bye!" in his best accent, and shot back into his car delighted when I returned him: "Na shledanou!"

The lift of the wooden prospect tower was labelled

largely: "Out of order", but as we stood confronted by this blow the car nevertheless came down, opened its doors, and a smiling workman with a bag of tools beckoned us in and took us up to the view platform. He declined a tip for his services.

"He is mending the lift," explained Helena gravely. "Now he tests with us, so we get our ride free." But his work had been good, and we arrived intact.

The day was a queer mixture of shower and shine, cold wind and sunny stillness, more suited to April than the last day of May; and on top of the tower we found the wind strong and the sky overcast, so that the lovely rolling prospect of forested mountains and valley villages, and the rich white town immediately below us, did not hold us for so long as it would otherwise have done. But the journey had been well worth while for the silent woodland walk back to the town, by zigzag paths dropping in easy stages, for the descent was steep. These are old, well-grown forests, mainly coniferous, but we found on these slopes some mixed woods also. The ground under them was too deeply sheltered from sun and light to bear grass or undergrowth, but is thick in leaf mould and needles, and smells rich and still.

Half-way down we came to the place of the Deer's Leap, marked by a statue of an ibex-like animal poised on a rock overhanging the valley. Here, in the fourteenth century, a stag hunted by the king is said to have made a prodigious leap into the fields below, and struck out in the spot where it alighted the first medicinal spring. The king in question was, of course, the Karel of Karlovy Vary, the great and ubiquitous Emperor Charles IV. The leap looks as impossible as most such phenomena do, but the legend persists —as all such legends do.

On re-entering the town we made an early lunch at a restaurant with the charming name of the House of a

Beautiful Queen. While we were lingering over our coffee two young people came in and settled themselves at a table near-by. Many times I had asked my friends for an analysis of those physical peculiarities which marked me out at a hundred yards as English. Now the mystery became deeper still as Helena took one glance at these two across the room, and said promptly: "English!"

She was right, for within two minutes an English-speaking waiter had been charmed up from nowhere for them, and they were ordering in my native language. But how had she known? They looked much like anyone else to me.

"But it is plain!" said Helena. "They are typically English!"

Yes, but on another occasion she had said the same of me, and I bore no resemblance whatever to these two. What was it, I insisted, which marked us out so clearly?

"Well," she said, "you are made on a smaller mould than our women; your bones are finer, more delicate, longer. I do not know what else one can say about it, but the difference is plain to see."

Other people, at various times, gave me different answers. Honza's was perhaps the most credible. "Have you ever seen a Czech woman wearing her hair short, as you wear yours? And then, all the clothes are made differently, both the cloth and the cut. Everything you have is in a fashion not quite the same." This I find more convincing, for every day lived and every mile travelled more clearly reveals the grand delusion of a national face or a national build; but differences of custom, be it only in the making of a dress, there is no denying.

After lunch we walked out of the spa into the older part of the town, where the permanent population live, and went to see the Russian Orthodox church, which was full of small gilded ikons, some of them very beautiful and very old. One or two were solid masses of gold, with only the two small human faces looking out as strangely as eyes through the slit of a mask; odd little narrow faces with big blank eyes, as pathetic in their way as the Child Jesus of Our Lady of Victory in Prague. The church over us went up in curving leaps to a dome lit with yellow-tinted glass, which filled the air with a kind of metallic artificial sunlight, and made the day look unnecessarily dull when we came out into fresh air again.

We spent part of the afternoon in a search for "oplatky", the flat wafer cakes filled with a sugar and spice mixture which are sold in all Czech spas. Helena knew the best maker of "oplatky" in Karlovy Vary, but unfortunately they had no more stock; so we went elsewhere, and in a quiet street found a shop which had them, newly made and still warm. We bought boxes, and were presented with one cake each to eat as we walked; and Helena confirmed my opinion that they were very good indeed, even if they were not the work of the crack confectioner of the town. They are the usual deep creamy colour of ice-cream wafers, and devotees consuming them unbroken—as we had to, being one-handed—look as if they were absent-mindedly devouring miniature bread-boards.

We had an appointment for tea at the Grand Hotel Pupp with a friend of Helena's, who was taking a cure in the town at a private sanatorium. I believe the hotel got its name from its founder, who was German, and a master of his business; it is enormous, and the most wedding-cake-like of all the hotels, white and sugary to the last pinnacle of its roof.

Mrs. Kubankova had voted here in Karlovy Vary, and reported that certainly at that particular polling station everyone had made use of the screen just as usual. There were boards up at the end of the mill colonnade to show the local results, and a few people were stopping to read the figures, but without any excitement.

After tea we went up the hillside to the sanatorium, to look at Mrs. Kubankova's rooms. High up the slope beyond was a big hotel, less of a crystallised fruit than the Grand Hotel Pupp, but equally monumental.

"That place," said Helena, "has been run by the Russians as a recreation centre for their troops on short leave from their zone of Germany; but often there have been only a few men there, and it must be terribly expensive to keep it open for so few."

"They are giving it up," said Mrs. Kubankova. "It cost far too much, so now they are building a smaller new place for themselves here, lower down. You see, the foundations are already laid. They are providing the labour themselves, and doing everything."

Our visit to the sanatorium had to be brief, for already it was almost time to go back to the square and board the return bus. We had time only for a quick glance at Mrs. Kubankova's very pleasant bed-sitting-room and bathroom, and then we had to be off down the hill again, by another little funicular which dropped us accurately into the square. Already our fellow-travellers were gathering, a few of them the same people who had come out with us in the morning, but most of them early holiday-makers going home, business people, and a few short-distance travellers, one a young policeman being moved out to a remote village, according to his own account because he had political differences with his superiors in the town force. But his grievance did not depress him very much, for he had the company in the rear of the bus laughing almost continuously until he reached his village and got out.

After an uncertain day we had a heavenly evening, settled, clear, lofty, primrose-coloured before the sunset, and lavender-grey after it; and everything on the earth seemed to draw from that light a bright translucence, as

D*

if its colours were lit from within. The red roofs of the villages and farm-houses were like lanterns, and the climbing tendrils of hops like thin green flames; and even the black of the pine-forests became a live, lustrous black like a cat's fur. By the time we approached the outskirts of Prague the sun was down, but the bright clarity lingered some while afterwards, and softened slowly into a dove-grey dusk.

"We won't go right into town," said Helena, "but get out at Malovanka, and take a tram from there; we can get a number which will drop me in Dejvice and take you on to Strossmayer Square."

We dropped off at the corner she indicated, and raced down into a side-street on the other side of the block of buildings, for this was a roundabout terminus for the tram we wanted. Here we found a new notice attached to the tram-stop post, and on seeing it Helena immediately set off back again to the main street, I obediently following.

"What does it say?" I asked.

"We have to take our tram after all from the main stop. It is only for some days—something they do with the lines."

So we waited, but our number did not come. When we grew tired of waiting we sought a passer-by, and made appropriate enquiries. He inclined to the belief that the tram started from round the corner as usual; but Helena was positive that the notice said it would start from here. However, after still more waiting we made another trip round the block to make doubly sure, and there stood a tram of the exact number we wanted, just filling up in leisurely style. At sight of it we ran, but there was no real need, for after we had reached it it continued to stand for a few minutes, long enough to allow Helena to get out and satisfy herself that the notice, and not she, was crazy. She came back guiltily smiling.

"What's the matter?" I asked. "Have you done it

again? Doesn't it say this tram will leave from Malovanka, after all?"

"Oh, yes!" she said. "I read that quite rightly. Only I didn't read quite all of the notice. As soon as I see that, naturally I turn back. Yes, for a few days they leave from Malovanka, instead of from here. Only it begins tomorrow!"

8

The Bat'a Legend

Honza put me into the single through coach for Zlin, at the end of an enormously long train for Bohumin and Warsaw, at Wilson station; just into it, and only just, for it was already full to the doors. The previous day I had had the extension of my visa confirmed, for longer, indeed, than I had requested; and now I was on my way to Marie's home in the shoe city of Moravia for a ten-day visit. Honza hoped, a little dubiously, that I should get a seat later on, and left me perforce wedged in the corridor with the rest of the latecomers. He no longer felt it necessary to commit me to the care of the guard.

At Kolin two people struggled out of the coach, but several got in, impossible as it already seemed to accommodate any more; at Pardubice more got out than entered, and we had room to breathe out again, but still none to sit down; but at Chocen, after two hours of steaming east, we reduced our numbers in the corridor to a mere handful, and I found a vacant place, and ensconced myself comfortably with the salami rolls and "buchty" which Mrs. Vesela had given me for the journey; and for the remaining five hours I sat watching alternately the passing scenery and my fellow-passengers.

There was a young mother with her two little girls, still wearing under their little blue frocks the sensible garment all infant Czechs wear in winter, white woolly stockings and pants in one; white for children as small as these, fawn-coloured, perhaps, for those a few years older. Like most children in trains, they were perpetually thirsty, and the mother was kept busy producing soft drinks from a seemingly inexhaustible supply of bottles in her bag. There was a family of Praguers, mother, son, and daughter in her teens, and a young man travelling alone, with whom the daughter had already made a decided hit, so that they spent much of their time viewing the scenery from the corridor, where they could talk animatedly without being heard by the whole family. The girl was pretty, vivacious, dressed to look older than her age, but sparkling with the unmistakable freshness of eighteen. When her mother brought out the inevitable food, and called her to come and share it, she declined to be interested in anything so earthy as "buchty" and sandwiches; but when the young man got out at Olomouc she reappeared in the compartment very promptly, hunted out all that was left, and despatched it with excellent appetite. Lastly, we had with us a plump, middle-aged lady who read solidly at a very serious-looking book, and for whom none of us really existed.

Seven hours is a long time to spend in a railway carriage in any country, but I cannot say that one minute of this journey palled on me, though I was certainly rather tired by the time we arrived in Zlin. From Olomouc we ran south-east to Prerov, thence south again, crossing and re-crossing a persistent highroad which used the same valley, and so into Zlin at half-past eight, dead on time. It was easy to see when we were approaching the town, because the line runs alongside the factory for the last half-mile or so, and those surprising red brick and concrete buildings begin to startle the sight as something jettisoned in this improbable spot by some cosmic mistake. Even the red, or perhaps more accurately the dark pink, of their brick-work came as a surprise to me, for photographs make them appear as whitish erections entirely of concrete, whereas they are concrete frames filled in with this bright, raw brick, doubly sharp to the eyes in Czechoslovakia, where naked brick is so little favoured. Their size, again, startles, particularly when the main administrative building comes into view with all its fifteen storeys; a modest enough height for New York or any other American city, perhaps, but truly a skyscraper here in the middle of Moravia; and the amount of ground they cover is roughly a third of the town.

Move a little out of this strayed industrial fragment of America dropped within sight of the Slovak mountains, and you are soon in the true Moravia, though here and there in surrounding small towns also the same influence suddenly confronts you, in Malenovice, in Otrokovice, with the authentic Bat'a hotel style, or a factory block on the Zlin pattern. Between these eruptions the fields and farms and rolling wooded hills assert themselves silently as more permanent and more significant. You can stand on a hillside on any hand from Zlin, on a higher level than the skyscraper, and get the place in proportion; but to be in it is, for me at least, an uneasy feeling, like trying to fit into a jigsaw puzzle a piece which does not belong to it.

Marie met me at the station, smiling and vivid in a hooded plastic raincoat, for it had been raining here, and the evening had cleared into the last thin sunshine only moistly and grudgingly, so that the sunset was like a tearful smile. We walked out to the nearest trolley-bus stop, and went round by the long way into the third third of Zlin, one great garden of small houses expanding uphill into the forest itself. The trolley-bus system here runs three or four circular routes which between them cover the whole town, so that we could have made our trip in either direction and still reached home safely.

Zlin extends along the valley, taking firm handholds of the hills on both sides; at the station end, the factory, the Community House hotel and the two enormous department stores, all products of Bat'a enterprise; in the middle old Zlin, the town centre, with its square and churches and shops and offices, and at the other end the garden city of small, flat-topped houses swarming up the hills to the very crest on one side, on the other giving place early to fields and rising woods. In one of these neat cube-shaped houses, built to accommodate two families, lived Marie and her parents. Space was limited, but good use was made of what there was. The flat roofs, they said, were inclined to be hot in summer and cold in winter, but they had the merit of being cheaper to build and much quicker to produce; and the look of them, as I saw them at this end of town going up in terraces to the top of the hill, was remarkably good.

For one thing, the many levels broke the sameness of the design; and for another, in laying out the site the planners had kept every tree it was possible to keep, incorporating them into the gardens, and in particular using them wherever possible alongside the paved footpaths which everywhere threaded the estates. There were many silver birches, many national limes, then just coming into honeyed bloom. Shade was easily accessible for everyone, and there was no need to walk among the traffic of the main roads, for the little paths between the houses were for common use. The result, because of the trees and also because the two houses in each block were entered from different sides, provided a pleasant sense of community without too much loss of privacy; and garden space was fairly generous. Often during my stay I walked along the crest of the hills opposite to this estate, and from that viewpoint, had the houses been white instead of red brick, it would have looked like a part of some Moorish town.

It was already growing dusk when we reached the house on this first evening, but the next day was brilliantly fine and warm, the first of a hot spell which charmed the children out of their winter stockings-cum-pants and into the most abbreviated of sun-suits in a couple of days; and as it was Saturday both Marie and her father, who was a schoolmaster, finished work at midday, so we were able to go for a long walk and look at the town from the high spots surrounding it.

Zlin has a housing problem like every other town. The Bat'a factory, renamed Svit since those days, is a national enterprise, and shares with the town authorities the responsibility for housing; and these two between them had on hand schemes which would house seven hundred and fifty families, apart from future plans not yet begun. But the waiting list, I was told, ran well ahead of the supply, somewhere in the thousands. Between the hillside garden city and the shopping town some great new blocks of flats were being built by the local authority; and at the extreme edge of the town in this direction, not far from Marie's home, new and similar blocks belonging to the Bat'a undertaking were also going up. They came in blocks of six, a neat, comprehensible size to look at; and we climbed up a wobbly plank to examine the interior of some just finished. They had two bedrooms, bathroom, store, small entrance-hall, good kitchen, and really large, handsomely windowed living-room, and were to be let at seven hundred and fifty crowns a month, including central heating; in English money, three pounds fifteen, and no heating bills to pay.

Higher up the slope, in the forest quarter, they were putting up some more pairs of houses, prefabricated in concrete blocks much like some of our own permanent prefabs. We investigated these, too. They had two bedrooms, bathroom and small boxroom upstairs, kitchen, hall and large living-room on the ground floor, and a fine cellar, coming a little above ground level so that it was lit with high windows. This floor comprised a laundry-room and a cool store. The rent for these houses was fixed at two hundred and fifty crowns a month, that is, twenty-five shillings, but here the heating bills would naturally be extra to this modest rental. They had a fine reassuring outlook over the town on one side, and a quick escape into the woods on the other; an important consideration in this community. There is always something disquieting about having to fit every part of your activities into the pattern of a factory signal, even when you own the factory; and at a period like the present, when the production drive has become hectic, and everyone is being urged to work harder, the problem of how to make the enthusiasm of owning national enterprises outweigh the oppression of being owned by them is by no means peculiar to the Czechs. Exactly the same problems confront nationalisation wherever it comes into force.

I wonder how much Zlin has really changed, now that that astonishing creation of one mind for one profit has become the property of all. The daily processes seem much the same. The townspeople still rise early and scurry away to the factory, work hard until the siren releases them, and stream out of the gates again in a formidable river of humanity to the trolley-buses. The repetition system seems inevitable where enormous numbers of a product must be turned out regularly, to feed a world which has never yet succeeded in satisfying the ordinary human needs of even half its millions; and this is surely the fundamental cause of the desperate urge to produce, however many sidelong considerations of export and import balances and hard-currency markets may obscure and complicate it.

There remains the sense of security, and all the imponderable psychological factor, so fatally easy to underestimate, perhaps possible to over-value also. The factory is theirs now, they are working for themselves. The day may go in exactly the same pressure and stress, but its energy when released flows into a new channel. For exactly how much that change counts we still do not know.

Tomas Bat'a, who made Zlin, or rather remade it in a new mould, for the town is a settlement four hundred and fifty years old, is buried in the new woodland cemetery, high in the hills above Zlin, a lovely place, less a cemetery than a forest strangely growing gravestones, instead of undergrowth of a more normal kind. I went there with Marie on Sunday morning, when scarcely anyone was about. Aside from the main path there is a colony of great recumbent slabs of polished granite guaranteed to hold down even the tumultuous energy of the Bat'a family; and under the greatest of them, as large as a cabaret dance-floor, lies Tomas. He was killed in a plane crash in 1932, and his pilot is allowed a place in the family necropolis, lying close beside him under an exactly similar stone, but naturally of smaller size. Tomas in death, like Tomas in life, is the centrepiece from which all immediate things radiate.

For a long time they kept the glass palace on the hill above Work Square as a museum to him, even his fatal plane was enshrined in it. It is the House of Art now, and shows live things to its visitors. But in any case the museum was unnecessary. You cannot go far in Zlin without being reminded of this much-reviled, much-praised, incomparably competent man.

He began, they say, with virtually nothing, himself a poor shoemaker, settled in Zlin with his family, and opened a shoe workshop towards the end of the nineteenth century. His touch was golden. Shoes were already being made in this valley, but it took a Bat'a to organise the trade, and he did it in the approved way, the only way known to his time, by appropriating it to himself. It flourished to such an extent that by 1910 he was employing fifteen hundred people, and in a few years more began to export. Shoes were not enough; he began to make the machinery which makes the shoes, went into rubber, toys and tyres. Zlin could not hold him. He spread his hotel system, his auxiliary workshops and his airfield to Otrokovice. And so potent is the force of his personality even now that some of the newest buildings in Zlin have the authentic flavour, as if Tomas himself had decreed them.

There seems little doubt, when all the differing opinions I collected have been added together, that according to the standards of his time Tomas was a good, enlightened and progressive man. Of all those who profited by his business obviously he profited most; but at least he recognised some of the needs of those who made his millions for him. It may have been because he cared in an entirely disinterested way for their welfare that he provided for them decent houses in well-laid-out estates, with gardens, trees, and parks, excellent schools, sports facilities, a hospital, and a five-day working week as early as 1930, when the five-day week in England was a distant dream; or it may have been that he was wise enough to realise that every penny laid out in these benefits was being paid back into the business and his own pocket with the double interest of increased output and patriarchal reputation. Or it may have been both considerations working together, in what proportion we are never likely to know, and I question if he knew himself.

But he did bestow upon the workers all these things, and many older people remember it to him for good. There is no doubt about the quality of his gifts. The houses I had already seen to be good, practical and well-built, if they were not lavish; the Masaryk Schools I saw later, airy, spacious, all glass and sunlight, with radio, film equipment, access to an enormous gymnasium, a beautiful new kitchen for teaching the girls cookery, sewing-machines, everything the heart of a teacher could desire; the parks are there for

all to see. There was, in fact, only one drawback attached
to his industrial paradise; every good thing in it stemmed
from him. It belonged to his people only because his people
belonged to him, those with fiercer memories will tell you
in soul as well as body. They had nothing of common
human right, everything because he gave it. In such a
situation, even if no conditions are laid down, or even
formulated in the minds of the people concerned, it is
folly to pretend that no conditions actually attach to the
gifts. It is a relationship which affects every action, almost
every word, of the beneficiary.

All that is changed now, the enthusiast will tell you. All
power is vested in the people; it is their factory, the living
conditions they suffer or enjoy are created by themselves,
and what they have they have of right, even if the weight
of responsibility has also grown heavy on them. It would
be easy to be cynical about this view; it is very easy to make
many and messy mistakes in aligning one's plans with it,
and I do not doubt that mistakes will be made in Zlin,
just as elsewhere. All the same, I think this is the heart of
the matter. It is not enough for a whole man to owe his
good to any patriarch, and the enlargement of man is
something which cannot be halted, however dangerous it
may be to try to hasten it.

After Tomas was killed, the proprietor of Zlin was his
stepbrother Jan, who was certainly no Tomas. He apparently admired Mussolini very much, studied the
pressure methods of German production chiefs, and tried
to squeeze Zlin into the same pattern. When the war
broke out he was in U.S.A., but he made even that hospitable country too hot to hold him by reason of the
warmth of his feelings towards Nazi Germany, and he was
expelled from U.S. territory, to find a congenial asylum
in the Argentine. At home the remaining Bat'as had to
trim their sails to the German wind, and console themselves

for the constriction of the occupation by making enormous war profits. But their boom had its end on an October day in 1944, when American super-forts flew a three-minute raid clean across Zlin, and blew out or burned out half the workshops and almost all the stocks of raw materials and chemicals. They keep marked maps in the school which show the track of the raid, and photographs of mountains of concrete rubble and twisted metal under stifling black clouds of smoke from burning rubber. It must have been a spectacular three minutes; and without, so far as I know, killing one member of the family, it effectively ended the Bat'a era of Zlin.

By this time the woods all round were full of partisans, for this was guerrilla country, hand in glove with the unquenchable outlaw areas of Slovakia, not far away. The factory, too, had its underground movement, in close touch with the free men in the hills. By early 1945 it was not safe for a German to venture out of the town. On the 2nd of May the Red Army came in as deliverers, and inside a fortnight the new National Committee had appointed a general manager to work the factory for the nation, and Works Councils were organising with all the enthusiasm of the newly liberated the resurgence of Zlin's decimated production. No one believed in impossibilities in the year of the German defeat.

Zlin's production is booming now, new shops have replaced the ones which were burned out, and shoes, rubber boots, stockings, tyres, are pouring out of the factories in their millions. The National Corporation claims that the conveyor belt processes have been replanned to relieve boredom and strain to the maximum extent, and the high output has been achieved not by slave-driving but by the better organisation of the work, and improved co-operation between departments.

Naturally I wanted to see inside the plant for myself, and

I went to the hotel one morning with Mr. Stransky to ask if a party was being shown round that day, and if possible to join them. There was a conducted tour every morning, it seemed, and I was welcome to attach myself to it without more notice; but the young man at the hotel desk had other ideas. He asked me to wait a moment, and flew to the 'phone; and presently came back to explain that no English-speaking guide would be with the morning party, but if I cared to wait until afternoon he would get time off to come with me and show me everything. I jumped at the chance, and at two-thirty in the afternoon Mrs. Stranska and I called for him, and we crossed the ominously named Work Square, and entered the gates of the factory.

We went first to the buildings where leather shoes were being made, following a handsome suède and kid walking shoe along the slowly moving belt through its accumulation of insole, waist, and sole. The noise of the machines seemed intense when we first entered, and I found I had to pitch my voice artificially to be heard, and stretch my ears to hear; but very quickly the senses adjust themselves, and the ordered clamour is tuned low, if it cannot quite be tuned out. The speed of the belts was not so hectic as to worry anyone overmuch, and no one here seemed to be entirely stationary, or embedded into the job too intently to exchange a few minutes of talk with us. One or two of the minor processes, like slapping glue over the insoles, were certainly not very exciting. Production is almost entirely by machines, and they have even machines for making the wood-pegged heavy shoes, making the holes, punching in the pegs, slicing them off, and polishing over the finished surface, all in one operation.

It rained a little, and we darted from building to building under cover of our guide's umbrella. Next, to the new block where rubber shoes are made. Wagons were running in at one end, laden with sheets of crêpe rubber, the colour of new blankets, and folded like them; and the smell of rubber hung over us from the moment we entered, insistent but to me, at any rate, not unpleasant. Here we saw in the making all kinds of sports shoes, fancy textile sandals, children's little plimsolls and canvas shoes, from the machinists' quick hands flicking off stitched uppers, to the heat and pressure processes which fitted the soles.

Men worked over these heat chambers stripped to the waist, smoothing the soft rubber over one last while the other shoe was cooking, whisking the second into the twin press as its fellow came out, trimming the finished one neatly off at the edges, and fitting a new upper on to the last to receive the next sole. The two small ovens, to call them by a convenient name, at which each man worked were within easy reach of his hands, the lasts moving in and out on a table at the right height for manipulation without stooping. The men's movements were so sure of themselves as to seem leisurely; indeed, the girl machinists seemed in more of a hurry.

We slipped out again through the thin rain, making for the stocking workshops. You could walk many miles by the roads which interlace the factory buildings. Railway sidings curve in among them, and small works wagons carry materials and packed goods from block to block. We passed the first-aid building, and turned in to the right, to watch machines the whole width of the great room knitting up fine stockings. Most of the operators here were girls, only a few men acting as supervisors and tending some of the machines. The stockings were seamed up on other machines at the sides of the room, and then washed, dyed, and ironed on plastic steam-heated frames which pointed their elegant toes skyward in ranks in one corner. They were almost all for export, but of several grades, and the yarn for each grade had its own distinctive colour, the finest being a rather startling yellow. But the finished products took on the most delicate dyes. I saw some boxed silons—they are like our nylons—cobweb-fine, in an almost invisible, shadowy iris-grey, guaranteed to slim the most ungainly leg. But Czech women find it difficult to buy this delectable hosiery, though they are turning them out here by thousands of pairs. The endless paradox of all for export irritates them, I fancy, as much as it does English-women.

Our tour lasted all afternoon, and ended on the roof of the administrative building, as every tour seemed to culminate in some lofty belvedere, natural or artificial. Five large lifts go up to the railed roof-terrace, where you can lean on space like a countryman leaning on a gate, and contemplate Zlin. The rain had stopped, but the air was still the colour of rain, soft and luminous as pearl.

Up the hill towards the two great Study Institutes there are large hostels for the boys and girls who work in the national enterprise. Zlin is aware of youth, and boasts of the provision made for these workers in their teens. Their hours of work are strictly guarded, their education continues; I am not sure that it is not a little overweighted in the direction of technical efficiency, but that is a danger to be faced here as well as there. There is no doubt that the town provides for them access to excellent art shows, good music, theatre, and every possible encouragement to take part in sport of all kinds. If, as a community, they can keep the factory in its place, as an asset and not a proprietor, their life can be a good and a full one. And it says much for the optimism of the generation now in possession that the whole town is full of children. In the little tree-shaded gardens, along the paved paths which thread the cottage-city, little things of a few years of age swarm and tumble in their thousands.

The preponderance of babies in any place is a barometer of their parents' belief in the future; and according to that gauge, Zlin confidently expects good things ahead, and is by no means afraid of the effort which will be needed to gain them.

9

Brno and the Zlin Woods

Marie would have liked to have more time off with me, but she was saving all her free days for the Sokol Festival, when she hoped to visit Prague; so she asked for only one day off during this week, and we made a coach trip to Brno together. The bus went from close beside the factory gates, very early in the morning.

We left town by the road which kept close company with the railway line all the way to Otrokovice; and then, instead of entering the outskirts of the Bat'ov quarter, we swung left, and headed for Napajedla, where there is one of the most famous of Czech stud-farms. Soon we were in the small towns of the picture region of Moravian Slovakia, Honza's "one whole piece of folklore", where they are not content with colour-washing their cottages in delicate blues, pastel pinks and yellows, but make garlands of the windows by framing them in painted flowers, and decorate the sides of the doorway in the same gay fashion. As every small town has its square, so every village has its duck-pond, the natural centre from which everything else radiates, green, ordered, old and populous. No community is complete without one.

The humming-top silhouette of close bodice and full, short skirt belongs in these villages to old and young alike, and the draped head brings all ages close together. You can follow what seems to be a young, light-footed girl, barefoot from choice, and walking like a nymph, to find, when you overtake her, that she is a grandmother in the sixties.

From Uherske Hradiste, the main town of this region, with brilliantly coloured flower-gardens flaming along the centre of a great elongated square, we turned due west again, and wound our way up into high ground; and after passing through Buchlovice our way became a pass through wooded hills, with the highest point in sight on our right hand for long stretches of the road, and poised on the crest of it like a crown, among its foaming trees, Hrad Buchlov. This castle I never saw at close quarters; perhaps it is a good plan not to try, for from the road it is like something from a fairy-tale, so aloof, so beautiful and so ominous that a nearer approach might only succeed in bringing it to earth. Czechoslovakia is full of such coronals of castle afloat in the piled hair of dramatic forested peaks. There are so many of them that they ought to grow commonplace; but they continue obstinately to charm even when the pattern is familiar, and every atmospheric change transforms them with some new and awful delight, as if they were indeed magical.

Soon the road crawled over the brow of the pass, and we began to coil our way down again into the valley at a great rate, leaving the closed forests behind, and welcomed again by open, rolling country of farm and small town. We passed through Slavkov-by-Brno, and the name struck some chord, though I could not at first capture the echo. There had been some battle here, I was sure, and westerners knew it by some other name; by no means surprisingly, since Austria used to fight half her major battles on Czech soil when these towns and villages bore only the Germanised names, when the language was submerged, and the people were vassals. As we left the town by upland fields, gently rolling in many minor hills and commanding wide views, Marie also harked back to the past to tell me that here Napoleon had once fought one of his greatest battles, and defeated the Austrian army; and aside on one of these hillocks was a monument to the field and its dead, and on another a plan of the lay-out of the battle.

"Austerlitz!" I said. But Marie knew it, of course, as the battle of Slavkov, and could not tell by what name it was known to the English history books, so I had to wait until we got home before I could confirm that I had rightly identified it.

From here to the outskirts of the textile town and capital of Moravia it is a long, open, descending drive, and the very slight haze of the city is visible for some time before you enter it. It is clear at once that this is a busy industrial centre, ringed with factories of many kinds; and soon after we reached the tram lines we began to see the marks of the war. Damage in the last fighting here was bitter and extensive; even in the heart of the town you can see whole cleared spaces half a street long, as in London after bombs, though guns did most of the damage in Brno. And where the street still stands, many of the buildings are badly marked with shell-splintering and machine-gun fire. Much has already been repaired, and what could not be replaced has been tidied away; but as in some of our English towns, gaunt, ghost-like ruins frown across the sunlight and make strange shadows on the white pavements of noon, constant reminders of recent warfare.

Brno is a very old settlement indeed. Even in Roman times a trade route passed northward here, joining the Danube lands with Bohemia and Germany; and by the eleventh century, when the records begin, there was already some sort of town here, and settlers from Germany and the Low Countries were turning it rapidly into an international commercial centre long before it became the capital of Moravia. As an important junction on an important road, it had to endure constant warfare throughout its history, and saw, probably with equal sick impatience, the manœuvring under its walls of Czech, Polish, German, Tartar, Hungarian, French and Swedish armies. These last, during the Thirty Years' War, held it in siege for sixteen weeks, and its earlier fall might easily have meant the fall of Vienna. The intensive fighting in 1945 between the Germans and the liberating Red Army, with hordes of partisans taking their due part in it, was nothing new to Brno; but it did damage much which earlier wars had left intact.

In the first republic the town grew enormously, and is growing still, engulfing its own suburbs at a great rate; and this growth has made it, like Prague, an extraordinary conglomeration of architectural styles, without quite the same perfect reconciliation between them which Prague seems to me to have achieved. There are some handsome modern buildings, and some beautiful old ones; but in the limited view I had of it I did not think they had accomplished a synthesis to the same extent. Trees redeem it from being what one understands by an industrial town; trees almost invariably save Czech towns from this fate, though I do not know Moravska Ostrava, which from all accounts may be the exception which proves the rule. Brno's surroundings, too, are fresh and green, and easily accessible, and their park-like woods reach into the suburbs and fill them with trees.

Two hills dominate the town from any view. On one of them stands the cathedral of St. Peter and St. Paul, with the two tallest, slenderest spires in central Europe; and on the other one the fortress of Spilberk, a level-roofed, low, sturdy castle covering the whole surface of the height. Under the Spilberk there are some of the most notorious prison dungeons in Europe, used again and again for infamous purposes through their unpleasant history, and during the occupation used again by the Germans for political prisoners, let us hope for the last time.

We spent most of our day shopping, or rather trying to shop, for in fact the shops of Brno were the emptiest I had seen yet in CSR. A textile town it might be, but it had no textiles, and very little in the way of ready-made clothes, either. As with us, all clothing was strictly rationed in CSR at this time, but with them some of the items in shortest supply, such as shoes and stockings, were issued on definite coupons, instead of being available on any, as in England. We found attractive dress accessories, but little besides; and after lunch we gave up the rest of our day to the cathedral, and the pleasant parks outside the city. Marie had been at school here during the occupation, and knew the district very well. And at the end of the afternoon we had just time to treat ourselves to ice-cream, the sweet, pretty but bodyless water-ice of a country where milk is gold, before we caught the bus for home.

From this day onward the weather was glorious all the time I was at Zlin. The playing children shed their clothes until they ran around in next to nothing, the littlest in absolutely nothing. The lime trees, from a shy bloom which only hinted at scent, burst into fullest flower along the avenues, and housewives came out with baskets and picked them full of the blossoms to make lime tea, one of the most favoured substitutes for the real thing, which was very scarce. The sun had a rebound we seldom feel in England, even in the highest midsummer, and on the half-made road which passed by the new houses the dust lay thick and fine as flour, and almost as pale. Then the best place was the forest, where there was both the heat I loved and the shade I needed, since I burn very readily.

Mr. Stransky had an afternoon free from school, and proposed that we should make a long walk through the woods to a certain miraculous spring called Svata Voda— Holy Water. Its story I do not know, the way to it we found none too easy to follow on the map, but I remember this walk as one of the loveliest days of the summer. Perhaps the woods looked more beautiful than other woods because we entered them straight from the hill above the factory end of the town; or perhaps the extraordinary calm of the day, which later threatened storm for a while but mildly withdrew the threat without a drop of rain, gave a super-lative sense of stillness and mystery under the fir trees. We walked, I am told, about fifteen kilometres, and most of that distance was in unbroken woodland, sometimes on wide tracks, sometimes on the slightest of grassy gypsy ways seen only as a dimpling and darkening of the grass. The routes were marked, as they always are in Czech woods, by small coloured blazes on the trees, so that by following the colour of the track you wanted you could safely hold to it no matter how involved the way might become.

Sometimes the woods were of a mixed character, thickly sprinkled with deciduous trees, and there a bright green young grass grew underfoot, and speckled orchids were just showing their heliotrope heads above the green, and brighter gold and red fungi clustered about the feet of the trees. Then we would come suddenly to a belt of thick conifers, velvet black, shutting out the light and holding down the heat of the earth under their branches in a richly scented twilight; and underfoot there would be nothing but the spicy silence of generations of pine needles. These belts of differing woodland met on as rigid a line as if their areas had been ruled out to the inch. From the borders of Zlin to a place where we came out for a time on to a road, only a few miles from Svata Voda, we did not see a single human being. Then there was a lonely meadow by the quiet road, and two women making hay.

We saw now for the first time that clouds had massed along one slope of the sky; but it would have been as long a trip to turn back as to go on, and we never liked going home by the same way. We had to ask our way several times, and the one person who ought to have known, a postman, confidently directed us in a way we were sure could not be the right one, so we ignored him and went on as we thought best, until we had found a small green cart-track deep in woods again, and descending sharply, and by the wayside a man and woman with a little wagon were loading wood.

"Svata Voda?" we asked, pointing ahead.

"Right on!" they said cheerfully, obviously sure of their country. So we went on, downhill into deeper, quieter woods sheltered even from a movement of the summer air, old woods where the trees had grown enormously tall, and interlaced so closely, high above our heads, that they kept the ground bare as surely as did the pines. And there at last was one solitary wooden house, long and snug under the steep slope, and the path continuing to drop past its door and zigzag away into the sheer silence of the valley. The spring we could not see yet, but we saw something which interested us just as much, for we were very thirsty, and I had gathered by this time that the only house at Svata Voda was the inn.

Fifteen kilometres is quite a sufficient distance, on a very hot day, to breed a thriving thirst, and I have never been more pleased to see beer in my life. Here it was a Moravian brew from Jarosov, which I am scornfully informed by Mr. Vesely is not, strictly speaking, beer at all; but it tasted like the real thing to me, at least on this day, when I was in ripe condition to enjoy even the usual English drink. We could not, however, linger to do it justice, for time was passing quickly, and that night I was going with Marie and a friend to see a company of visiting Russian actors perform a nineteenth-century comedy called: *Krejcinsky's Wedding*. So we set off again down the hill, and right at the foot of it the road curled under a bank built up with a low wall, and making a narrow bend began to climb again. Here at this lowest point gushed out the holy spring, filling a small, clear well before the overflow took it away as a thread-fine brook.

In the angle of the wall, looking over the singing spring, was a small shrine, ringed round with carved and painted flowers, with an image of the Virgin. Often in the woods one could see little pictures or figures of saints attached to trees, in the most unexpected places, their sudden garish colours like improbable orchid growths parasitical to the trunks. This Virgin was more cleanly pastel-shaded than most of them, and glowed like a pale, bright flower against the russet-brown bare earth and the dun-coloured wall. Fresh flowers had been laid at her feet some time this same day, they were only now beginning to fade. The Virgin of Svata Voda grants wishes to those who drink of the water of her spring; I drank, and found it piercingly cold. My wish was granted, but it was the same one I had entrusted to Rabbi Löw in the Jewish cemetery, and in any case its issue was in little doubt, so perhaps it was hardly a fair test.

From the well the path set off steeply uphill, climbing back in a comparable distance all the many yards it had slithered down into the valley. Soon we emerged from the perpetual twilight of this secret little place, and the forest thinned and grew green round us, and finally fell back from us altogether and left us walking over the crest of a large field, between rising grain. A cart-track ran straight across, cut deeply into the ground from centuries of use, so that if we had walked in it we could have seen nothing but the banks on either side; but trodden tracks wavered alongside on either hand, balancing on the edge of the decline, and on these we walked, as it was obvious did every other pedestrian, for they were trodden hard and bright. We crossed the brow of the rolling down, and there below us was a small town, or perhaps more truly a large

E

village, in a valley, and beyond it the waving, undulating distances of Moravia running away evenly to the skyline.

The village was Malenovice. It was near enough to Zlin to carry some suggestion of a Bat'a outline on one side, where there were factories; but it had also, in a fine position half-way up the slope of a wooded hill, sheltered from wind and weather, a great castle, which seemed to be at any rate partially Romanesque, and in fairly good preservation. I believe a part of it was still being lived in, though part was approaching the ruined stage. Its stone was whitish, wonderful against the olive-green bank of trees.

But Malenovice had what was of more interest to us at that precise moment, a bus back to Zlin. We boarded it, and went to meet Marie at the factory gates as the siren blew, our return timed accidentally at the perfect moment.

This was a fascinating and appalling sight, all the more as the town happened to be suffering from an extreme attack of road safety consciousness that week. For five minutes before the hour, policemen would mass in Work Square, putting on the white bands they wear for traffic work; and as the siren went they would take up their posts in the centre of the pedestrian crossing-places. For perhaps one minute after the signal there would be peace, ominous and brittle, like the hush before the storm, then the first few human drops of the storm itself would materialise within the gates, scurry through, and cross the road. Then more and more human beings, the stream rapidly thickening, and then a solid mass of people, the whole pavement area moving into the road, resolving itself into two rivers, and pouring across towards the trolley-bus stands. These rivers were as tightly packed to the width of the pedestrian crossings as queues outside a London sale before opening time, but moved at the speed of a tube escalator in the rush hour. From time to time the policeman's levelled arm would cut the worm in two, the rear end would halt instantly, the front end would continue to rush forward at the same speed, oblivious of the fate of its tail. This rapid advance of the severed half, and its dissolution on the pavement, where it flew apart with the vigour of a good firework, was the most surprising thing to watch of the whole remarkable show.

Marie came, and we scrambled aboard our bus and went home for a quick supper and change before the theatre show, which was to take place in the large cinema here on Work Square. Zlin has a theatre of its own, considered perhaps a shade too experimental and propagandist by some of the older people, but the visit of the Russian company was something special. The play would be in Russian, of which language Marie understood a little; and she had already seen the same play done twice before, for it was quite a popular comedy. We had also programmes which gave a generous outline of the action in Czech, and these we spent the intervals feverishly translating into English; so I was well prepared to follow only a leap or two behind, even if the actual words were beyond me.

It was not the kind of play the average Briton would expect to see a company of Russian actors putting on in one of the factory towns of a neighbour country, for too often we make the mistake of thinking they do nothing without some propaganda end in view. This was just good fun mixed with quite a lot of shrewd good sense, and set in the Moscow of 1869. The story concerned a well-to-do farmer who had been persuaded by his women folk, against his better judgment, to leave the country and give his daughter Lida the advantages of a town season. All he himself really wanted was his good, solid country life, and to see Lida happily married to the young farmer whose land bordered theirs, and who had been in love with her for some time; but his flighty sister wanted a town life, and made Lida, who was not unwilling to try the delights of

Moscow, the excuse. And there both the women fell under the spell of a plausible, handsome, self-confident adventurer, the Krejcinsky of the title, who saw his way to a comfortable fortune by marrying the impressionable Lida.

Naturally the wedding never came off, Lida was saved at the last moment from making so ridiculous a mistake, and married her young farmer instead. Krejcinsky, however, came out of it intact, as his kind usually do, being as resilient as sinuous; and indeed, one had to like him at times, which is true of his kind also, and their most dangerous characteristic.

But the best part in the play was that of his downtrodden, adoring, bungling camp-follower, Raspljujev, who messed up every smallest job which was entrusted to him, and yet came back every time on the rebound as eager to help as ever, and with as ready an eye to the main chance. He was a delight even when one had to translate him from Russian through Czech to English.

The company of actors stood up well to most standards I know. I would rate them above most of the comparable travelling or provincial companies we see here. It was a conventional and static setting, of course; nothing else would have been suitable. Most inconspicuous but memorable of virtues, the cast wore their costumes of the 1860's as if they were not used to wearing any others.

Entertainment in Zlin was notably international. I saw there one Czech film, the lovely *Spalicek*, a puppet film made up of country songs, legends, customs, running through the whole year; one Russian film; and two American ones of very uneven quality. American films were popular, I think, for the slickness of their making, even when the plot could be pulled to pieces with one hand, and the settings belonged to nowhere but Cloudcuckooland, and the characters to nowhere but a psychiatrist's nightmare, as was certainly the case with *Gilda*, which Marie wanted to see but with her usual Czech sanity rejected scornfully afterwards.

Marie had had a piece of unexpected luck just at this time. Two places at a Trade Union recreation centre in the Giant Mountains had been allotted to her office to be handed out for good work, and one of them had been given to her. This meant, of course, not an entirely free holiday, but an opportunity for an unusually cheap one, and she promptly accepted it. She was to travel on Sunday, so we could go together all the way to Pardubice, the greater part of the journey.

Sunday was not a good day to leave Zlin in one respect, for there were no early trolley-buses, but with the help of Mr. and Mrs. Stransky we manhandled our own luggage the twenty-five-minute walk to the station. Though it was only six o'clock the platforms were already swarming with people, and we anticipated a scrimmage for places, and squared our elbows accordingly, but it turned out to be a very easy journey. The coach next to ours was reserved for a brigade of young people, and their songs resounded all the way to Otrokovice.

"Well, they sound happy about it, anyhow," I remarked.

"They'll be going home," said Marie cynically; and it appeared that she was right. The outburst of song marked the end, not the beginning, of their brigade. However, their spirits did not seem to have suffered at all during its course, to judge by the amount of ebullient energy they displayed throughout this journey.

We had to change at Otrokovice, and again at Prerov, where we boarded a really fast train; and in spite of the two changes my return trip to Prague was faster than the outward journey. At Pardubice Marie left me on her way north to the mountains, and we promised to meet again in Prague during the Slet. Then I went on to Wilson, to find that this time Honza had taken me at my word, and left

me to make my way home alone. He had left me a note
in the flat, to say that he had gone out for the day swimming,
but would be home in the evening; and in the meantime
Mrs. Burianova produced lunch for me as if by magic
within three minutes of my key turning in the lock. After
nearly seven hours in trains pork, cabbage and dumplings
appeared to me a perfect welcome home.

10

THE WRITERS' CASTLE

IT was while I was in Zlin that the news of President Benes' resignation suddenly filled the headlines. Everyone had known that he was ill, but the shock was profound for all that; nor do I think of it as a shock for only one part of the community. He belonged to all; those who agreed with him in everything and those who disagreed widely on some issues regretted him with equal sincerity. It was his misfortune, I believe, to be a symbol of dissension when he would infinitely have preferred to be a means of reconciliation. I talked with people of many shades of opinion politically, but never did I hear anyone speak of him as an enemy, or show satisfaction in his retirement.

But very little showed on the surface by the time I returned to Prague. The weather continued golden, and everyone went about his business or pleasure in a matter-of-fact way, as always; one could scarcely feel that anything out of the ordinary had happened. In Zlin the emotional impact had been more noticeable.

On the day following my return Klement Gottwald became president, the only nomination for the office. I had heard one or two other names mentioned as possibilities during the intervening days, but I imagine the issue had never been in very much doubt. There were celebrations in St. Vitus that morning, at which Archbishop Beran officiated, and some mild celebrations in the streets, of which I saw little. It was on the whole a very quiet day;

and the most vivid memory I have of it is of walking back with Honza at half-past eleven at night from a concert in town, and seeing from Stefanik Bridge the floodlit Hradcany afloat high above the earth, magical and lovely, every reflected surface of light an inverted flame in the water of Vltava far below it. By that vision any day would be marked and remembered.

We were now half-way through June, and soon the Sokol Slet would begin, with the early performances by the schoolchildren, tuned down to suit them into games and dances and innocent little drills. Foreign visitors could get tickets through a special bureau in Wenceslas Square, and there we went to file our order. Already the square had a festival look about it, with many shops decorated in the national colours, and with Sokol flags and emblems; everywhere the hawk was appearing, from the little badges in coat lapels to the enormous symbols flaunting from the upper storeys of the Bat'a shop. Traffic was intense, and the pavements had acquired a character even more cosmopolitan than usual with the influx of foreigners, among whom Americans easily predominated, though the French also were notably and audibly present in considerable numbers. In the brilliant weather everyone wandered coatless, and light summer frocks and Sokol uniforms made the scene one of perpetual holiday.

In connection with the festival, advertisers had cooperated in publishing a series of small stamps showing the many positions of the exercises we should see at the stadium, and there would be prizes for those who collected the complete set. Consequently all the small boys and girls of Prague, and half the grown-ups, were engaged in feverish trade, swopping their duplicates for the stamps they lacked. The most favoured stamp exchange for this traffic was the pavements of Wenceslas Square, which were dotted with groups of devotees, haggling, comparing and bargaining for dear life. No one interfered with them; the pavements were wide, and they gathered mainly under the shade of the trees, where they did not block the way. Practical in all that they did, many of them had brought out camp-stools, and were settling down to business in comfort.

The counters for foreign visitors in the banks were doing a brisk trade. The Sokol bureau for foreigners was also extremely busy, but we logged our application for seats for the main Sunday display, the final celebration day, and Army Day, and succeeded in getting all three. Foreigners were greatly favoured in the question of Slet tickets, I may say, understandably so, since currency was a matter of national concern; but it seemed a little hard on some Czechs, who had put in early orders through their own Sokol organisation, and in the end were not able to get what they wanted. Mr. and Mrs. Vesely made endless journeys for their tickets in vain, and finally it proved easier for me to rush into town again and enlist the help of the foreign bookings bureau, who soon got me the extra seats I wanted. But many Sokol members, I am afraid, were fobbed off with standing room.

Helena's friend, Mr. Kubanek, had offered to drive us out to the Writers' Castle at Dobris, owned by the Syndicate of Czech Authors, and run as a sort of super-hotel, with the important function of providing ideal writing conditions at a reasonable price, and accommodating, also at a reasonable price, foreign writers visiting the country for such occasions as the Slet. Various associations, trades unions, guilds had such places at their disposal, but this was the most famous of them all.

Honza came with us, and Mrs. Kubankova, who was home from Karlovy Vary in blooming health. We left Prague in the late afternoon, and drove out southward through the industrial suburbs and under the cliff of Barrandov, through the village of the sixty-five murdered

E*

hostages, uphill through the square of Zbraslav, leaving the castle on our right hand; and so away from the river, into the meadow and forest country of our last year's haunts. We crossed the woodland road by which we had walked from Trnova-Mechenice to Vsenory on Corpus Christi, and which ran for a long way through forests stained here and there by a distressing brownness of dead trees. I had seen the same marks in many spots round Prague, and also in Karlovy Vary, but in the region of Opocno and the Polish border the stains were absent.

They were due to a serious disease, caused by some insect under the bark, I was told; Bohemia was full of the same trouble, but probably the great open space of the Hradec Kralove plain, with its comparatively scarce trees, had prevented the disease from spreading further east. Voluntary workers were urgently needed to help in fighting the pest, since the only possible treatment was to cut out the affected timber at once and burn it; but it was not a very popular brigade because the job proved particularly unpleasant to handle. However, it had to be done, for the forests are one of Czechoslovakia's most valuable assets, and already more than sufficiently depreciated by the neglect and misuse of the occupation.

Presently we left the closest of the woods, and the first landmark of Dobris, the vast white bulk of the Masaryk Sanatorium, loomed up on the right hand, looking down on us from high ground beyond the town. Then the road branched, and we turned to the right, curving round the end of a lake, and deeply dipping under a steep bank opposite to it. Two bends of the road under encroaching trees, and we emerged in front of the castle.

Very much a castle for gracious living, this, "zamek", not "hrad", though a section of dry moat, turfed as smoothly as velvet, crosses the front of it and is spanned by a bridge. In front are two ellipses of lawn set with flower-beds, and ringed round from the road by low white posts linked with a chain. The frontage of the castle is low, only three storeys, and long, and symmetrical about a central section which contains the great entrance doors, through which cars can drive directly into the courtyard. Moulded pillars flank the doorway, and over it rises a triangular tympanum, crowned with heraldic stone figures; and on either side extend the twin main masses of the buildings, regularly pierced with uniform windows, those on the second floor being oval dormers projecting from the roof. What one chiefly notices on first acquaintance is its colour; it is a pink palace, a deep, soft rose-pink, with all its columns and window-frames and doorways outlined in white.

The doors were closed when we drove up, but Helena entered through a wicket, and began negotiations with the castellan, and soon they opened before us, and we drove through into a large courtyard, open on the right, and light and sunny by reason of its size and the low height of the buildings. Directly across from the outer doors where we entered there was a way through into the garden, but for the moment we were occupied with the castle itself. All round the inside of the court passes a kind of cloister, glazed in from the weather, so that you can walk right round past the main staircase, side staircase, kitchens and dining-room, and so into the garden hall without going outside. The grand staircase is not normally used, but is open on party occasions. Later I stayed for two days at Dobris, and found life there very free and easy, something of an achievement in the presence of so much magnificence.

The state rooms of Dobris are very beautiful, but I think the best moment in it is that in which one emerges on to the balcony of the main salon, and sees the ornamental garden spread out below in an intricate pattern of toy hedges a few inches high, like a green brocade, or an aerial photograph of a box maze, about the feet of many statues, with green lawns and bright flower-beds sleek on either side, and a fountain playing beyond. This first reach of the garden is enclosed at both ends by a thick arcading of trees grown into a dark green cloister. Beyond, it rises in a series of terraces, first by two paths which mount like ramps to a level above the fountain, where a company of stone putti look down at the playing water, and an expanse of turf moves away to the next terrace; then by more brocade of tiny hedges, by twin pleached alleys inside which you can walk or sit secure from the heat of the sun, by an enormous group of Neptune and his improbable court, and so beyond them by narrowing reaches to the balancing group of the theatre, which gazes down at the house across a descending vista of spacious and leisured beauty. This was a private theatre belonging to the castle, its outer walls painted in scenic murals, often renewed, and the present ones as recent as 1938.

When you have walked so far, however, you still have not begun to see Dobris. There remains the park, the lake, and the sudden silent green meadows opening like an arena among the more remote groves of trees. But we did not yet move on to these, for Helena, practical as ever, wanted first to make discreet enquiries as to the possibilities of supper, and disappeared in search of the responsible party. She came back to report contentedly that they could supply us; and thereupon, satisfied that the most essential need was already guaranteed, we would gladly have gone on into the park, if it had not at that precise minute begun to rain. So we returned to the garden hall, and sat there for a time waiting for the desultory fall to stop, and discussing guild castles and their uses.

It was remarkable how few people were visible at all; but as I found out later, it is one of the virtues of Dobris that it is large enough both inside and out to absorb and hide any amount of people. At meal-times you wonder where they all emerge from. We speculated wildly on the few guests whom we did see, debating whether they did or did not look like writers. It was early yet for the busy and fashionable festival atmosphere which came with the actual beginning of the Slet. Children were more in evidence than anyone else, scuffling along arcades in charge of harassed nurses. After studying them for some time it occurred to us to wonder if, in fact, writers ever really come here to work at all.

"I think," said Helena, "they send here their families, so that they can get peace to work at home."

It is a tenable theory. The Syndicate goes out of its way to create and maintain ideal conditions for writing; but what are ideal conditions? I spent most of my off-duty time during the war years sharing a single common-room with anything up to thirty other people, and was able to work with intense concentration while three or four conversations, a wireless programme and a ping-pong game were carried on simultaneously at short range round me, and I had just enough elbow-room to move the pen; but I am quite sure I could not work at Dobris, in the quiet, calm and dignity which ought to produce masterpieces. Perhaps the Czech author is equally perverse; perhaps he sends his children to enjoy Dobris, while he writes happily at home in a miniature Prague flat, with the telephone ringing, and all the washing-up piling up in the sink. A certain amount of mental peace is necessary, but it is a part of our own curious nature in what particular circumstances we find it.

Honza and Helena and I had all been at Roztez, near Kutna Hora, the previous year, where the journalists had their own castle in a former German hunting-lodge. Honza and I disagreed about most matters of taste, but agreed in preferring Roztez to Dobris, at least for the purpose they were both serving, on account of its greater intimacy and compactness. I remember the light crimson carpets and white woodwork of Roztez with pleasure, and the comfortable gallery above the wide well of the stairway. Besides, it stood on top of a hill, a position I always like best in a house. But it had not the magnificent grounds of Dobris.

The rain continued until about six o'clock, and then allowed us a little way into the park. Helena was in high spirits, and had constituted herself guide. We had only to go aside out of the trimmed alleys of trees to the left, and there beyond a diving slope of grass was the lake, running away far beyond the edge of the grounds and into the distant meadows on the road to Pribram. A long, wavering water it was, end on to us where we stood; and just across the shallows of its beginning the ground rose again abruptly in a rocky cliff, with some great building on top, probably a granary, pierced over its whole face with small ventilator windows. It looked old, and if it was a granary it had been placed with the dramatic dignity of a fortress. Through a tangle of half-wild garden under it an overgrown brook entered the lake.

I have said that the lake was end-on to us here, but we found when we moved away to the right that it was an L in shape, the long stem moving directly away out of the park to the meadows far distant along the road, the base, pinned to it by a small, round green island, running off to the right for some way before it narrowed, grew shallow and stagnant, and finally dwindled into a creek, and was crossed by a small stone bridge. By which time it had left behind the ordered garden and the last glimpse of the house, and penetrated deeply into the park.

"You see?" said Helena. "I told you it is very fine. We have here beautiful walks, across the water, and right to the end of the estate. This is the best thing about Dobris."

We agreed it was very fine.

"But it would take a long time to walk all that way," said

Helena, with a business-like eye on her watch, "and now in any case you have seen it already. The rest of the park is the same." She turned back on her tracks, and put on speed. "Now it is time for supper."

We were hungry, too, so we went. The dining-room was on the ground floor, and already the invisible people were drifting into it from all the elusive spots where up to now they had been hiding. Children were still in the majority, and became steadily more numerous as more groups appeared. We, as non-residents, were found places together at one end of a large table, otherwise occupied almost exclusively by children, with one untroubled lady of middle age in charge. They were nice children, but they were disconcerting company at table. Sometimes they were sitting at it, like little cherubim, sometimes they were underneath, sometimes they abandoned it altogether and went for a walk round to visit their friends, both young and old, at other tables. Most of them were only about three or four years old, some even younger, and their conversation was limited but confident. When they were tired of sitting on their chairs they stood on them and surveyed the room, plunging into profound meditation for some minutes before they slithered abruptly back to their plates. Helena's face became a study in mild apprehension, since at no moment could one reasonably determine what would happen next, and she was nearest; but Mrs. Kubankova, who talks to animals as if they were children, and to children as if they were contemporaries and equals, was charmed. Helena's theory that Dobris creates ideal conditions for writers by removing their families became increasingly feasible.

Afterwards we went back into the park, for even if it was all the same we did not intend to miss anything. The paths receded ever more deeply into solitude and silence, by deep reaches of woodland, and sudden isolated green ovals of meadow. We crossed the water, and walked beside it on the other side almost to the edge of the estate. There were no people, and no sound but from birds and the small things that run in the grass. Here and there one of the unexpected shrines would appear, fixed to the trunk of a tree, showing some saint in prayer, including St. Jerome complete with lion. Later, when I was here alone, there always seemed to be a flock of sheep picking thin pasture inside the park, a shepherd and his dog with them. On one day, when I was sitting in the park, a sudden wind-storm blew up from nowhere, tore madly through the trees and hurled branches to the ground in a litter of falling leaves and rustling twigs. In half an hour it was all over, the tree-tops were quite still; but when I went out again I found the paths cumbered with shattered boughs.

It was a place, I thought, which might more suitably have been a castle for naturalists. I saw here butterflies I had never seen before, and the names of which I do not know; and there was plentiful life in and about the water. Once, walking along the path beyond the creek, I almost stepped on a snake about two and a half feet long, which was doing its slow best to swallow a fish about three times the breadth of its own head. The fish was half inside, the snake's mouth enormously distended to take it in, and the effect was like a small king cobra with its hood inflated. I did not see them until the snake threshed uneasily at my near tread, for the path was littered with brushings from trees, after woodsmen had been busy there; and the movement was so sudden that I almost fell into the lake. The fish was dead, and the snake appeared to be pretty well exhausted; but he got him down, for when I came back they were gone.

We left at dusk, and drove back to Prague along the forest roads, singing Czech songs to pass the time. When I came back along the same route by bus after my later visit I did so in the middle of the afternoon, and all along the forest part of the way people were climbing aboard with piled-up baskets of mushrooms, the big, plump-stemmed "houby" like lightly-baked cottage loaves, which grow in the bare brown ground of the forests. I had already seen them spread out for sale on the pavements of the square at Zlin, and many times had eaten soup prepared with them. Other people seemed to find them in great quantities, but for some reason I never could. In Zlin we had tried once all the evening, and I, obstinately English, had brought back, of all the improbable kinds to find in a wood, only the familiar mushroom of the English meadows in September, or something so like it that I could not tell the difference.

In town we parted from the Kubaneks at Jirasek Bridge, and returned to our suburb by tram through the neon-lighted wonderland of Prague by night.

11

Melnik and Kokorin Valley

Honza was now safely through his immediate examination worries, and so, as we heard from his village near Melnik, was Pavel; so we planned to meet him for a day out in his own part of the world.

Across Hlavka Bridge, in the street called Florence, they were just preparing a big new bus station, with numbered stands and every convenience. It was not quite ready when we went along to look up the buses, but on the day when we rose early to set out at seven o'clock it was already in action.

Later we developed a technique in dealing with buses. The thing to do with a fellow of Honza's height was to move right to the back, where in case of overcrowding he could not possibly rise and surrender his seat; or if that was out of the question, to remain somewhere within reach of the sliding section of the roof, so that when his nice nature got the better of him, as it invariably did, he could at least stand in comfort, with the top of his lofty head protruding into fresh air. Otherwise he travelled in torture, and emerged bent double, or at the very best with a bad crick in his neck. But I had not yet considered the possibilities, and on this occasion we had one of the few remaining seats, half-way down the bus.

Melnik, the wine town of Czechoslovakia, lies due north of Prague, and about an hour away by road. We left town by way of Karlin and Kobylisy, skirting the bend of the

Vltava, and climbed out of the valley to rolling upland villages, leaving the military airfield away on our right hand. The factories of the north-eastern suburbs slipped behind us, and there was the true Bohemia, the clean, colour-washed houses, the ponds and greens and orchards of a garden and meadow country, made for the sun and the summer; and the day was opening in warm splendour, the very day for which the land was made. Strips of poppies, white and red, the white tinted at the roots of the petals with mauve, made gay patterns across the fields; geese were encamped in the stony little beaches of ponds like miraculous drifts of fresh snow.

When two-thirds of the journey was over, we reached the villages which used Melnik as their shopping centre, and the bus bulged with marketing women and their baskets. Up went Honza and soon was thrust back towards the rear of the bus by more and more people crowding in at the front. Czech buses do not believe in leaving people behind. The limit is the limit of cubic content when everyone aboard is holding his breath.

Shortly before entering Melnik we crossed the river Labe, which later becomes the Elbe. Then the road began to rise into the town, and soon we reached the square, and began to breathe again as the first of our number alighted. Honza was not much crumpled, the bus being one of the loftier ones; and as he had been standing only a short time the few creases would soon come out.

"I see Pavel waiting for us," he said; and there outside the window was the unforgotten, incandescent grin which blinded one to the rest of Pavel's appearance. He is the most Slavonic Slav I know in looks, with the light, bright, positive blue eyes, the bold, well-shaped bones, the impassive gravity, and the sudden blazing smile proper, at least, to the idea of the Slav. Neither of us had seen him for a year, and we were both glad to meet with him again.

"There is a bus to my village," he said, when we had greeted one another, "in just over half an hour. So until then we can go for a little walk round by the castle, and perhaps see the wine cellars, and we can talk as we go. Then you will catch the bus, and I have my bike here, I shall be home as soon as you."

We had indeed plenty to say as we walked up from the square, and rounded a corner to emerge on the terrace of the castle, which now contains one of the most famous restaurants in the country, naturally known everywhere for its wine. It is set in a magnificent position, above a steep slope of vineyards which drops to the confluence of the rivers Vltava and Labe. They run here as level and smooth-edged as canals, and merge gracefully, a long point of grass holding them apart until it dwindles imperceptibly away to nothing, and the two rivers are one river. The castle extends all along the terrace above, looking out over this green and gentle expanse of country; one of those long-roofed, evenly windowed, undramatic castles, like Hrad-cany itself, turned into a thing of loveliness by the accuracy of its assembly into the whole scene, by its correct placing on the hill-top, its level reproduction of the lines of the vine-terraces below, and the sudden lofty vertical counter-balance of the tower of the church, which sits cunningly so close that it might be part of it, and shoots up to more than double the height of the castle roofs. I have often noticed in Bohemia how such assemblies of buildings appear to have been conceived as a group; but whether this is ever indeed so, or whether in every case some genius came along, found one attempt incomplete, and added the transforming church, or tower, or wing, I do not know.

We walked round to the courtyard of the castle, and asked if we could go down into the wine cellars. Pavel's smile was irresistible, and we could. They led us down many dark stairways and passages to an underworld of busy people bottling and casing the famous local wines, and beyond, into more obscure and reverend places where enormous casks were stored, the round ends which fronted us topping even Honza by several feet. These casks were things beautiful in themselves, very old, their wood grown richly dark, and on each one its name and its patron saint carved as lovingly as the misereres and bench-ends of any cathedral. Saints took care of them every one, for they were precious, not to be entrusted to ordinary men. The cellars smelled heady with wine-fumes, and pleasantly sleepy; but with the bus in mind we could not linger there for long.

Pavel gave us quick directions in Czech when we emerged again into the square, for our bus was already in, and beginning to fill. Honza relayed them to me at leisure when we were installed in the back seat, our feet stretched out among assorted baskets and bundles, for in this bus there was a space for luggage in the back. At the last moment Pavel came tapping at the window, and handed in to us a large, flat, floppy parcel wrapped in brown paper, which we were strictly enjoined to take care of, and deliver safely to his mother at Bosyne, on pain of his displeasure. He did not see why he should carry it on his bicycle, when we were travelling by bus. He was wise, for its floppiness proved a problem after we alighted; however one carried it, it sagged, and Honza ended with it balanced on one spread palm, like a waiter with a tray. We speculated on what it could be, and decided it was the family laundry; nothing else makes quite the same sort of parcel.

We had still some rolls, and some sliced sausage to go with them, and on the way we demolished the lot. Then we began to look out for the place where we had to alight.

"We shall pass the road-sign," said Honza, "and then we get out at the turning on the right, and that brings us into the village. We have to find Pavel's house by the number, but in a village like that it may be anywhere, because when the next house goes up it takes the next number, not by roads or streets."

We passed the convenient road-sign which always gives the name of the village you are approaching, and knew our time. Alighting, we took the road on the right as we had been told, up through a winding village of small farms and cottages and orchards, keeping a close watch on the numbers of the houses as we went. As Honza had prophesied, some ran in order, others cropped up in the oddest corners. However, one road seemed to serve the whole village, though it twisted enough for three in the process, so we were sure of finding our goal at last. We turned a corner, and came upon a stretch of road which consisted at the moment entirely of the rough underlayer of stones, as big as clenched fists.

"We're on the right track," said Honza positively. "This is the road Pavel has been helping to make." For he had shown us proudly the blisters of his latest brigade.

We didn't think much of his work by the time we had walked a hundred yards upon it. We told him so, when he came peddling along madly behind us on the grass verge, just before we reached his own door. He objected indignantly that it wasn't finished yet. We hoped not, indeed!

No one else was at home that morning except his mother, who welcomed us with the warmth and kindness I met everywhere, but spoke no English. Pavel himself was just beginning to be comfortable in that language, after many months of using, in general, only his own; and we spent the rest of the morning giving each other full accounts of the year which had passed since we last met, sitting all three together round the table in the cottage parlour, with our elbows comfortably spread and our tongues going at full speed. He had planned a walk through the valley of Kokorin for the afternoon, and a visit to the castle, so the interlude of sitting still was acceptable.

The cottage had two storeys, and a beautiful outlook from a small wooden balcony upstairs, since it stood somewhat higher than the houses opposite, and could look clean over them across the valley beyond. Pavel had all kinds of plans about the decorating he was going to do, now that his examination was safely over. If he got through half of them I think he would have done his duty nobly by his family.

His mother was kindness itself, and like all Czech mothers, anxious to feed us beyond the capacity of even our appetites, not to speak of the disastrous effect upon the rations. She gave us dinner, and before we set out for Kokorin made up for us many packets of her own cakes, the Czech "kolace" made like large tarts, but with a different kind of pastry, filled with cherries or bilberries, and sprinkled with sugar. By this time Honza had shed his wind-jacket, and we had in our mesh bag not only that and the mackintosh and the cameras, but now several packages of food, and Honza was afraid the whole thing would collapse. We had endeavoured to reduce the food supplies, but without success; so when Pavel's mother was not looking we quietly deposited the largest parcel in a corner where it would not be immediately noticed, and the bag ceased to sag quite so ominously.

"We will explain to Pavel afterwards," said Honza, "and he will make our apologies for us."

We set out at last, taking leave of Mrs. Novotna, and went on through the village almost into open country, and then turned abruptly to the left, and dived down into a narrow cleft which presently widened into a wooded valley, deep and silent. All trace of the village disappeared at once. The path twisted gently, but bore mainly in the same direction, and constantly the valley grew a little

wider, to a point where the woods fell back, and we
emerged into a green meadow filling the floor of a deep
limestone bowl, the walls of which were broken up into fantastic columnar shapes, weathered in pillars and stems and
smooth cliff-faces, with trees and bushes precariously clawing
a foothold in the crevices. Holiday huts, not too conspicuous,
some of them built back against the rock, began to appear.
Often one could well have done without them, but I never
saw any quite so noisome as some of the bungaloid growths
which deface our own coastal beauty spots. Here they were
not enough to offend, and were of wood, which helped
them to fit well into their background, though the Czechs
make exactly the same disrespectful comments on the
phenomenon which we make in England.

Here the curve of the road brought us out into the floor
of a wider valley, and directly on to a road which ran
along the shore of a sizeable lake. There was a hotel, and a
few people were sunning themselves in swimming costumes,
and one or two were in the water. Pavel pronounced the
pool rather weedy for swimming, though it would do at
a pinch. On the other side of it trees climbed, and the
rock walls which everywhere enclosed these surprising,
level arenas. We went alongside the lake for a time, and
then left the road again for another valley path which
turned off to the right; and again we were shut in by trees
and the enfolding pillars of rock, and again it was warm
and very silent.

This valley went on and on, and grew steadily, the cliff
walls receding to enclose fields, a stream, scattered houses,
and the neat, coloured crops of strip-farming made
patterns in the level ground. We kept under the right-hand
wall for a time, and passed by many villas disposed into
the sheltered corners of it; then we crossed over and took
the left-hand side instead, crossing a road which threaded
the valley, and again preferring a footpath which quickly

detached itself to walk under the trees. Here there was a whole village of houses, though many of these, too, appeared to be holiday villas; and in the afternoon heat many families were sunbathing on the grassy slopes above the brook, and many children were wading in it naked. It was grassily overgrown, but the water was clear; and over it like animated fragments of lapis lazuli flickered great numbers of some blue-winged fly, shaped as a dragon-fly, but smaller. I never saw them anywhere but over this one small stream in Kokorin Valley.

This is the country of "May", and of Karel Hynek Macha, of star-crossed, stormy love and hectic romanticism; for it was this beautiful and strange valley which moved the young romantic poet Macha to write his most famous poem. I think every Czech knows it, but I confess that I do not. I know of no translation into English, and I never had the Czech copy in my hands long enough to extract anything from it beyond an impression of short lines pressing ahead with the impetus of fever, and a recurrent couplet setting the scene for a drama, which, so far as I am concerned, still waits to be performed.

Byron was an influence in this part of the world, and Macha is regarded as one of his followers; either that, or the time and the circumstances and the aspirations of his brief life tugged him in the same direction, for I am chary of over-simplifying. Some singular energy of his own, I fancy, was needed to leave so vivid an impression from so few years of living, for 1810 to 1836, according to his statue on Petrin, was all the time he had. He was not even quite twenty-six when he died. You see him in this monument as a handsome, pensive young man leaning back upon a low wall, turning momentarily away from his poem to regard with tender melancholy the nosegay in his left hand; the perfect prototype of the early nineteenth-century romantic, quickly withdrawn into the shades before his indignant promise of greatness could either transform or betray him. Perhaps saved, perhaps cheated; who knows which?

We walked on towards the still invisible castle by a path between woods and water, the brook grown into a long, slender pool on our right hand, banks of bilberries on the left, which we ate as we went until we had the purple-black tongues of good chows. Now we could see the lime-stone walls of our valley only on the far side, a long way off, with here and there buildings, the most noticeable a little church, placed fantastically along the edge, on another level of the world.

We came out at length on a good motor road, made in the first republic, which began to climb steeply on our left, leaving behind at the foot of the hill a hotel and swimming-pool. We climbed with it, and now we were actually under the castle, though we still could not see it, for woods en-folded the road. We turned aside as soon as possible by a sharper and shorter path, up through the silent aisles of the trees, and presently we were walking under the looming masonry of the outer walls of the castle.

A flight of stone stairs, narrow and without handrail, but in good repair, climbed along the wall to a large door-way. Honza and Pavel invited me to mount first, and assured me that this was the quickest way in; and did it so well, and with so little false emphasis, that like a fool I believed them. I did not observe until I was half-way up that they were not following, but moving onward very gently by the path below, and watching me with pleased satisfaction and surprise. I dare say it was a long time since they'd had any success with this gag. I returned to earth with less complacency than I had left it, for I am not really partial to unrailed heights; but I was warned now that anything could happen, and should not bite so easily next time.

The path wound round the outer wall and entered a wide gate, and we were in the courtyard, which was small and narrow, and almost entirely shaded by a large cherry tree; from which, as we were quick to notice, almost all the accessible cherries were already gone. There was a spot on the watch-platform from which the branches could be reached, but little to gather from them. I don't know why the first instinct of quite law-abiding people at sight of fruit trees should be a predatory one.

Kokorin is much restored, and makes no great claims to be an authentic piece of history; but as always it crowns its hill and completes the valley scene to perfection. The whole castle is contained within a high, crenellated wall, along the inner side of which the watch-platform runs at a height which enables you to look out over the whole great cleft of the valley from cliff to cliff. But it is even better to climb the stair which spirals upward inside the round grey tower, and to enjoy the much wider view from the top, where you can walk all round a conical roof like a witch's hat, and look out in all directions from the many deep embrasures of the battlements. The most delightful thing about the whole place was that no one showed us round; we were let in and turned loose, and when we had investigated everything we went down at leisure and sat at a wooden table in the courtyard, under a tree, writing postcards and eating our supplies of cakes.

I remembered the package we had left behind, and asked Honza if he had yet told Pavel about it.

"Oh, yes," he said, "I told him some time ago."

"And what did he say?"

"He named me in a very familiar way," said Honza austerely, and presented me with the last cake.

Our day in the sun was drawing towards evening already, and we had almost finished with Kokorin. All that remained was to climb out of it by the motor road, which in the course of its sinuous journey to the upper levels of the world offered many increasingly fine glimpses of the castle. The best, I think, is to be seen from the very crest of the rise, where the road levels out with a sigh of relief along the high, flat land towards the village. There you must turn again where the trees part and show you the enfolding wall, the compact, doll's-house block with its high red roof on the right, the tall tower in its witch's hat on the left, with a lower red-tiled roof tucked under it; here you are on a level with it, though the wooded valley holds you off like an olive-green moat protecting a fairy place. No wonder that some of the Czech children's books I have seen excel in the illustration of fairy tales; all those charmed towers and remote palaces on magical mountains might have come straight from the everyday life of Bohemia.

The walk into the village was now level and sunny, upon a white country road bordered with cherry trees. The white and rose fruit leaned down to us temptingly. We had eaten well, but had had nothing to drink since dinner, and we had walked a long way in the heat, and were very thirsty. Often I had marvelled at the rows of unravished fruit trees along Czech highways, and admired the virtue of a nation which could resist the lure. Now we hesitated, but the sight of a couple of men with ladders and baskets, engaged in the lawful harvesting of this crop, somehow clinched the matter. We helped ourselves; only to modest handfuls to eat as we walked, and with special pleasure at doing it neatly and smoothly under the very noses of the custodians, but the crime was none the less regrettable. However, nothing I ever ate tasted better than those stolen cherries.

At Kokorin village we caught a bus back to Melnik, and dropped Pavel on the way, with many regrets that the time had been so short, and many thanks for the much we had packed into it. As always after a whole day in the fresh air, I was half asleep by this time in the evening, but the bus was proof against sleep, and by the time we pulled into the square at Melnik I was again thirsty, and demanded something to drink.

"You can have," said Honza, looking at the crowd of people waiting for our bus back to Prague, "either a seat in the bus or a drink; but you won't have both."

I chose the drink; but he proved right about the seat, for by the time we came back the bus was already in, and full. However, we stood in fair comfort, for it was a high-roofed one, and an hour of hanging on to the rack was not much to complain about in a day as near perfect as one can reasonably hope for in this world.

12

A Place of Pilgrimage

THE Slet proper was to begin on Saturday, June 19th, with the display of the youngest children, and to this great day already thousands of little people were looking forward with intense anticipation. We had bought tickets for the performance of the fourteens to eighteens, as well as two full Sokol displays and Army Day, and since something had to be missed I reluctantly decided to miss the children, and go instead to Brandys-on-Labe and Stara Boleslav, at the kind invitation of another family of friends, the Smoliks. This was another bus journey from Florence, and I set out, as usual, at an ungodly hour in the morning, for the Czech day habitually begins earlier than ours.

When Honza and I walked over Hlavka Bridge that morning the day had every appearance of promising good weather and no worries, and already the town was alive with small, earnest Sokols, effulgent with excitement; but by the time the bus had reached Stara Boleslav the sky was overcast, and within another hour it was beginning to rain. This, after the brilliance of Easter, and Whitsun, and Corpus Christi, and all the other holidays of the year, seemed incredible; was it possible that the weather could suddenly decide to be unkind to the children? It was. The rain, which began desultorily, soon settled down to its work in determined fashion, and the day ended in grey, solid, unrelenting drizzle. In Prague I believe it had patches of brightness, but the rain soon made a damp mess of the arena, and the heroic children, who would naturally rather have died than cancelled their performance, drilled and played in the wet sand as well as they could, were dried out behind the scenes as often and as thoroughly as time allowed, and consumed as much as possible of the extra food and sweets and fruit which had been thoughtfully provided for them; and came up smiling at the end of their gruelling day, when the teachers, instructors and Sokol officials who had had charge of them were one and all prostrate. This was the only performance for the six and seven year olds, so everyone tried to compensate them for the failure of the weather.

Stara Boleslav lies north from Prague, perhaps three-quarters of an hour away by bus, holding hands with Brandys across the Labe, some distance upstream from its confluence with the Vltava at Melnik. Brandys is the business town, Stara Boleslav the dormitory town, full of gracious houses redolent of retirement and the professions, not exactly wealthy, but what might be described as comfortably off. Some of the roads there, the houses and gardens which border them, could easily belong to the remoter and more exclusive suburbs of some English city. Any walk out from it will take you very quickly into the familiar green and pastel-coloured villages again; but the general impression one receives is that much of the population of Stara Boleslav itself has closer ties with Prague than with the countryside.

It is much more than a dormitory town, however, being one of the holiest of Czech holy places, the scene of St. Vaclav's murder. It seems strange that they should have chosen to christen the place, not for the saint, but for his murderer, for Boleslav was his brother, who struck him down in the very act of clutching at the sanctuary ring of the church door, and promptly took over his principality. It is perhaps not very important, but at that time it was not a kingdom, and Good King Wenceslas was not, in fact, a king, but a ruling prince. The ancient church which witnessed this tragedy of the patron of the land is now enshrined in the heart of St. Vaclav's cathedral here, for the greater church was entirely built over and around it, a casket about a diamond.

But not content with one cathedral, Stara Boleslav has also a second one, St. Mary the Virgin, within a stone's throw of the first; and not content with drawing pilgrims to the one for a glimpse of the blood and bones of St. Vaclav, it draws them as vigorously to the other to adore the miraculous picture of Virgin and Child known as the Palladium of the Czech Lands, a small rectangular gold relief which has been submerged time and again in the course of history, and always come safely out of the hands of its enemies to resume an honourable place in the life of the nation. So on any fine Sunday can be safely guaranteed in Stara Boleslav at least one band, and many national costumes, and if you are lucky a procession, as well as a perpetual flavour of a religious fair, with stalls, garish pictures, coloured mementoes of your visit, sweet cakes and sweeter drinks. And this side of the town is older than the charming villas and the English gardens, and has survived many changes and much growth, and will as placidly survive any amount more.

Petr Smolik boarded the bus in the square of Brandys to see me safely home to his wife Jitka, though he had thereafter to return to the office and finish the morning's work.

Jitka was Moravian, vivacious and vigorous in body and mind. She was the mother of three children, but sometimes, haring about on a bicycle with her hair down, she looked like their slightly older sister. She approached all human creatures with perfect warmth, confidence and fearlessness, attracted liking as a magnet does metal, and gave it as unreservedly as a stream gives water. Intellectually she was like cut crystal, as clear, as definite and as glitteringly honest. Emotionally she was affectionate, impetuous and impatient, but she balanced all these explosive qualities with an enormous sense of humour. If she disagrees with this summing-up her sense of justice will still allow me my point of view, and her sense of fun will delight in the results.

There were three children, two little girls of eight and six, Ana and Antonie, and a little boy of two, Venousek; but Ana and Antonie were in Prague for the day, for they were ardent Sokols, and had been looking forward for weeks to their appearance at Strahov.

"We don't expect them home until after nine this evening," said Jitka. "They will come home very tired and wet, and we shall have to put them straight to bed. But here is Venousek to say how do you do."

He was small but sturdy, with fair hair and the light, bright Slav eyes of extreme seriousness. His greeting was a grave and wobbly bow, and when he had several visitors he would stand in the middle, face each one in turn, and perform the same courtly evolution, sticking out his small seat behind, and ducking his fair topknot in front. His instinct, upon entering a room, was to make a bee-line for anything eatable which happened to be in it at the time; and to do this with the aplomb of an arrow leaving the bow he did not appear to have to employ any of the usual senses, but only a sixth one which connected him invisibly with food. But having reached it he would distribute it scrupulously among the whole company, not content to consume his own biscuit until everyone else had been presented with one. Naturally he didn't think it necessary to hand them round on a plate, but used the more reliable steerage method, and if he was short he would bestow on someone the biscuit on which he had already commenced operations. The great thing was that every-

F

one should be fed. He never walked anywhere, even if it was only three steps away, but always ran full tilt. Petr thought him the most wonderful child who had ever astonished the world; he didn't say so, but he didn't need to say it.

He was accustomed to visitors, and treated them graciously, for it was a poor day when at least ten different people did not at some time or other invade the house. Petr and Jitka had both the gift for friendship highly developed, and their small circle over coffee, for instance, would be expanded gradually during the first cup to take in half a dozen extra persons who had just happened to wander in to see them at the right moment. The conversation would expand with the circle, until it took in politics, religion, social problems, literature, art, and the whole business of living.

The two small wet Sokols returned from their watery triumph in Prague at about nine o'clock, as Jitka had prophesied, but not in quite the state we had foreseen. Excitement had kept them keyed to the top pressure of activity. "They will be too tired to creep," Jitka had said. They erupted into the hall like Chinese firecrackers, sat on the floor to tear off their muddy boots, shed their raincoats wherever they fell, leaped upon their parents, talked both at once in a continuous and crescendo flood, and when Petr was unwise enough to sit down in a big chair, climbed all over him and almost pulled him to pieces. Ana was dark, and changing her teeth, so that she had an engaging gap at the moment. Antonie was fair like Venousek, and had her father's features. They both appeared to be made mainly of india-rubber and whalebone. They described their day ecstatically, the perfect way they had drilled, the nice things they had had to eat, how they had spent their money. They demonstrated some of their exercises, singing breathlessly the music to them. They behaved exactly as all children behave at the end of a day which has transcended their wildest dreams; the only marvel was that they had energy left even to be aware of their own happiness, much less convey it to others.

The rain did not appear to be worth considering, for they passed it off with nonchalant shrugs. Oh, yes, it had rained, but that had spoiled nothing at all. They were whisked off up the stairs to hot baths, and put to bed, the recital still continuing diminuendo as they vanished.

The last anxiety was about tomorrow's Sunday-school. They were reluctant to consider the possibility of having to rise in time for this very early institution, after such a long day; but Petr was a stickler for duty, and disposed to insist that a day's pleasure, however hard one had to work in the course of it, was no excuse for missing Sunday-school next day. However, Jitka despatched the children with soothing words, and then arranged everything. Considering, she said cheerfully, that almost all the children involved had been in Prague, and would be going to bed very late, it was a practical certainty that if Ana and Antonie went they would have instruction alone; and it was long odds that this would have occurred to the teachers, and that they would tacitly consider Sunday-school to be off.

Petr seldom missed attending his church on Sunday morning, but on this particular day the marriage of the Communist and Social Democrat parties was being solemnised in Stara Boleslav, though the official date for the country was later; and there was a joint meeting on the occasion, at which he had been asked to speak. He was out of the house before I was out of bed, and I did not see him during the morning; meetings, like processions, went on for hours in CSR.

In the late afternoon, when the light rain had stopped, I went with Petr to see the cathedral, while Jitka began to prepare the supper. The day had been wet up to now, so wet in Prague that the children's procession through the city was cancelled, to their great disappointment; but here in the early evening there was some sun, and the roads and even the trees soon dried. The air was sweet and fresh with the scent of lime flowers.

We passed by the brightly coloured stalls which stood outside the gates of St. Vaclav's, selling little china hearts, crosses, pendants painted with tuppence-coloured religious pictures, of that childish and crude quality which I find so hard to reconcile with the Roman Catholic church's standards of beauty in the sister art of music. Why should one so perfectly understand how to move the minds of a mass of people through their ears with sounds of impeccable taste and austere loveliness, and at the same time find it necessary to appeal to their eyes on the lowest possible level? It is a thing which has often puzzled me. But the effect of the stalls themselves was by no means the same as the effect of their individual wares. Hung with their masses of red and white and blue and sugar-pink spiritual confectionery, they made a glow of spangled brightness under the deep green of the trees, against the yellowish-brown wall, and were curiously pleasant to behold.

We entered the cathedral, and looked for the verger, for Petr was determined that we should see everything, and did not claim to know it all by heart. St. Vaclav's as it stands now is a long baroque church, with two curving staircases leading up from the nave to the much higher level of the choir, and between these the doorway to the old church, leading down by several steps into the small, dark interior of the Romanesque holy of holies, St. Cosmas and Damian. We found the lights and switched them on. Plain stone pillars support a shallow-vaulted roof, withdrawing into a greater length than at first you suppose. At this west end there have been some later reconstructions, but they say that the altar end is actually the body of the church of the martyrdom, a thousand years old. Here in a narrow slit window Cosmas and Damian stand cramped for space; and here was the first burial place of St. Vaclav after the murder, before he was taken away, and most of his treasures and relics with him, to lie in St. Vitus on Hradcany, as the possession of the whole country, and ultimately its patron saint.

It is silent and dim here, and awe comes in; even a sceptic could be moved, I think, by the thought that he was standing on the site of a martyrdom whose memory ten centuries have not obscured. On the left, as we faced the altar, there was a window through into the main church, and a lamp burning over it, hung by chains from the roof. This was the very spot where once was the door to which the saint clung as he was killed; but this one sees best from outside.

The verger came, and led us round to the side aisle and chapels which flank the choir; and there was the outer side of the window, ringed round with a protective screen of wrought iron, and within it a group of life-size figures re-enacted the thousand-year-old tragedy. The saint knelt, just fallen forward to catch at the ring; the murderer's sword was on the point of piercing his side, the accomplices crowded eagerly in, and the lamp above cast a soft rose-coloured glow over their baroque violence and agitation. Baroque can be terrifying; sometimes it seems in such positive motion that one feels the silence is not really silence, but the suspension of a sense.

Above the window was a painted stone relief of a company of knights riding out with the Prince at their head. This, the verger told us, had been carefully represented during the occupation to be merely a complimentary portrait of Vaclav and his army, so that it should escape otherwise certain destruction; for what it really meant, of course, was the ride of the magical armies of Blanik, coming out to the help of the country in time of need. And the Germans had failed to see the inner significance of it, and let it alone, an inspiration to those who understood it, until the time of liberation came.

Relics of the saint are kept here still, in a cupboard in the panelling of the choir. We climbed the curving stair-case past the gorgeous gilt and marble pulpit, and the verger unlocked the shrine, and showed us crystal vases of Charles IV, containing some almost indistinguishable scraps of hair and bone, and some fragments of wood, now crumbling towards dust, stained dull brown with his illustrious blood. Many such relics repel, I find. The battered skulls of St. Ursula's virgin companions, in their glass case in St. George's on Hradcany, the reclining skeletons of St. Vincent Martyr and St. Felix Martyr in the great church of Sedlec near Kutna Hora, clothed and with waxen faces, turn one's mind rather to a consideration of the ghoulish quality of human imagination than to any heavenly thoughts; even the Abbess-Princess Mlada in St. George's, though she lies like a tomb sculpture, reposefully, and not on one elbow like a Roman at a feast, and though the mask which covers her face is young and beautiful, appeals to the morbidity in us all rather than to our reverence. But these minute and fragile things in their crystal cups, hardly more than cobweb and dust, are so slight that they succeed in being suggestive instead of threatening, pathetic instead of grim; the very fact that their delicacy has survived a thousand years—or even that one is asked to believe it has done so—invites the mind to wonder and awe. St. Vaclav becomes triumphantly real to the imaginative here, simply because so little of his substance remains to get in the way.

Along the upper reaches of the walls there are painted scenes from his life, and a short life it was, of charity and gentleness and piety. He was twenty-two when he was killed, but a creature so reverend that most painters and sculptors who have been moved to portray him, even here in his own country, have given him a beard, and the foreign ones have even made it a long and a white beard. Here he is himself baking the bread and pressing the wine for the sacrament, and here as the English know him best, carrying food and drink through the snow to the poor, his half-frozen page walking in his miraculous footprints and regaining warmth and vigour at their touch.

Whether the young prince was as efficient as he was pious is a matter for doubt. When we were speaking of him once Honza said provocatively: "But you know, I am not sure it was so bad a thing Boleslav did when he killed him. He was not a very wise ruler; he paid tribute money to the Germans when they threatened, and after Boleslav succeeded him he didn't go on doing that. I think he made a better job of things than his brother."

Perhaps, then, when the Czechs rest their minds on the promise of Blanik they are relying on the myth which time has made out of Vaclav, rather than on a historically true figure. The tribute money has been washed away somewhere by the tides of man's mass forgetfulness, and the halo catches the transfiguring light of his mass optimism.

Because of the enclosed church under it, the cathedral has a shape and character almost unique, though St. George's church in Prague enfolds its crypt in precisely the same way, climbing over it by two staircases; but there the choir does not remove itself on the higher level almost from sight of the nave, as it does here, detaching the inner half of the service, I should imagine, from the bulk of the people. Still I like this place, it has an eccentric and inconvenient beauty, and is not so awesomely overweighted with decoration, with black marble and gilt altars and baroque monuments, as many Czech churches are. After it, the other cathedral of the Blessed Virgin, for all its treasure of the small gold palladium, looks ostentatious and has a spiky glitter of ornate altars and much gilding and silver, striking at the eyes from all sides at once in an uncomfortable fashion. I do not find baroque at its most exuberant at all conducive to worship; it seems much more adapted to impressing the passer-by with man's own arrogance in the flourishes of his palace fronts, as palladian did in England during the assertive eighteenth century. But it can be extremely exciting.

"The house of the canons here has a nice garden," said Petr when we emerged from the church. "We can go and look at it." And though it was a private garden, into it we went, through a corner of the cathedral grounds. It was large, and full of fruit trees and some rather sad, battered but very sweet roses, ill-used by the rain. The house of canons stood just outside its gates, and suddenly in the middle of a pathway we met one of them, an old man in decent black and a dog-collar, who could have come straight out of Trollope. He had the authentic clean-shaven, classical gentleness of the nicer Barcastrians and was reading a book as he ambled along between the damp bushes; and on seeing us he naturally shut the book upon a guarding finger, and asked if we were looking for anyone. Petr made me the excuse for our trespass; I was English, and must be shown everything, and we had entered to admire the garden.

The old man made us free of it at once, and regretted that much of the early fruit was either gathered or damaged, and the apples not yet ready. I must come back in a few weeks, and visit him again. Then he asked if I would do him a small favour. He had received a present of an American razor, and was not getting on with it as well as he could have wished; and he wondered if perhaps he was not using it correctly. There was a paper enclosed with it which might, if we would translate it for him, give him some tips for getting the best out of the gift. Naturally we said we would be happy to try to help, and he begged us to eat as much fruit as we liked while he fetched the paper from the house.

We needed no second telling, for there were still fine currants, gooseberries and even some cherries, and we investigated every tree in the garden. Petr had a boy's appetite, and his instinct when confronted with anything growing on a tree was to ask himself at once: "What's this? Is it eatable?"

Unfortunately we were not of much use to the old man. When he returned with the paper we found that all we had to translate was the usual advertising matter, and I am afraid he got little good from that, and has probably gone back to his old razor by now. However, we had some little conversation with him, and before we left he cut for me what roses were left, and we took them home to Jitka with the pleasantest memories of the canons' garden and at least one of the canons.

There were some attractive walks round Brandys, as I was able to discover during the next day or two, for the weather improved, and sometimes alone, sometimes with Jitka and Venousek when the two little girls were at school, I walked in the water meadows of the Labe, among charming natural parks, and round the old, small streets of the town. Brandys looks very fine from the bridge which connects it with Stara Boleslav. One would be cheated without a castle, but there it stands, on higher ground overlooking the river, quite near to the bridge, a deep cream castle, urban and urbane, with a single tower. The Labe offers good bathing in hot weather; many people come out even from Prague on summer week-ends to Kostelec and Melnik and other Labe towns, preferring it to the crowded city pools of Vltava.

F*

It was Jitka's part, in the discussions which went on ceaselessly in the Smolik household and circle, whether on art, music, politics or any other subject, to uphold the honour of Moravia in this corner of sophisticated Bohemia. "You will find," she warned me, "that Moravians are dreadful local patriots." I had just made the acquaintance of the operas of Leos Janacek, beginning with what was probably not the best choice, *The Trips of Mr. Broucek*; but already getting tickets for Prague theatres was largely a matter of grabbing without quibble at whatever offered, or missing everything.

"Oh, Janacek is not appreciated here," said Jitka, "because he is Moravian. To be fashionable in Prague you must also be a Praguer. He will be acknowledged abroad before he gets his due here."

I had heard advanced as another reason for his late recognition the fact that his natural leanings were to the east, and not instinctively western as in the cases of Smetana and Dvorak. About that I am not competent to speak. But as a voice from the auditorium only I can say that he is not a composer with whom the ordinary listener can instantly feel on good terms; one has to get to know him by respectful stages. I had seen *Mr. Broucek* at the Grand Opera of the 5th of May, and found it hard going until something familiar caught my ear in the second act.

It is a satirical opera based on a novel of Svatopluk Čech, in which the earthy, limited and insensitive Prague landlord, stumbling home drunk from the Vikarka tavern— a real one, folded into the arm of Hradcany, just round the corner of St. Vitus—is transported into some situations as remarkable as he himself is commonplace. The first trip is to the moon, whose creatures of air and spirit are at a loss how to find any common ground with this gross piece of matter. The stage had a wonderful moon, which revolved all through the act, but unhappily creaked softly the whole time. The second trip is to the heroic days of the Hussite wars, to an embattled Prague erect with the spirit of Zizka, where again this hunk of twentieth-century practicality at its lowest falls ignominiously short of standard. And it was here that my ear began to pick up majestic echoes of the old war chorales which served the Hussite legions as the psalms of David served Cromwell. Czech music is full of them, and rightly, for Czech history and character would have been different without them. They have a splendour which is not of defiance, not of hope, not of triumph, but of absolute and immovable certainty; they assert that faith really is a rock, a thing in itself, not affected by its manifest justification or apparent emptiness.

"But where Praguers are concerned," says Jitka, with a provocative twinkle in her eye, "the mistake he made was in being born out of Bohemia."

When I left Stara Boleslav she was just expecting her father for a visit. The house was never without visitors. Ana came with us to the square to see me off and to welcome her grandfather. When she was excited her eyes and her whole face shone like stars, and already so much of this small person was thoughts and feelings and sensitivities that I didn't wonder she was thin as a willow. Antonie was more placid and substantial, and also more shy. They were unending fun together, and there was always some new story about them. Later in the summer they went away to a school camp, and on their return Antonie confided to her mother that she had enjoyed herself very much, but all the same she was very glad to come home again.

"Whom did you miss most?" asked Jitka, impulsively fishing. It is one of her favourite stories, and I think she liked the answer she got much better than the one for which she was angling.

"My bicycle!" said Antonie.

13

"Not For Glory, Not For Gain!"

I RETURNED to a Prague now fully en fête, crowded with visitors, billowing with bunting, and full of music. Sokol uniforms and brass bands were everywhere, and the town had burst into an orgy of exhibitions, Manes water-colours at Kramar's house, prints and maps of the Hradcany throughout its history at the Belvedere, fifty years of Czech films at the museum on Letna, the Radio Exhibition still in full flower near Stromovka, and the Agricultural Exhibition just dwindling away into the background after entertaining millions. It was difficult to get into a theatre at all, for whole performances at the National Theatre were booked up for Sokol or other organisations, though foreigners had ways and means of getting their own way. With the town in a perpetually festive mood, like this, it was impossible to settle to anything more serious than enjoyment. We went the round of the galleries, saw some films, and *St. Joan* in Czech at the Vinohrady Theatre, and Professor Skupa's puppets, who were just back from touring Britain; and the festival of the Sokol youth, the fourteens to eighteens, came round very quickly.

Their procession was on Sunday, the 27th of June, and they opened with a full-dress display at Strahov the same afternoon. We had seats in the south tribune, and were fairly warned that the trams would be bursting with people for probably two hours before the show began, so that it was questionable if we dared stay long enough on the streets to see the whole procession through. However, we set off early in the morning, Mrs. Vesela and Honza and I, to find a good place, and chose a corner of the Little Town Square, just where Neruda Street climbs out of it towards the Hradcany. Here we had the arcades solidly at our backs, the street just narrowing before us, and no possibility of interlopers taking station in front because the space was only sufficient to allow passage to the procession, and the police would see to it that no one stole another inch. We parked determinedly on the extreme edge of the pavement, planted Mrs. Vesela's little folding stool, and settled down to wait. Already thousands of other people were doing the same, and as usual they whiled away the time by opening immediate conversations with their neighbours. Soon the stool was in occupation by a lady who had spent the night in the train, and was feeling the effects now. We had our raincoats, for the weather was uncertain, though in the end there was little rain; our pockets were full of biscuits; and Honza left us to keep his place while he fetched newspapers. What more could we need?

Sometimes the processions were less interesting than the entertaining hours we spent waiting for them, for the crowds were lively and in good humour. A little group of Sokols stood opposite, across the narrow neck of the street, kept in constant laughter by an irrepressible lady who spent most of the procession hours rushing into the street to embrace acquaintances among the young people, and was several times all but swept away. We had two policemen on this strategic corner, and they had their hands full, once the procession began to circle the square and move up towards the Hradcany, in preventing the spectators from breaking through and cutting across their path. Much depended on how it was done, and many people crossed discreetly and caused no confusion, merely by waiting until the official backs were turned. But with the older policeman it became a matter of principle to prevent these small offences, and the more people who slipped by him, the more irritated he became. His young companion was disposed to turn a blind eye, and had difficulty in controlling his grin whenever some enterprising youth sneaked across and shot into the crowd on the other side, to a round of applause. As for us, we were delighted. Gales of laughter saluted every defeat in the officer's gallant campaign to be everywhere at once, and everyone who contemplated the crossing was assured of hundreds of accomplices. Best of all was when our Horatius pursued one trespasser, only to turn from him just in time to see another one disappearing at the end of a successful run. Not that anything happened to the ones he caught in time, except that they had to stay where they were until the next opportunity offered; the game was simply to keep them from crossing; if he did it, he scored a point, if he failed, the point was theirs.

Here, as in countries nearer home, existed the person adept at arriving late but somehow reaching the front rank—usually plus the largest possible hat, or the widest pair of shoulders. Also the optimist who, without the enterprise to copy this example, yet expects the large people who came early to see the justice of his claim to a place in front of them. Crowds of people are much the same everywhere, especially on procession routes, but in England we tend rather to attempt to improve our position by oblique reference than by direct attack, to remark audibly to our companions on the hat which obscures our vision rather than, quite simply, to remove it and hand it to its owner. The Czechs use direct methods. If they want you to move aside, they ask you to do so. If you don't wish to comply, you remain deaf, or if your Czech is up to the test, state with equal firmness your intention of remaining exactly where you are. Belligerent rights are yours from the start, and the national sense of balance ensures them to you to the end.

A crescendo of shouting at the distant corner of the square warned us that the head of the procession was in sight, and we saw over the heads of the crowd the first rank of Sokol standards advancing. Lime-wreathed banners told us from what town or district each group came, and usually their instructors walked with them in full uniform, the boys and girls marching behind in exercise dress, the boys in their white singlets and red shorts, the girls in white blouses and full red skirts, carrying their white exercise rings, or bunches of ribbons or paper streamers, which they shook in the air as they came with a dazzle of colour. Some groups wore the khaki uniform of shorts and battle-dress blouse. Sometimes bands led them, sometimes breathless young white-gloved trumpeters, scarlet in the face. We were badly placed for the bands, for they could hardly be expected to play their way up the steep slope of Neruda Street, so that their marches usually petered out at the corner of the square, and they passed us in silence.

The word, however, seems out of place; for there was such a gay din eddying upward between the tall houses from street to gable that we scarcely missed the bands. The young people laughed, and shook their favours at us, and yelled "Nazdar!" at the full stretch of their lungs, and we yelled back as lustily. Close beside my left ear was a youngster about eighteen, I should think just old enough to be a full Sokol, who could have made a sensation at the annual town-criers' contest in England. He had not only range, but stamina, for after more than four hours he was only reaching his best performance, and seemed capable of keeping it up all day without much deterioration.

The boys and girls were chanting in unison rhymed couplets, which drew roars of cheering from the crowd.

It took me some time to work out any of them, but I gathered at length that they were mainly about President Benes, or in some cases harked back to Masaryk himself. I heard: "We are the children of Hana——" ostensibly the Hana region of Moravia, from some who certainly were not, and concluded that the Hana really referred to was Mrs. Benesova, as beloved as her husband. The implication was that they were asserting the excellence of Benes and Masaryk and their republic, in the face of what they—or more properly their parents, I suppose—considered to be an affront to these ideas. I don't wish to suggest that boys and girls of seventeen have not ideas of their own, but the very formation of these must depend in some degree on what they absorb from their parents, even when they have rejected much. The young Sokols waved, and laughed, and cried their defiance of all who would separate them from the love of Masaryk; and the crowd cheered, and laughed, and waved back.

No one attempted to interfere with them, at least in my sight. Our policeman was still fully occupied with the escaping club, and in the intervals of being baited by them, relaxed and beamed at the ranks of handsome young things marching by him. The strange, expressive incident, a whole morning long, went by almost without an echo in the mind, leaving me quite at a loss how to relate it with full truth to the normality of life around me; it was as if its proportions, its significance and its real quality eluded measurement no matter how closely one tried to observe and understand. For which reason I merely state it as I saw it, and make no further comment.

Two little girls had somehow made their way to the front, since everyone here gives the children first place, and stood hand in hand in front of me, periodically snatched back by the shoulders from falling into the street, one or another of us catching up crumbs of responsibility for them. They had been there some time, when the smaller one began to be uneasy, and presently to knuckle forlornly at her eyes. I asked her what was the matter. She made small, indistinct noises, and her sister explained rather scornfully that she wanted her mummy.

"And where is Mummy?"

"Over there," said the child, unmoved, and waved a hand airily towards the rear of the crowd, while the smaller one continued to cry quietly into her glove and make no fuss. But very decidedly she wanted her mummy.

Honza took over where my supply of Czech failed, and firmly detaching her from her sister, handed her back through the crowd from person to person until somewhere on the outskirts she reached her parents safely; for presently there was passed back, by the same method, a summons to the elder one, who was by no means pleased at having to leave her vantage point, but obeyed with a good grace.

"There will be a lot of lost children today," said Honza, smiling after her. "Our policeman will be very busy."

Soon afterwards we ourselves had to leave, though the districts were still passing merrily, waving their sprigs of lime towards the upper windows of the palaces of Neruda Street, and advancing their banners like a conquering army upon Hradcany. Policemen and others leaned out from the crowd as the girls went by, and caught at their hands for a moment, and the young things looked back laughing as they extricated themselves, and tossed their long, fair hair. But by half-past two we had to be in our places at Strahov, and it was high time for us to go.

We walked home; it was easier, for the trams were heavily laden already. In the early afternoon we went out all together, five of us with Mr. Vesely and an uncle from the country, and were lucky enough to find space in a car almost on the doorstep, in Strossmayer Square where the trams on this route did not normally stop. We groaned

our way up the hill on to the crest of Letna, at every stop
more tightly packed, and through Dejvice and on past
Hradcany, always uphill, until the car turned into the
special terminal station under the lee of Strahov, and we
tumbled out and joined the solid mass of people thronging
up towards the stadium.

It was an impressive sight. A footbridge with several
stairways up to it spanned the mesh of tramlines where
cars went in and out ceaselessly; and the pathway up the
grassy slope, wide as a good road, was closely filled from
verge to verge with people, from here until it crossed the
brow of the hill and passed from sight. The stream moved
unhurriedly but steadily; and the sun came out on our
backs as we climbed, and warned us that in spite of all the
morning symptoms it was going to be very hot. We had
come out prepared for anything, with coats and raincoats,
the men in hooded oilskins, for the south tribune is not
yet covered from the weather, and its upper reaches can
be very exposed indeed if the wind is right.

A long entrance gate of many divisions passed us through
on to the plateau of Strahov, and in the broad approach
to the stadium the cramped stream of people was able
to gush apart and vary its speed. To reach our places we
had to walk the whole length of the main tribune, under a
brave blazoning of Sokol flags flying from the topmost
crests of the walls, alongside a white carriage-way where
the cars of the important passed ceaselessly. A covered
terrace ran along each tribune, numbered entrances
directed everyone accurately to his own place, and frequent
stalls selling sandwiches, soft drinks, beer, sausages, insured
him against hunger. Hundreds of thousands of people
were handled as if they had numbered merely dozens;
on the showing of this day Sokol scored high marks for
efficiency.

We were shown to our places on the back row but one, a

good position rather nearer to the main tribune than the opposite one, which is important, as the drills are naturally designed to present their main effect to the president's box. We settled down resolutely for a stay of hours, rescued the packages of cakes and cherries from our pockets, assembled field-glasses, cameras—not banned, but you must pay for the privilege of using them here—and prepared to enjoy ourselves. The sun was full on us, and the raincoats soon began to come off and disappear under the seats; it grew hotter, and our coats and Honza's wind-jacket followed them; hotter still, and he removed his pullover and rolled up his shirt-sleeves. The strip-tease ended there, for we could shed no more clothes with propriety.

Now, inside the stadium for the first time, I could see its full awesome size, the vast white floor perforated at regular intervals with circular grids. These later solved the problem of how the music came from everywhere at once, and was brought simultaneously to all the performers, for if they had had to rely on distribution from the tribunes there would have been a decided time-lag before the notes reached the people in the centre. I am told that at some earlier Slets this method was used, and that the resultant effect was that of a wave gradually curling across the arena and breaking, unique and in some ways to be regretted now that it had been sacrificed to uniformity. I should think, however, that it carried the risk of serious confusion, as well as this pleasing eccentricity.

There had been some speculation as to whether President Gottwald would attend today's display. Now we suddenly observed his flag being run up at its own staff above the box, and the fanfares which open the overture to *Libuse* flashed out to announce his arrival. Out came the field-glasses, and were trained on the scene in the box; the President was quite easily distinguished, Mr. Truhlar, the head of Sokol, was with him, some uniforms, a lady, probably Mrs. Gottwaldova, but my view of her was obscured by some of the people in between. And since the arrival of the great was the signal for the performance to begin, we quickly turned the glasses on the opposite tribune, with its great central entrance from which everything stems. A line of colour, the reds and whites and navy blues of display dresses, had advanced to fill the gateways, a gay and hopeful music wafted them forward, and they advanced across the arena carrying outspread between them the Czechoslovak flag, with the hoisting of which every performance begins.

As it climbed the staff we all rose, with the surge of a big sea breaking, and the national anthem was played. "Kde Domov Muj?"—"Where is my home? Where is my home? Waters whisper in the meadows, pine-woods murmur among the rocks; our orchards gush with flowers, an earthly paradise to the sight. This is that lovely country, the Czech land, my homeland!" And for Slovakia the stormy outcry of: "It lightens over Tatra, and the thunders crash——" We settled ourselves again in our seats as the flag-bearers withdrew, and in a ruled line of red and white the boys came out to exercise.

First the mass exercises, without apparatus, those simple unison movements on the spot which achieve their beautiful effect only at this respectful distance. Light played over the stadium as they used their arms, their faces, their young bending bodies to reflect it, exactly as the many ears of a cornfield in the wind take the silver of the sunlight, or even the tint of the sky's blue, and give it back to the watching eyes translated. Some of the music I remembered from Val, some of the entrances I had seen there, though on a small scale; but here, so high above them, it was really like watching a complex red and white flower grow out of the members' tribune before one's eyes, and send out petals and tendrils into all the corners of the arena; and when they ended their performance and drew back their ranks into concentrated groups again, closing towards the exits into which their thousands vanished as if by magic, it was like seeing the same flower turn back from blooming, and fold up again into the ground.

The girls came, a blue flower this time, and expanded to fill the whole space, and I saw again the dance of the white rings. The swaying movements of the arms, the rhythmic rise and fall of the rings, have an almost hypnotic effect; I believe that one could be soothed to sleep like this through the vision, if one concentrated entirely on the stadium, and foreswore contact with one's immediate neighbours; but there was plenty going on among the tiers of seats, too. Sellers of soft drinks and sandwiches tightrope-walked along the concrete rims between the rows, swinging trays from wooden handles. Periodically some hungry or thirsty soul who had failed to get his favourite snacks brought to him climbed out to fetch them, and came back balancing half a dozen "chlebicky" precariously on one hand, and a waxed cardboard tumbler of beer in the other. The "chlebicky" were ovals of bread loaded with cream cheese, tomatoes and pickled cucumber, sometimes with snacks of salt fish also. The beer was poor stuff, black and much too sweet; for once we all agreed about this, and furtively poured it away gradually on the sunbaked concrete, where it steamed off in a few minutes. When we had neither cherries, tumblers nor cakes in our hands we applauded; the applause went on in small, reverberant waves the whole time, rising to a peak at the exits. I think it would have been better saved for these altogether, for it must make the exercises far more difficult when spasms of clapping cut across the rhythm of the music.

Between the mass effects we watched people, every one as unique as his own fingerprints; the alert stretcher-bearers who hung about the barriers, and were off like hares between the ranks as soon as some child collapsed

from heat or excitement, whisking her away so lightly and
promptly that if one looked away from the operation for
a second one could not find them again; the sad little
casualties themselves, regaining consciousness on the
stretchers to break their hearts over their failure; the
dropped white ring lying just out of its owner's reach between
the lines, and the anxious artifice by which she regained
it; the quick, anguished recovery after some mistake which
in one small corner, for one breathless moment, broke the
rhythm. Oh, yes, they were human beings none the less
for being parts of a pattern. Slips, failures, were few but
reassuring; just enough to keep contact with our affectionate
sympathy as well as our detached admiration.

For their final appearance the girls entered in longer
dresses, their skirts in pale pastel yellows and blues, their
hair loose, and many of them barefooted, spaced their
delicate colourings about the whole arena, and performed
national dances, to the music of many Czech and Slovak
songs which were already familiar to me. There are few
epic songs among the national legacy of the people of CSR,
no rattling of swords, no celebration of battles; their songs
are deeply concerned with more practical and permanent
things, the seasons, the harvest, poverty, geese at pasture,
horses, love faithful and unfaithful, and the passion for
home.

The boys had the last word. They brought in with them
all kinds of curious and fascinating things, small sectional
bridges, archery butts, boomerangs, and tenting equipment; and in a few minutes they covered the stadium with
a convoluted pattern made up of little khaki tents. The
sound of a thousand small hammers chinking away at
tent-pegs eddied upward between the tribunes with an
extraordinarily remote effect, seeming quite unconnected
with the movements of the boys. Inevitably there was one
tent which would not go up at first, and when it did consent

to do so waited only until its proprietors' backs were turned to subside; but they quickly got it up again, and so impressed it with their determination that from then on it gave up the struggle, and behaved admirably.

This was the end of my first full-scale Sokol display. We went home discussing it, and after a late supper ended the day at the open-air cinema on Letna, watching cartoon and news films and ancient comedies from the film archives, including a 1914 Charlie Chaplin which was not very funny, and one of the same year featuring some obscure couple I never even heard of, which was extremely funny. So much fresh air in one day proved too much for us; we nodded on one another's shoulders, and were not sorry to go home to bed.

A week later came the full Sokol performances, and again we were in the stadium for the Sunday display. By this time delegations had arrived from many other countries, Russia, Poland, Yugoslavia, France, Vienna, even America. The full Sokols, both men and women, naturally showed a precision and perfection which the youngsters could not yet match, and the effect at times was breath-taking. I was confirmed in my first reaction that I liked the exercises with apparatus less, no matter how well they were done; but one item which won special applause and deserved it was the show put on by the older men, in exercises specially designed to stay comfortably within their scope. I thought this typical; no one ought to feel that he has no longer a worthy contribution to make.

The women chose Indian clubs for their second appearance, and gave a performance which so far as I could discover was faultless. By and large, I think they reached a higher all-round standard than any other section, and they later justified this opinion by winning the gymnastics Gold Medal for women at the Olympiad in London.

Next came the Yugoslavs, first a picked group of seven

hundred sailors, in white trousers, navy sashes and the familiar white summer cap common to all navies. They were matched like a theatrical chorus, all of one height and colouring, and tanned to an even shade of coppery brown. Against that tan their brilliant white grins were visible, even from the centre of the arena, without glasses. They were followed by the young men and women of the Yugoslav Physical Culture Organisation, the girls in brief tunics of a very soft, clear speedwell blue, the boys in red shorts and white singlets. I think they used these colours in their circular dancing with the most beautiful visual effect of the whole Slet, though they had not the austere and moving unanimity of Sokol, the delicate and humane balance one always felt there between the member and the whole.

After another appearance by the Sokol men we had a surprise item, a foretaste of Army Day, in some parachute jumping. Marks were spread in the arena, the planes made their runs, conveniently for us, from over the opposite tribune, and the small dark bundles projected themselves into the air, always, it seemed, minutes later than they should have done for an accurate drop, and opened into pale convolvulus flowers as they drifted earthward. Sometimes they seemed to jump when the plane was actually leaving the area of the stadium, but the descent proved each time that this was an optical illusion, for their landings were remarkably accurate, and one at least came down precisely on the mark. But we had only just enough of this to whet our appetites, and had to wait until the following Thursday to see more of it.

Now came the Russians. They were not a large group, and used apparatus and plenty of it, motor-cycles, rings, parallel bars, high bars, everything which was portable. And certainly they handled everything like experts. Their acrobatics were flawless, and had some of our neighbours in the stands gasping and shouting for more. One boneless wonder revolving by his hands on the high bar, for all the world like childhood's familiar monkey-on-a-stick, did things which I would not have believed the human body could be induced to do. There were girls among them, in close exercise costumes of clear green, and they were as nonchalant as the men in handling motor-cycles at speed, or standing on one palm on the parallel bars. Their show concluded with a rapid drive round the arena, taking various jumps by the way, two and three tiers of young people erected upon one cycle, and a vast silken banner streaming above them into the wind. Acrobatics, of course, are not Sokol, but that must not be read as criticism, for they were not pretending to be Sokols, but making their contribution as guests to a national festival, and making it as brilliant and complimentary as they could.

It was already evening by this time, and officially the performance was over, but we stayed in our places for fear of missing something, for soldiers had appeared in the entrances, and were manhandling some light field guns into position in the extreme corners of the arena, and it seemed that something was about to happen.

"They are perhaps going to rehearse something for Army Day," said Honza hopefully.

I thought so, too, and was by no means sure that we should be well advised to stay, for at this time Honza had an injury to one eardrum, and for two days had been flinching even at the sound of a cup going down briskly into a saucer. Nothing would move him tonight, however. We sat through the thorny crackle of small arms fire, the grinding of tanks and the explosions of shells without any apparent inconvenience to the damaged ear; and only when the Army manifested its intention of going home to supper could Honza be induced to do likewise.

14

The Great Sokol Procession

Throughout the festival, Prague was one continual glitter, and its streets too crowded for comfortable walking, but the entertainment to be had on such vantage points as Wenceslas Square was too good to miss, and we were always out struggling through the crowds as best we could, and enjoying them. I would not have been a traffic policeman there for any money, but they seemed to like the job, and the foot of the square was an ideal spot for watching them. Often very young officers were on duty there. They took themselves very seriously, and had us as well-drilled as schoolchildren in the proper use of pedestrian crossings. I found their attitude, even when they pounced on evildoers, curiously paternal, and treasure a delightful memory of a boy of about twenty lecturing an elderly and influential-looking owner-driver who had transgressed, leaning down to the window of his car and actually using a schoolmasterish forefinger to drive home his admonitions. They are allowed to levy small fines on the spot for minor traffic offences like crossing in an unauthorised spot, and whenever we were tempted to try it Honza would depute me to answer if we were challenged, so that my nationality should infallibly get us out of trouble. It happens that it was never put to the test, but I am sure it would have worked. The same defence was employed when we tried to use tram tickets after a change which did not quite fulfil the conditions laid down.

"I'm not sure if we can really use it from here," he would say doubtfully. "But give it to him yourself, and then he won't say anything."

Meanwhile we continued our round of the exhibitions, dropping crowns into the slots of working models in the Film Museum on Letna, admiring lovely early glass and ceramics and furnishings in the Museum of Industrial Art, and visiting all the picture galleries. What interested me perhaps most of all was the exhibition of the work of Max Svabinsky held at the Manes gallery in celebration of his seventy-fifth birthday. He is the grand old man of Czech painting, and I do not understand why his work is not known in England; speaking for myself, the more I see of it, the more I like it. One of the magnificent windows of St. Vitus—perhaps more than one, but I speak of the one I remember best, with the Czech kings—is his, and the cartoon for it was here among his collected work. From enormous canvases glowing with the strange paradisal jungles and majestic nudes of the 1920s period, when in the establishment of the young republic his mind seems to have found a promise of Eden recovered, to the late small drawings of landscape, only a few inches square, evoking the spirits of willows and poplars with a touch as light as their spring leaves; from the austere ceremonial portraits of Masaryk and Benes to the stamp designs for the Sokol Slet; from the early costume portraits with their exquisitely finished laces and elegant silken textures to the spare, pale "Annunciation", in which the angel is as sudden and dazzling as an explosion of light in the mind: he does all things with an equal, dedicated intensity. A set of illustrations to the "Satyr" of Victor Hugo was, for me, among the most beautiful and haunting things in this diverse collection.

One-man shows can be exceedingly dull, since every-thing in them must come out of the same mind, and there is no more fatal way of revealing its limitations. This man can stand it; his mind appears to have explored seventy-five years without coming up against its limits yet in any direction. A more competent critic must examine the limitations of his art; but I know that I left Manes as fresh as I entered, with much reluctance, and having no trace of the mental indigestion which usually afflicts me after looking at too many pictures in one afternoon.

Monday and Tuesday, the 5th and 6th of July, were public holidays, being the feasts of St. Cyril and Methodius, the Christian missionaries of Czechoslovakia, who with unique foresight brought eastern Christianity but were under papal jurisdiction, so originating the bridge tradition which only force of unbearable circumstances has temporarily broken; and the martyrdom of John Hus. On this latter day was to take place the main Sokol procession through the city. On the former we decided to book tickets for a half-day coach tour to Lidice and Lany. To visit these places of pilgrimage in company with a charabanc-load of holiday-making Czechs at a time of national festivity may seem rather going out of one's way to court the wrong conditions, but it did not turn out that way for me.

We boarded the bus at the Powder Tower, after lunch, a cream-coloured coach of unimpressive appearance but very respectable performance, with a large, cheerful, leather-coated and rosy-faced driver. We occupied the seat immediately behind him, which had only one drawback, that it was also the passage to the doorway; but even this carried with it the compensating thought that we could always without reproach be last back from anywhere, because we must of necessity be last into the bus. Our load was a mixed crowd of people, such as you might find leaving any capital city by bus on a bank holiday.

We left town by the now familiar way out towards Kladno, leaving Hvezda on our right, and were heading out merrily through open country when the driver suddenly slowed down, and we saw that a policeman was waving us to a standstill, and another one ahead was speaking to the driver of a stationary car.

"They want to see our papers," said someone philosophically, already feeling for his own.

Honza groaned. There, as here, one is legally obliged to carry one's identification papers still; and there, as here, one doesn't trouble to observe the regulations by any means rigidly. He had often laughed at me because my passport always stayed ready to hand in my bag; now it was my turn to laugh, for he was caught completely without legitimations. He went through all his pockets in the hope of finding some student papers which might serve, but was not unduly concerned about his misdemeanour, and explained to the policeman quite frankly that he had simply not troubled to bring the thing out with him. The policeman was equally unconcerned, and declined even to lecture. He had already politely excused the women from accounting for themselves; now he glanced over the papers of the rest of the men, saluted us, and waved us on. We held no one of the slightest interest to him.

"Well, whoever they are looking for," said Honza, "must be a man, and somebody not my age nor at all like me in appearance." But there ended all the conclusions we could draw from the incident.

This had happened to me once before, in company with a bus-load of Czech and foreign writers on the way out to a reception at Dobris; but on that occasion, as soon as they heard who we were, and where bound, they allowed us to go ahead; and in fact, the only times I needed my passport were when I drew money from the bank, or a new supply of food tickets from the magistrate's office.

Both Lidice and Lany are in the Kladno region of mines, and the village which has by now almost given its name as a new word to the dictionary was a mining community. We went there first, driving down a dusty byroad into a wide and shallow valley, where in an emptiness broken only by one or two unobtrusive wooden pavilions we got out of the bus. I knew already, everyone must know, that what one goes to Lidice to see is that there is nothing there; but still the arrival is a sickening shock, however well prepared you may believe yourself to be. A shock of blankness, not of horror; the horror comes later, when your imagination begins to work on that blankness.

We stood in the centre of the shallow bowl, broken, barren, thin-grassed land going away from us in every direction, in a stony desolation bearing no colours but the dull greens of poor turf blanching to straw colour, and the sandy greyish whiteness of soil. On our left, moving slightly uphill, a sad cemetery, unfenced, hardly distinguishable from the waste ground; for the Germans desired to wipe out even the traces of the dead, and no stones remain, only new small wooden crosses set to mark the resting-places freshly identified. On our right the ground dipped slightly, a hollow within the hollow, crossing the ghosts of fields and the shadow of a brook, and where it again began to rise there was a square of turf fenced round with a low chain and small green shrubs, and rising from it a tall cross, with a crown of thorns hung upon it. A strip of garden, piled with wreaths, was laid out in the foreground. This is where the murdered men lie, the whole of the male population of Lidice from the age of fifteen upward. From there you could throw a stone into the yard of Horak's farm, where they were stood against a mattress-covered wall and shot down in batches, about a hundred and ninety people. The fact that the farm also is a ghost, only a piece of its cellar newly excavated and showing a rubble of brick in the pale grass, does not help to smooth the horror from one's mind, but rather accentuates it.

What you see here is something worse than the vicious instinct to kill, it is a kind of blasphemy against both God and man, an arrogance absolutely without limit, which set this scene to say in effect to all future witnesses: "I Am, I can alone do and undo, and what I destroy is destroyed utterly and without memorial, body, soul and seed."

To deny this is not enough; it is necessary to remember that the challenge was made, and to realise that it could be made again. No plan for the future can have the faintest hope of success unless it includes in the range of its vision the keen recollection of the past.

For that reason the new Lidice will be built not on exactly the same site, but further up the slope, overlooking this place, which will remain, and rightly, a memorial and a warning. Already at this time the roads for the new village were laid, and by now I think houses are going up. Then there were no buildings but the sheds which hold pictures of the lost community, and the few poor relics recovered from the foundations of the houses; and up the hill the new canteen for the workmen, where we bought lemonade, and sheltered from a sudden squall of rain. Life goes on. On this day there were many coaches here, and many Czech people walking among the desert fields; there were Sokol families in uniform, father pointing out to the children the place where once the large Bohemian baroque church stood, or the school, very small boys playing over the waste where the other boys died. I had expected to find this holiday atmosphere, practical and grave though it was, an interference with understanding; instead, it preserved a balance and perspective in the mind, which might otherwise have been damaged. It would be very easy to be overbalanced into mere hate here, and that, like half-baked magnanimity, is by no means enough; but on the whole I think it does less damage of the two.

After the murders, the work of levelling Lidice with the

ground, buildings, trees, cemetery monuments, everything, was given to members of the Nazi Youth; and I have seen some private snapshots—it does not matter where, or whose, but they were made secretly from the negatives of a German officer, and without his knowledge—of the gangs at work, lusty young men stripped to the waist, beaming, puffing out their chests, proud to be photographed wielding pick and shovel for the fatherland on such an assignment. The blood of the other young men was then hardly dried into the ground at Horak's farm.

We walked up the hill to the site of the future town to board the bus again, and left this unforgettable place by the new bright roads which will some day be the streets of Lidice. The blankness here is exciting in its potentialities, like the paper on which an artist has just begun to sketch. The skeleton is impressive; I hope some day to go back and see the flesh beautifully covering its bones.

From here to Lany is only a short drive. A road under repair brought us first to the little grey-walled cemetery I had once recognised from the main road to Karlovy Vary, and we went in through the gates in company with crowds of other charabanc visitors. The Masaryk graves are in a distant corner, in the lee of the stone wall, with fields extending beyond; a low fence of wooden palings surrounds them, with a little gate in it, through which people were constantly leaning to lay fresh flowers, favours, Sokol emblems, on the edge of the low green plateau of the graves. There could be no more modest place of burial.

When we came near, the corner was quite hidden by the mass of people crowding closely in to the fence on all sides. There was a great quietness, in which the voice of a guide was reciting what I suppose was the usual list of facts and dates one gets at places of national interest. Apart from this there was no sound. Newcomers joining the audience came almost on tiptoe, and no one wished to move away.

Remote from us on the road the ordinary movement and murmur of life went on, but here the crowd seemed to hold its breath. It was extraordinary to look round at them, and see that almost every person was in tears.

The guide had to ask them, at last, to make way for others following; and we resolved ourselves into a long, reluctant queue, moving slowly round the three sides of the fenced enclosure. The graves are raised only a few inches from the level of the path which surrounds them, T.G. Masaryk in the centre, his wife on his right, his son on his left. Trophies lean against their clear edges, and are hung on the wall behind. The purple and red and white paper ribbons grow faded and sad, and their gilt inscriptions wither away. But there are always fresh flowers, and at this time there were very many, for Sokols from all over the country, in Prague for the Slet and therefore within reach of this place for perhaps the first, perhaps the only, time, had brought tributes on behalf of their towns and villages, almost hiding the grass. St. Vaclav's gem-encrusted tomb in the dim, hushed treasury of its chapel in St. Vitus is moving in one way, this in quite another. We moved slowly along the rail, I watching the still, intent faces and silently flooding eyes of my neighbours as closely as the graves. When we came here again there was what one usually associates with Lany, a green, retired calm, hushed, without people; but I am glad that was not my only visit.

In this corner of the cemetery stands a small building in which is kept the visitors' book, and many tributes and trophies keep it company. The guide had found that I was English, and drew me in to sign the book. Then we left, and from the gate of the cemetery walked through the village. It sells, of course, Masaryk postcards; but it does it with an amateurish air, and a pride and directness, which keep even the postcard stalls serenely in the picture.

G

It is a nice village, growing steadily more attractive as it recedes from the main road; and in its school are kept a famous ceremonial portrait of the President-Liberator, and some personal relics of his life. The picture is life-size, and shows him mounted on Hector—a name as familiar in CSR as Bucephalus in Alexander's Macedon—in the framework of autumnal branches in the park of Lany. They say that the setting was of his own choosing, and the autumn colourings he insisted on as the fit expression for his own sere and yellow leaf.

From here we walked on to where the walls of the park begin, and in due time were shown round the exterior of the castle, which is small as castles go, and welcoming, and surrounded by charming gardens. It is easy to understand why he chose it as his favourite residence. At this time it was suggested that it might be given to President Benes on his retirement, but most people thought that he would not accept it, preferring to remain at Sezimovo Usti. Most unhappily for everyone, the question did not arise.

Said Honza, as we drove home: "We must go to bed early tonight, because we have to start out very, very early tomorrow, or we shall not get a good place for the procession."

"How early?"

"Half-past six! And you will need the alarm-clock!"

On these occasions I always had to borrow it; it had a voice as soft as a purring cat, but it invariably worked, thus adding efficiency to tact. This time I set it for half-past five, and before half-past six was round at the Vesely flat, where everyone was in a bustle between breakfast and preparations. Honza and I were ready before the rest, and set off on our own, with the usual provisions in our pockets, for this was one of those days when lunch might be at four o'clock in the afternoon. We took a tram to the Powder Tower, and hurried along into the Old Town Square; we had come quite without plans, but this looked as good a place as any, and we were early enough to be able to stake a claim firmly on the edge of the pavement, and behind the shoulders of a conveniently short policeman, so that we could not be victimised by the hopeful latecomers who here, as everywhere, tend to form up in front instead of behind.

Across the wide expanse of the square, right before us, was the shell of the Old Town Hall tower, and beside it stood the covered tribune for the President and government, and the diplomatic corps. At our backs were the arcades of the Tyn School, with the church soaring behind, and on our right, out in the open space of the square, the bronze memorial group of John Hus, with the shallow bowls on either side, where his symbolic fire should burn on this day of his martyrdom. Within this space before the tribune the foreign delegations would take station as they reached it at the head of the procession; and we were in a fair way to see whatever was to be seen, including all the celebrities.

It began to rain, and at once umbrellas were fished out from nowhere, and a curious black and brown and tartan roof sprang up over the entire crowd. No one forgoes such a show in Prague, however, for a little thing like rain; we stood stolidly, thankful for our forethought in the matter of hoods and raincoats, and squared our shoulders against the increasing pressure from behind. Everywhere there were people; up the scaffolding of the tower, hanging out of the windows, on the roofs, everywhere that a foothold offered. The tribune began to fill with diplomatic corps representatives and members of the government; some we recognised, about some we asked our Slovak policeman, and about some he had to ask us. Two Indian ladies scurried across from a car, shielding their saris under plastic raincoats and umbrellas, but the unfamiliar dress caught his eye, and he asked who they could be.

"More diplomatic wives," we said, "from India or Pakistan—more likely India."

"Oh, some more bolsheviks!" said the policeman surprisingly.

We doubted it, but he merely smiled, retaining his own unexplained ideas.

Half the members of the government were already in their seats in the tribunes, and we took this as a sign that the procession could reasonably be expected soon; consequently a spirited dialogue had begun between the front and rear ranks.

"Velky do zadu!" bellowed the people behind. "Big 'uns to the back!" Obviously this was aimed at Honza, but he remained deaf and withdrawn into the depths of his hood.

"Umbrellas down!" they shouted. And our stout neighbours continued to hold them aloft like standards, and shouted back: "When they come—not before!" And faithfully they held to this, for as soon as the first inclined banners appeared at the corner by St. Nicholas' cathedral, down went all the umbrellas.

"But the more radical ones," said Honza, chuckling, "are crying: Sit down in front!"

He was in some trouble at close range with a particularly erratic umbrella, held by a tall lady with an unsteady hand; and as the spokes came just on a level with his eyes I began to think I should have to lead him home. After he had dodged several lunges I asked him if he wouldn't like to change places with me; he said he certainly wouldn't object, and I slid him past me and took his position, an admirable arrangement, for where he had risked impalement I fitted neatly under the umbrella out of the rain. He drew a breath of relief, too, but less pleased was the woman who had been standing behind me, and who now raised a wail of dismay, and burst into voluble protests.

Contemplating the massive rear view of Honza in a black oilskin coat with a large hood, head and shoulders taller than most of his fellows, I must admit I felt some sympathy with her.

Someone behind me kept very quiet, by no means displeased with the change; for him the wind was not so ill; but the unlucky lady accused us bitterly. We stuck to it that we had come early, the two places were ours, and we could exchange if we liked. She said it wasn't handsome of us; she went on saying it at fretful intervals, but we relapsed into deafness, and thereupon she found another grievance, and demanded peremptorily that Honza should at least remove his hood. This he was willing to do, but saw no sense in getting wet until there was some reason for it; but she could not wait to get at least this fragment of her own way, and she hauled the hood back on his shoulders in a way which finally provoked him into a wordy battle far too rapid for me to follow. The people behind said it wasn't handsome, meaning, I think, that Honza should be allowed to measure nearly two metres; but he had no choice in the matter.

The battle subsided because the bands began to make a colourful noise even through the rain at St. Nicholas' corner, and we all faced front at once. Some men were trying to kindle John Hus' fire in its two bronze bowls, which I think concealed gas jets, and for a short time a gaudy flame and a rapid ascending smoke did add a sombre splendour to the scene; but the rain was too heavy for them, and they had to be put out again.

After the Sokol detachment with the national banners, pride of place was given to the foreign delegations. Lime-wreathed, flower-decked, beribboned, the banners crossed the tribune, and swung round to encircle the square, passing us closely. Then the Russian athletes, in their loose blue overall suits, carrying their beautiful flags, fine and transparent as silk, light as lawn, so that they really flew, even in a mere breath of wind. They were in their usual high good humour, these young men and women from sixteen different Soviet republics; often we had met some of them in the streets, and never without a grin.

Some French delegates followed, the women in regional costumes; but this was a small group. Then the very large contingent of Yugoslavs, led by the white-clad sailors we had seen on the stadium, under a forest of banners, and almost warming the rain into steam with the glow of their jubilant self-confidence. The young people of the physical culture organisation, following them in their grey uniforms, rather reminiscent of the R.A.F., carried the same aura with them. They had a sort of untidy splendour, exuberant, coltish but dynamic, and most significantly at one; and I take them to be a pretty fair microcosm of their country, very naturally intoxicated still with the new wine of unity and freedom, doing things in a big, whole-hogging way, perhaps sometimes in a silly and assertive way, but as one man, and with a warmth and faith which ought, given fair play, to survive the stage of costly mistakes and treading on other people's toes. They were a tall group, on the whole, and because of this glow they had were so pleasant to look upon that I thought them good-looking, but cannot now be sure how much of this was due to their features, and how much to the instinctive response I felt to their joyful belief in themselves.

Tito's quarrel with the Cominform was new in those days, and reactions had not set in at all accurately; but when these young people carried round the square a huge portrait of their national hero the crowd managed to raise a louder roar for him. I do not seriously think it could be classed as a political demonstration, and I am quite sure it did not come exclusively from anti-Communists; I think it represented more truly a contra-suggestible people saluting with particular appreciation a contrary man. I noticed that the Russian athletes, who were now drawn up in the open centre of the square before the tribune, cheered as loudly as anyone. They had no grudge against anybody.

A separate delegation came from Trieste, bearing a little sailing ship in the corner of their standards; a group from Vienna; the Bulgarians with a handsome portrait of Dimitrov; the Poles, less laden with banners, I think, than the rest, and having in the mass a curious, dramatic dignity. Their women walked like queens.

Places were found for all these guests in the square, still leaving a passage round the outskirts for the Sokol detachments which now began to arrive. First came the Slovak districts, then the Czech lands, and finally the capital city of Prague, and the mounted Sokols. Rain had brought out the black hooded cloaks, which the tall men wore like brigands. They had sprigs of flowering lime in their hats, they sang together, they flung up their arms and shook handkerchiefs, favours, flowers in the rain, and thundered: "Nazdar!" and crowds and arcades, the step-gables of the Tyn School, the lofty bulk of the church behind, all re-echoed the shouts across the square. Presently we saw that they carried other small trophies, postcards which they held for us to see, pictures of Masaryk and Benes, and small flags, including British and American, which they displayed with a specially significant flourish. So, at least, the spectators thought, and storms of applause greeted them.

The morning became a repetition of the scenes during the Sokol Youth procession. The same slogans echoed before the president's tribune, chanted loudly and clearly, and the onlookers took them up and called them back again with delight.

"We are the children of Masaryk——"

"All the world knows that we want Benes back!"

"No one can dictate to us whom we shall love!"

Again the theme was not so exactly politics as Benes, and the effect, though they laughed and cheered, was of an outburst of grief and anger at the loss of the most beloved creature in the world. Both the government and its opponents seem to me to have tried to exaggerate and distort its significance afterwards, probably from honest conviction. I record only what I saw and heard.

The demonstration, to call it by the convenient name, went on probably for four hours and more. Across the heads of the marching Sokols all this time I could see the members of the government talking together in the tribune, and calmly watching the procession pass. "Long live President Benes!" shouted some sections of the crowd, and the cry became constant, though President Gottwald was seated not fifty yards away. The Slovaks passed, and district delegations from the Czech lands came, all in perfect normality but for that flying exchange which continued between marchers and onlookers.

There was no interruption in the order of things, no attempt whatever to silence the demonstrators. Just as before in the Little Town Square, the police went on doing their job with a placidity ruffled only by the growing weight of the thrust from the pavement, which by now had pushed us a yard or two into the roadway. No one was actively pushing, it was just the cumulative thrust of thousands of people all craning forward in one direction, and it had us, in front, so nicely braced against it that if one of the rank shifted a foot to ease his cramp at the wrong moment the mass overbalanced, and we all lurched forward another pace, threatening to wash away our unfortunate little Slovak policeman once for all. To order us back was futile, and they did not try it, having sense to see that we couldn't move back if we tried; all we could do, with their help, all they could do with ours, was to lean back hard and try to hold the present position. When the bulge in one spot became too dangerous they moved some of us further along, to a sector which hadn't yet given way. By degrees we stole half the passage room which they were trying to keep clear for the Sokols, and with all the thrusting, and the exhaustion of resisting it, tempers became a little frayed. But the chorus of chanted couplets continued undisturbed, and apparently unresented.

By half-past twelve I had to admit I was tired, principally from bracing myself to keep my place, sometimes cramped into an uncomfortable position into the bargain; and Honza suggested that we should try to work our way through to the rear, and move to a new position. In the process we happened upon the fringes of a verbal battle, which was in full spate when we came into range. A well-dressed middle-aged man was taking violent exception to the cries of "Long live President Benes!" and accusing one of his neighbours of joining in them. What he objected to was not the fervour of love expressed for Benes, but the use of the word president; he was a purist, and wanted that title kept for its present owner. Witnesses on both sides quarrelled over whether the word had, in fact, been used, the defenders asserting that it had been "Brother Benes", a perfectly correct salutation from a fellow-Sokol, but one which could hardly be mistaken for president, I thought. We stopped, naturally, to see what happened, but it came to nothing. There was no doubt whatever about the middle-aged man's sincerity, though his logic was not beyond criticism.

"Millions of Russians," he cried to the grinning but not unfriendly crowd, "died in the war to liberate you, and now this is how you behave!"

The man who had caused the clash, growing bored with the argument, suddenly put his head back and roared at the full stretch of enormous lungs: "Long live *Brother*

Benes!'' And the onlookers laughed and cheered, and the angry old man subsided, muttering.

We moved on, more freely when once we had worked our way to the back, for pressure had carried the whole mass forward, and left a clear passage under the Tyn arcades. We stayed for almost an hour longer, but saw no more such arguments, only a great deal of pushing for places still, and always the same spasmodic duet of procession and crowds upon the name of Dr. Benes. The people in the tribune continued calm and apparently content, though probably they were feeling hungry by now, for they could hardly pull out hefty sandwiches from their mackintosh pockets and eat them while they watched, as we presently did. We tried two or three other viewpoints, and then decided we had had enough; it was then about half-past one, and I think the march must have continued for about another hour after we left.

We walked home, to wear off the stiffness of standing in one spot for so long; and as the rest of the family was still missing, made ourselves a pot of tea and foraged for some cake, to keep us going until they should come. To fill in time we went up to the nearest cinema and booked seats for *Monsieur Verdoux* for the early evening show, and when we came back with our tickets the family were just letting themselves into the flat. Over a four o'clock dinner we compared notes on the procession. They had been installed near the Jewish cemetery, and had seen very much the same scenes there as we had witnessed on the Old Town Square, including some spirited squabbles among the crowd, though none of the protagonists had actually come to blows. None of us had seen any interference from police or others; those who quarrelled over the issue quarrelled upon equal terms.

We ended the day with our Chaplin film, very contentedly; the second time I had seen it, but much more emerged than I had noticed on first acquaintance. The brisk synchronisation of step and music in the boulevard scenes early in the film, and the shocking effect of the same bright little tune used later against the same background, with the lame gait of the broken man crossing it like a wound; and some of the three-word phrases at the end which carry the whole weight of enormous thoughts balanced on them so accurately that there is not even a tremor of uncertainty to shake the effect. I still remember the cool, still voice saying: "Numbers sanctify, my friend!"

There may have been better pictures; I do not remember ever seeing another one with quite so much of the world's wrongs compressed into it. It seems a superfluity of riches that it should also be extremely funny; but if you took out some of the laughs some of the thoughts would be found to have gone with them. So far as I am concerned, in fact, this film is the mixture as never before.

15

The End of the Slet

We had tickets for both the final days of the festival, the "dozinky", merry-making, harvest festival, call it by any name you can think of which means a good job culminating in an outburst of revelry, and the Army's display; but somehow the whole thing, even with the bounteous noise and activity of Army Day, began to decline after the procession. Rumours on the following day said that there had been some disturbances beyond what we had seen, and even some arrests, but to this day I have no grounds but rumour for thinking so. I went about the town alone on that Wednesday morning, taking photographs round Hradcany, in the Golden Lane and the courts of the castle, and down in the Little Town, and saw nothing but normality, the natural reluctance to open the shops again after a long week-end, and some heavy eyes from a sequence of late nights; but nothing more.

Mrs. Vesela was to have come with us to the stadium that afternoon, but circumstances made it impossible, so another friend was hurriedly called upon to make use of the ticket, and we went creaking and clanging up to Strahov in our bulging tram, and installed ourselves warily with a good supply of raincoats and umbrellas; for the weather was breaking down completely, and this was perhaps partly responsible for the impression one had that the Slet itself was finishing a too stiff course with a broken wind. The expected rain drove us from our seats to cover once during the afternoon, and so broke what continuity there was; but we all three found the spectacle curiously flat and dull after the taut and exciting patterns of the main displays. I was bored, and inclined to suppose that the fault was in me, until I caught Honza's eye and perceived that he was no less so. And on enquiry it was clear that our friend shared our feelings to the full.

What had gone wrong? We could not guess. The stands were filled, as usual; the atmosphere had been rather spoiled by the rain, but that did not account for everything. In the arena there were probably as many as thirty thousand people, in the most gorgeous colours, dancing, raising a giant Maypole, going through all the motions of gaiety; but the effect was confused and uncertain, too much moving about, too many properties, and too little design. The range of the stadium was not made for detail, but for bold effects. The clear block colours of mass Sokol drills stand out splendidly in it, the intricacies of national costume do not. Magical in the street or on a normal stage, they dwindle into insignificance here, and are lost. Those who put on this display were attempting the impossible.

Many inquests must have been held on that performance. Some people concluded simply that the thing had been badly done, and left it at that. Some said that there had been official interference in some way with the programme as planned, and that what we saw had been hurriedly put together to fill the gaps. Some hinted that the Sokol authorities had fallen foul of the civil authorities, with the result that some of the key people necessary to the success of the display were missing. But I never found any evidence to support any of the theories, and the afternoon remains a disappointment and a mystery.

The emotional temperature in Prague was certainly high that day, and on a delayed reaction to the scenes of the previous day the government was rather inclined to look

for trouble even where it was not. The air of the town had
a tremor of uneasiness and heat, like the wind blowing
from a fire. When we left the stadium at about half-past
five, after a short as well as an unsatisfying performance,
we saw a rank of empty cars drawn up on the least con-
gested approach, and considerably more policemen about
than usual, some of them carrying automatic rifles as well
as the quite usual revolver. If there had been any untoward
incident we had heard nothing about it; but it was evident
that the authorities were rather uneasy about public order,
and taking no chances.

The display on Army Day began later, at four o'clock,
and by this time we had become a little over-confident,
perhaps, about being in our places in time; consequently
we arrived at Strahov, and made our way hurriedly along
the road outside the main tribune, with only ten minutes
to spare, and were dismayed to find, half-way along, that
we had come to a dead stop. Here, of course, was the
entrance to the central part of the main tribune, with all
the important boxes, and it happened that the cars of the
great ones were just arriving, with the result that the
approach to the doors had been cordoned off to allow them
to come right in; and there were we, in company with
crowds of other irate ticket-holders, barred from reaching
the south tribune until the cordon was removed. An almost
continual stream of cars was still arriving, and there was
no indication of when they would stop. We had a wild idea
of cutting back and walking all round the stadium, but
it would have taken too long, so we edged our way gradually
through the crowd to the carriage-way, and began to
prospect for the best place to cut across the cordon when
no one was looking.

Others were already on the same quest, scouting up and
down the lines for the most gullible-looking policeman or
the least interested young soldier, for both were engaged

in keeping the way clear of just such incursions. The crowd was very angry, and made no bones about saying so. "We've bought tickets, too!" they shouted, and flourished them under the harassed policemen's noses. Between the cars adventurers ducked under the ropes and ran for it, pursued by indignant shouts and threats from the overworked guardians of the law. Twice we found a likely-looking place and ducked the ropes, only to have our nearest officer turn at the wrong moment and order us furiously back. The third time we stepped back with deceptive obedience, but did not quit the route, and Honza said cheerfully in my ear:

"Wait until a few more people join us, and we'll all go together." He added shrewdly: "Make for that soldier yonder; he just isn't interested."

The boy in question was young enough to have more sympathy with the transgressors than the law, and was studiously looking the wrong way when anyone risked the passage. We waited until our angry policeman was bellowing at someone in the opposite direction, and then headed a raid of half a dozen people, and swooped under the soldier's arms to lose ourselves in the crowd on the far side, wafted through the ropes by the redoubled bellow the policeman not unnaturally loosed after us when he turned to see our heels tilted at him in this disrespectful fashion. Giggling, we scurried away to our places in the south tribune, and left the rest to work it out their own way.

We were only a few minutes late; the flag was up, and the President seated, in uniform today, I think for the first time, as Commander-in-Chief of the Czechoslovak Forces. Our friend was in her place, and had been looking anxiously for us. She told us that there had been some cheering and counter-cheering from the two long tribunes, the main tribune, which was full of solid trades-unionists, crying: "Long live President Gottwald!" while the members' tribune answered with: "Long live President Benes!" A few minutes later it began again in full voice; I am not sure which side began it, but neither was willing to give way first, and it went on until the performance got under way and became sufficiently interesting to make them forget their rivalry.

Then the rain began in earnest. We were determined not to stir a step for it this time, and hoisted our hoods and sat close under one umbrella, while lakes formed in our laps and ran off us at every movement in rivulets. For an hour and a half it rained hard, but the soldiers went ahead with their mass exercises, gymnastic displays and obstacle racing under fire as if the weather were ideal; all it did was to slow them down somewhat on the racing. Mrs. Burianova's brother was in the mass display, and I saw his exercise shoes in the bathroom afterwards, solid lumps of caked sand, as if they had been under the springs of Karlovy Vary for a term of years.

Emil Zatopek took a leading part in one demonstration, which was designed to show that a relay of average men could outrun and outstay the exceptional one; but I cannot help feeling that it was also designed to show that in Zatopek the Czech Army had someone very decidedly exceptional. He ran several long laps against pairs of men operating in relays, and lost very little ground by the end of the course. They ran in full uniform and army boots, and on that heavy ground, sodden now almost into a series of shallow pools, it must have been a killing ordeal.

Later the arena became a battlefield for riflemen, field-guns and tanks, and we saw again the advance we had seen rehearsed after the main Sunday display. While we were watching it the rain stopped, and imperceptibly but quickly the tribunes dried off, and even the sand ceased to look quite so like a level beach just after ebb-tide. The clouds lifted, and the light improved, and we began to hope that, after all, the stunt flying and parachute jumping would not have to be cancelled. Again the runs would be made from over the north tribune, and soldiers with flares suddenly appeared behind us on the crest of the stadium wall, and became a counter-attraction for us as they watched the sky and tested the wind. Apparently the conditions were good, for the display took place as planned, and throughout it our friends sat on top of the wall, dangling their boots over our heads, and lighting spectacular rose-coloured flares to indicate the course and force of the wind to the pilots. There was some formation flying afterwards, and then a hair-raising display of stunt flying by the crack pilot Horak, and as a climax to the aerial show a parachute attack on an imaginary enemy airfield, with a great racket of small-arms fire.

We dried out during all this activity, and Honza fetched some sausages, and we sat eating them happily in our fingers, scooping up pools of mild mustard and filling out the meal with crescent-shaped rolls. But towards the end the sky blackened again ominously, and even while we were congratulating ourselves that the storm would come too late to ruin the end, with a sudden swoop which carried it ahead of our calculations the storm came, pouncing down over the rim of the north tribune and emptying itself into our laps. It was not rain this time, but hail, stones as big as the nail of my little finger, that rattled off the concrete and the hurriedly raised umbrellas like renewed gunfire, and washed up in drifts in all the corners inside five minutes. It came crescendo, not relaxing from the first pounce, but steadily improving on it, and we, who had sat through the original assault stolidly, determined to see out the last parade, soon picked ourselves up and scuttled with the rest for shelter. The hail battered us triumphantly as we went, and when we reached the covered colonnades below we had to empty half-coagulated blocks of ice out of all the folds of our coats. Luckily it passed as quickly as it had come, but it had lowered the temperature many degrees in the ten minutes it lasted, and we were really shivering with cold, even inside our many coats, and were glad to leave the stadium, and walk back sharply along the glazed roadway and down the hill to the tram-station, in order to get warm again.

Never did one have to wait more than a minute for one's tram here, they simply came in, filled up, and pulled out, to be followed at once by more empty ones coming in. There was nothing the matter with the traffic organisation, it worked like freshly-oiled machinery.

In the tram we warmed up slowly, and went gratefully home to drink hot tea and make a hearty supper afterwards. We had just one day's interval, and then we were setting out with a coach party for a holiday in the Tatras, and so far we had not even considered our packing, though Mrs. Vesela, more provident, had already baked some long cakes, like the plaited continental loaves we used to see pre-war, and made bountiful provision for our appetites. No Czech, I found, would dream of booking a coach holiday and trusting to the company to provide him with sufficient food; their interpretation of full board was a sort of basic minimum, which they took care to supplement with plenty of between-meal snacks brought from home. In this case our caution was not altogether necessary, but we had no difficulty in eating everything we took with us.

There was a lot to be done in that one day, and because of all the bustle the ending of the Slet passed into the background of our minds, and was never, I think, the subject of much discussion. Before I came to CSR Mr. Vesely had urged that I ought to see the displays, saying that they were something one should never forget. Having seen them, I understand what he meant, for he was thinking of the pure, clear, mass effects which most impressed me, and which are precisely the effects most directly due to the traditional Sokol idea. This is indeed "All for one, and one for all". Premier Zapotocky is credited with having remarked of the 1948 Slet that: "Its success proved the insignificance of the individual". With all goodwill I must disagree with him. For me the best of what I saw proved again and again the interdependence of the individual and the whole, the responsibility of the individual to the whole, and the fact that the acceptance of this responsibility in full turns it into a privilege. The anxious young girl at Val, biting her lip in grim concentration on her white ring, was as essential to the success of the Slet as the designer of the most intricate entrance. She and the wonderful shimmering expanse of colour and movement were like peace, indivisible.

This is my last word on the Eleventh All-Sokol Slet; for at the time I had to devote my attention rather to orgies of hair-washing and stocking-washing, in a bathroom turned into the hob of hell by its coke-fired geyser, and where I always contrived to get the shower flowing either too hot or too cold. I pay now to the national movement the tribute I had no time to consider then.

The next day we set out by coach for the mountains.

16

To the Tatras!

WE caught our coach early in the morning at the Hotel Paris, near the Powder Tower, and the first surprise was that it turned out to be the same cream-coloured bus which had taken us to Lidice and Lany; the second was that it had the same large, leather-coated driver; but the coincidence became preposterous when we found that we had also been allocated the same places in it, just behind the driver, and consequently could never settle in, however prompt to our hour we came, until every other soul in the front part of the coach was safely seated.

However, we got used to nipping in at the last moment, and liked our places for various strategic reasons. The step, for instance, provided an admirable position for the large bag of food which we had brought with us; out of our way, but available when we wanted anything out of it, for Honza had only to lean and unzip it and reach inside, and we had arranged it so that what we wanted to use first was on top. The only occasion when this failed was when I hoisted the bag on to its step inside the door with the closed end of the zip forward instead of the open one, and Honza had practically to worm his way under the seat to get hold of it and yank it open; which he did not fail to point out, with emphasis, when he emerged scarlet and crumpled.

Our companions were a mixed bag, not very different from any holiday party anywhere: a middle-aged father and mother and their daughter, perhaps trades-people, a young doctor and his wife and little boy, one or two young couples, two girls going away together, perhaps for the first time without their families, a thoughtful-looking young Girl Guide, some settled married people, one or two solitary young men who would not be solitary for long. Everyone was naturally studying everyone else, for we had to spend ten days together, and the group becomes important in these circumstances. I hope they all felt they might have done worse; take it by and large, we got on pretty well together. We had also our organiser and his wife, who sat beside the driver and nursed a very English-looking fox-terrier.

We left on time, pulling out of town due east on the road to Podebrady, which we reached and passed through in about an hour, a gleam of white spa buildings and a shimmer of green parks, and then we were out rolling across the north Bohemian plain, wide lifted fields undulating only softly in the bright sunlight of mid-morning, fields with a baked golden appearance I shall always associate with the Bohemian summer. Through Chlumec, and on to Hradec Kralove, a well-planned modern town with handsome wide streets and a twentieth-century briskness about it, where we crossed the Labe and turned south-eastward on the long run to Svitavy. Here we stopped for lunch, and already we were on the edge of Moravia in one morning's travelling and without apparent haste or effort. Our respect for our unimpressive but very competent bus increased; it was comfortable, too; all it lacked was the chromium and plush polish often found in coaches of lesser performance.

There was just time after lunch to walk round and stretch our legs; then we were off again across the plateau and down into the valley of the Morava, into the rich black farming country of Hana, and after that into the forested uplands of Beskydy, where we began to encounter many road diversions due to work in progress, and effectively lost ourselves on the way to Velke Karlovice. Everyone had become cheerful, friendly and noisy by this time, and advice was offered from all directions, and maps came out and were consulted in rivalry over routes; during which process the driver went placidly on by every likely-looking road, and we emerged triumphantly at Cadca, and began to cruise along the left side of a wide, deep valley, looking down over a rocky descent and scattered villages and fields at the southward-flowing Kysuca. Somewhere on this stretch of road and river and railway, for all are forced to share the same bed, we entered Slovakia; but I have to admit that at the time I was asleep. I was never more anxious to stay awake, for now we were in country really unfamiliar even in outlines, the very villages different in character from anything I knew; but I had reached the stage when I could not keep my eyes open.

Some time in the early evening, before we drove into Zilina, I awoke, and gazed eagerly at the scene, and asked: "Are we in Slovakia yet?"

"Oh, yes, a long time ago," said Honza. He added provokingly: "We have passed through the beautifullest scenery."

"Why didn't you wake me?" I asked indignantly.

"I didn't dare," said Honza demurely.

At Zilina the Kysuca empties into the Vah, and this mountain river, which in its many tributaries draws off the waters of both the High and the Low Tatras as it flows westward between them, was running high and wild as I know only flood rivers in winter, though it was July and lovely weather. Perhaps it is always so, or perhaps in the mountains they had had more rains than we even knew of, for I found out very soon how it can rain there while the plains sun themselves in unclouded warmth. But for this first day we had finished wandering. We stayed the night at a pleasant hotel opposite the railway station, I sharing a room with the two girl friends, Honza with a young clerk in government service, who was travelling alone.

In the evening we went out to have a look at the town, which has a most imposing paved square with bright gardens, soaring upward on the further side by flights of steps to concrete terraces, where the church and city hall stand close together, with the double cross of Slovakia shining over them. Looking beyond these white modern buildings one can see always the background of the Fatra hills, wild, beautiful and violently different. Often when even the most prosaic town—which this certainly is not— is dropped into such surroundings, one is not conscious of the contrast from the streets, but here the hills are always in view, inescapable and challenging; almost one expects to awake and find either the town or the hills have been dreamed, so impossible do they seem together.

During the occupation the Germans tried very hard to make use of separatist feelings in Slovakia, by such acts as the setting up of the puppet government, which was dressed to look like a state in its own right, though actually it had no more rights than any other non-German group under the thumb of Germany. What they hoped, I suppose, was to leave alone as much as possible this part of the country, which was of little industrial use to them, and to dismember what remained of the feeling of country in the Czechoslovak nation. With the great mass of the people they created, instead, the very solidarity they had hoped to break in pieces. Even ardent former separatists, I should think, took to the hills in Slovakia during 1944, and began with dour thoroughness their own campaign of the war; and when you see their hill country you can realise how the soil which kept them faithful made it possible also for them to be effective.

We left early next morning, and followed the Vah's course upstream, the road running closely along the floor of the valley by the river. Here the Vah has no banks; simply on a level the water and the green meadows meet, and in places the current has eaten pieces out of the land almost to the edge of the road. We saw again how high was the flow, and how rapid and turgid, bringing down bushes and small trees and lodging them in the curves of its tumbled bed. Yet long villages of wooden houses, small and narrow and without the opulent colours of Bohemia, sit beside the road without apparent care for the incalculable neighbour on their doorsteps.

Throughout the length of our drive through Slovakia, perhaps a hundred and twenty miles, we were continually being pushed from the main road, which was fairly good, on to narrower tracks which would just take us in, because almost every stretch of roadway was under repair. There are years of lost time to be made up, for during the occupation nothing was done. In all this distance, a maze of rivers, we did not cross one bridge which was not a temporary affair of wood, all the old ones having been shattered by one side or the other in the partisan war and the last desperate efforts of the Germans to prevent the advance of the Red Army.

In all this distance, also, we did not pass through one village without seeing new small brick houses going up on at least one site; nor through one community large enough to be called a small town, without noticing in addition to the cottages new or half-finished factory buildings. There is a great drive on to bring Slovakia up to the Czech standard of living and population by dispersing industry into its undeveloped regions. This was Honza's first visit, as well as mine, and he was much impressed by this spate of building.

Presently we climbed higher above the river, leaving

the floor of the valley, and headed into the Little Fatras, those hills which had provided such a tantalising backcloth to the smart white square of Zilina. Beautiful hills, rolling, wooded, shaggy, rising to forested peaks, as dramatic in a different way as the mountains themselves. Road, river and railway are forced together through the solitary pass between their two main masses, a gorge everywhere narrow, but at one point closing in in overhanging rocks, first on our right, then on the left. On these two vantage points are the ruins of two castles, stone ghosts leaning on space far above the river. In their heyday this pass must have been impregnable indeed. We reached first the one on our own side of the gorge, and gasped at the sight of it, for this is no fairy-tale palace with Gothic roofs, but a grim, grey skeleton clinging to the jutting rocks with claws of stone, cliff and wall rising sheer together, bleached and weathered to the point where no one can tell their meeting-place. We had no sooner crept past under the hanging shadow of this fortress than we saw the second one, on just such another crag ahead of us, on the other side of the valley. Our road ran on a high shelf of the slope, and the railway was below us, so close that we could not see it at this stage, but a little later the valley widened just enough to allow both to proceed without, so to speak, edging their way along with their eyes shut and their fingers and toes gripping the face of the rock. Then we saw a debris of iron strewn along the side of the line, far below, the remains of locomotives, road trucks, all kinds of rolling stock and transport, some of it wrecked there and hurriedly cleared out of the way, some pushed over from the road; the relics again of the partisan activities which flourished here, and of the final advance of the Red Army. Traces of those battles are everywhere.

Presently the valley widened, and we came down nearer to the river again, and cruised through the northern foothills of the Great Fatras, sometimes crossing and recrossing the Vah, but never leaving it for long. It is a land of wide, folded hills, dappled and tufted with drying flax under the smoother slopes, and of grazing cattle in the low pastures, but of limited agriculture because of the narrow levels and the hard conditions. Everywhere the forested slopes rise wave on wave at the skyline, and the whole colouring of the land seems harsher and darker than in golden Bohemia; black and dark greens of conifers, leaf-brown of the river, hard greys of the outcrop rocks and the stony lower slopes, the palette is different.

We passed through Ruzomberok, which is the chief centre of the region, a cotton and textile town, with many wide new streets and imposing civic buildings, sitting in a curve of the river on a broad level site, with all about it an apparent emptiness of pastures, and then the hills. And from this point we were within sight of the peaks of Tatra; they rose before us on the left, a cluster of jagged heads, beautifully compact and sudden and aloof. On our right were the Low Tatras, second only to their big brothers, and in some ways as lovely; but we could look only one way, for our eyes were held by those half-veiled summits remote and white in the sky, and the chiselled faces of rock below, pied with snowfields and polished with sun. They were still a long way off, for the road here does not approach them closely, and between the ranges the river valley widens into an open plain, perhaps fifteen kilometres broad. A few towns are strung along the road like a chain of beads. At one of them, Liptovsky Svaty Mikulas, we stopped for lunch.

This St. Nicholas is not the usual one, but a local saint, hence the identifying adjective "of Liptov". We had just time to walk through the big square of the town, and look at his church and statue, and then we were off out of town again on a detour southward, to pay a flying visit to the caverns of Demanova, in the foothills of the Low Tatras.

Ahead of us now were the highest peaks of the range, but we were shut into a narrow and lovely valley by two soaring slopes of rock and forest, shut in with only the road and the tumbling, clear mountain stream Lucanka, which comes out of the caverns themselves and scurries north to join the Vah. It is a rocky stream, one which dances and sings in small fountains of spray between leaning trees, like a morsel of Scotland, and fills the narrow valley with echoing sound and scintillating light.

We came to a clearing with the usual pavilion or two selling postcards and souvenirs, parked the bus, and prepared to foot it up the wooded hills, for you must climb to enter the grottoes, though as soon as you are in you immediately descend endless steps again. We were forewarned that it was always cold inside, and wet from many miniature streams and springs, and therefore everyone emerged clutching raincoats and hoods and scarves, and Honza hauled out his case from the luggage recess in order to put on an extra pullover. Thus wrapped up like eskimos, we walked up the zigzag path, and paid our way into the caves.

It was certainly wet, drips from the roof began to flop heavily on our hoods at once, but we did not find it particularly cold. A brisk guide gathered us together upon a promontory of soap-coloured rock glazed with the stalagmitic formation of centuries. Over us the roof was an intricate draping of tinted stalactites, low-arched; and over the fenced rim of our platform there was a sharp descent of spray-filled air, lit from hidden lamps, walled in with curving and undulating planes of coated rock, like surfaces of iced cake. A long staircase cut in the stone led us down into it, until we reached a level way and a sound of water, and were wandering side by side with the river again.

From here the real colours begin, and you are in an Arabian Nights world. The path winds and undulates through softly lit labyrinths slenderly strung off from hollows of water on both sides by a cord, sometimes climbing a few steps, sometimes descending, but maintaining for some distance roughly the same level. Four kilometres of pathway, they say, is now sufficiently smoothed out for visitors, and we walked the whole of it; but the caverns wander for more than double this distance, and some day the whole length will be opened for us, nearly seven miles of a world between the catacombs and fairyland. The roof leans down in curtain folds and bosses and chandeliers of stone, intricate beyond belief, and shading from clear, greenish white through all the delicacies of saffron and coral and rose to a deep, glowing orange, and every surface has two ways of reflecting light, from the glaze of its own smoothness, and severally from the crystals of which it is formed, in a mica-like glitter. The floor rises to meet it in tiered fountains and pagodas and small frozen fir trees, giving back the same sparkle and glow, sometimes touching and uniting in new recessional arcadings, retiring greenly from the light. Here the walls close in to make polished corridors about you, and there expand into vaulted Gothic halls.

Through this maze the river wanders with a purposeful, unhurried sound, deep, clear and glitteringly cold, of a gem-like brilliance. The waters here are virgin, without blemish, for there is literally nothing to soil them; whatever dust or earth or sand enters comes only on the shoes of visitors, and is soon washed away and lost on the first descent, among the small incidental rivulets which make for themselves channels through the stone. Here below, the hollows beside the pathway contain small lakes limpid as crystal, and shading from sapphire blue in the deepest places through aquamarine to the flushed gold of the shallows. They are full of stone flowers, lapis lazuli lilies, petrified amber weed. In recollecting Demanova one recites colours with fair accuracy; but there is no way of expressing intelligibly forms which copy no familiar forms, for the patient, cold and industrious stone of which this wonderland is made used only original ideas.

Our level path ended by encircling a broad white ski-ing slope of rock, and turning on its tracks. We walked back a little way, and turning off by another path, began to climb upward through the five ascending storeys which honeycomb the hill. By elaborate spiral staircases and little closed corridors and sudden clearings in the translucent forest we mounted steadily, and the sound of the river fell away from us. One of the most grandiose of the levels is the President Masaryk gallery, where walls and ceiling are richly rose-coloured.

We reached the highest level, and emerged into daylight by another door in the rock, blinking at the greenness of the woods and the bright surge of air above us. We did not discuss what we had seen; we seldom did, so soon after seeing it, and sometimes we never talked about it at all. Honza liked a lapse for due consideration, time for his ideas to crystallise, and grew quite cross occasionally if he was asked to give an opinion before he was ready.

We drove back into Liptovsky Svaty Mikulas, and turned eastward again by the main road; and again we were travelling along the open plain, parallel with that wonderful crested dragon of the Tatra range, for so long a time that it began to look as if we were going to drive absent-mindedly past and forget to turn in towards it. The whole comb is scarcely more than twenty-five miles long, and so sudden and resolute in its ascent that in a distance of about ten miles it climbs from this valley level of two thousand feet to eight thousand, and crowds into the few monstrous miles of its length peak upon peak, buttressed together, reared heads of granite and gneiss furrowed with snow-fields and scoured and glazed with wind. The frontier hills near Poland have rounded, shaggy heads of forest, the Little Fatras have often ragged, crumbled rocky outlines, melodramatic and swaggering, brigands of mountains; but these are the hard, diamond-hard, diamond-bright silhouettes of Alpine peaks, the pure, polished residue of adamantine rock after all its inessentials have been weathered away. Their beauty is the spare, bleached beauty of bone. In sunlight all their lines spring into dazzling clarity, dark blue-grey like steel, spear-edged, against a sky unbelievably lucid and blue; in cloud they retire sullen and abrupt, filming every plane of light and shadow to one smoky greyness, and looking out darkly between the folds, whirl the heavily-draped sky about them again, and hide their own grandeur and definiteness in its shifting uncertainty.

When it seemed that we were almost abreast of the extreme end of the range we turned suddenly to the left, and drove full tilt at it, and as we reached the first foothills our total view became shortened into a partial one, troubled only occasionally by glimpses of the heights. On the map the High Tatra range appears as a shallow crescent, open to the north, and at about two-thirds of the way along its curve there begins a wonderful road which runs along its moraines at a height of from three to four thousand feet; they call it the Freedom Road. Here are strung out like pearls on a thread the many famous resorts of Tatra, Strbske Pleso, Smokovec, Tatranska Polianka, Vysne Hagy, Tatranska Lomnica, almost one continuous rich community, since you can scarcely tell where one ends and the next begins, but everywhere so graciously spaced that not one of them offends by being in the usual sense of the word a town. Along the roadside shops and white hotels alternate with meadow and forest; everywhere you can walk out of your lodgings and straight into the woods and the first spicy slopes of the mountains. Just below the road a miniature railway line runs alongside.

To this road we now climbed by a breathless zigzag ascent, and turned along it, and began to think of supper and rest. Booking in these resorts is done, since the nationalisation of the big hotels, through a district bureau, which seems to be a good idea; but we ran into a slight tangle and delay because there had been a mistake over our rooms, and we were, technically, homeless. Our unlucky organiser had a wearying evening trying to find us new accommodation, and saw us safely stowed for the night at last in a hotel at Tatranska Polianka, with the intention of tackling the problem of permanent quarters—so to speak—in the morning. Actually the expected and desired happened, and we stayed there the rest of the week, which suited us admirably, for it proved a very comfortable hotel. It was an annexe of a much larger and more palatial one across the way, where we went for our meals; the large block was classed as an A hotel, and lived up to its classification in every way, notably in its excellent and friendly service; our rooms were in a much older house, without the modern convenience of running water in every room, but a most comfortable and cheerful place to live in, which is more important. From curiosity we made enquiries about the actual prices chargeable here, and learned that the highest, with full board—and that really meant full!— was the equivalent of twenty-five shillings a day. To those bereft of running water and telephones by banishment to our quarters, twenty shillings. And this in one of the loveliest centres in the country.

By this time our company was sorting itself out naturally into convenient parties. We had found that the Girl Guide, whose name was Magda, spoke a little English, and she and I shared a room. Honza was still with his room-mate of last night, the young clerk, Jan, who had a lean and melancholy look and a guileless manner much belied by a deep twinkle in his eye and a certain tone in his gentle and mellifluous voice. He was adept at playing the clown, which is a thing only a cultivated and intelligent person can do with infallible success; and not all of his patrons, I fancy, noticed the twinkle or the tone, so that we had more than one kind of clown in our circle very often. He took them—perhaps I should say "us"—apart, however, only as an academic exercise for his own amusement, and that of those who happened to be able to catch at the undercurrents, never for a general Tatra holiday.

We four set off up the nearest mountain slope on our first morning, in glorious sunshine, with the peaks in dazzling black and white and blue so near and clear to us that they seemed within touch. It was natural that my friends should lapse into Czech very often, and frequently I did not know where I was going, but where all was new and equally beautiful this mattered very little. We tramped uphill by the shortest, steepest ways we could find, singing "The Uist Tramping Song" at the tops of our voices. Robert Wilson's record of it was Honza's favourite of all the discs I had brought from England, and we had the words by heart after many playings. So far up the mountains there is a slight resemblance to Scotland in the profuse pine-woods, and the outcrop rocks, and the leaping, dancing, turbulent little rivers, which have trout in them, but offer you little chance of taking them out. One such river, not so little now that I remember the wild cleft of its bed and the force of its falls, came tumbling down the mountainside here in a spectacular series of cascades, and a path, tenuous and uncertain in appearance, followed it downhill. We debated whether we had better return by the beaten track, or could take this way and still be back for dinner; and since everyone was willing to risk it, off we went in a series of standing leaps, like the river itself, on our devious way home.

Our luck was magical, and our faith perhaps earned it. The river appeared to us to wind more and more to the left, and though we knew that track and river alike must ultimately meet the Freedom Road, we began to think that it would be at a spot somewhere near Lomnica, miles from our lunch; but we went on untroubled, even when the path dropped literally into the river, climbed a little higher through the jungle, and pushed on. The water did our singing for us, and justified its confident tone by bringing us out only on the far side of Smokovec with a sharp walk home and a large meal at the end of it.

In the afternoon we added to our party another couple, a young husband and wife named Zdenek and Jana. They were Jews; almost the first thing I noticed about them both was the concentration camp numbers tattooed on their left forearms. They had married very young, in the hope at least of being together in captivity, but in spite of that, had been separated, and found each other again only after the liberation.

Jana suggested that we should take the little train to Lomnica, and go up in the funicular to Lomnic Peak, or at least to the midway station of Skalnate Pleso, for at this time the upper section which climbs right to the peak was not open to the public. We were not sure of the times of the miniature trains, and set off to walk along the road, only to see a train coming when, as usual, we were midway between the tiny stations. However, at least we caused a lot of amusement to some of our friends who were already on board it, by tearing hell-for-leather along the road to the next stop, where we caught it by the skin of our teeth. There was no tiresome delay to book tickets, for the guard comes round as in a tram, and issues them as you go.

H

Tatranska Lomnica seems to be more of a town than any of the other centres, with many hotels and shops and a fine park; but we did not wait to see very much of it, preferring to make straight for the funicular; and we were wise, for even so we had to wait over an hour for a place in the car. Tickets were issued in numbered batches, and the holders admitted strictly according to the order of issue. We sat on the steps only a yard from the doors, to make sure that we were not cheated; and Honza went down and fetched us some ices to eat while we waited. I am allergic to waiting for anything, being inadequately provided with patience, and began to wonder if it was worth it; but in due course I found that it was worth that and more.

The line goes up to the peak, the second highest in the range, in two leaps, and the higher was denied to us, for the present at least. On the first stage nine great pylons—if I kept accurate count of the number—carry the cables a distance of four kilometres, with a rise of one in three; but the second, which mounts to the summit, makes a single bound of nearly two kilometres, without any supports at all, and with a gradient of one in two, and at the last stage even three in five. Consequently the free cable has to be slung at an enormous height, and the sight of the car in motion on this stretch fairly makes one's inside turn over. I was almost as glad not to be in it as I was sorry.

The peak, seen from the direct line of the funicular, is shapely to the point of symmetry, and soars to a point almost as spear-sharp as the Matterhorn. A deep groove marks its upper face in accurate line with the cable, and accentuates the classic regularity of its features. I, whose stomach turns at the mere idea of climbing mountains beyond the levels to which the dizziest amateur can proceed at a safe walk, never tire of looking at their beauty; and that sky behind the summit, so deeply blue as to be near the colour of gentians, surrounded the lovely, cold profile with a softness and radiance which should have melted its snows.

Our turn came, and we hurried into the car to secure for ourselves a space of window, and look down on the lost world. I am told, and can believe, that many people who don't mind flying are very sick in funiculars, for on passing every pylon there is a sudden drop which makes you wonder where you have left your internal economy, and whether you will ever recover it. I think, however, I was too interested to pay much attention, and recorded the sensation without feeling much physical effect from it. The cleared channel below the cable unrolled beneath us down the slope, we emerged from the trees, and climbed. For a time we saw only the near-by mountainside, stippled with the green crests of its enormous conifers; then a wider and wider expanse beneath, and away beyond the town from which we had come, far below, the sunny toy meadows of the plain, infinitely distant.

Even before one reaches Skalnate Pleso, the trees beneath have dwindled from their magnificence, and there is only rough heath-turf, and dwarf conifers no higher than scrub. As the slopes undulated under us we swung sometimes near enough to see plainly every detail of the ground, and suddenly Honza gasped, and gulped, and pointed downward to where a narrow, cleared track through these scrub trees went headlong down the mountain, curving slightly as it descended.

"What is it?" I asked, concluding that no one human was meant to walk down it.

"It is a ski-run!" he said, quite positively, but as if he himself found it a considerable shock to contemplate this undoubted truth. "But *I* would not like to try it!" And this, coming from Honza, and with so much decision, would seem to indicate that the ski-slopes on Lomnic Peak are little short of suicide.

The last reaches of our journey saw even the dwarf trees recede, unwilling to climb higher in the cold, unable to root longer in the thin soil. Now there was only rock and turf, and where the winds gouged at the slopes only rock. A last sweeping ascent, and we had arrived.

The large, square, tower-like building which houses the funicular station holds also a hotel and a restaurant, and stands on the outer rim of a glacial valley, looking one way far down to the shelf of the moraine road, and the lower world beyond, and the other way into the mirror-smooth, steel-blue water of Skalnate Pleso itself, one of those characteristic Tatra lakes above the tree-line, in the palm of the hand of this granite-walled valley, a hand as cold, as beautiful and as austere as the Snow Queen's. The lake has no shore, no softening of its stone outlines, only a double frigid splendour of its own, a piercing still clarity which reveals the subtle shades of blues and greens and greys in the rock below, and the reflected sapphire of the sky with the soft drift of clouds in it, afloat upon the motionless surface. This blueness again casts upward, along the glazed stone planes ascending from the valley, a shadowy reflected colour and light. When one looks at details, there are boulders and scattered stones here, some thin, pale turf in the sheltered places; but the general impression is of a hollow of dark rock scoured as clean and sterile as the facets of a cut-crystal bowl.

Easy paths trace their way up the mountainside from this point. We began to climb by one of them, and Honza suddenly gave a whoop, and shot away at a run to bury his hands in the lowest snow-bank, which lingered, like the highest grass and the last surviving flowers, in a deep, sheltered hollow under a slope of rock. Young Magda was off after him, and in a moment the snowballs were flying. Magda read much, and had a grave dignity older than her age, but she punctured it at the most unexpected moments by bounding about as incalculably as a Saint Bernard puppy.

We climbed well above the valley, with the great bare faces above, a single wall when seen from below, separating themselves into many complicated clefts and couloirs, all outlined with long-lying snow. Then we sat down on a bank of turf, and looked back at Skalnate Pleso, and realised that we were not going to be able to climb much higher, for half the sky had filled with clouds, purple and stormy, and rain was already scudding up from the south-west. However, it can remove as quickly as it appears, so we waited the event, and even debated going higher. In the meantime, we were content to stare our fill.

At our feet the mountainside fell away into the bowl of the valley, and the funicular station sat on the shallowly lifting rim beyond, darkly outlined against the air. On the left, at some little distance, was the only other building here, a small observatory, with a globe-like dome. Between them the line of the valley dipped to its lowest, so that only the hairline of black rock seemed to prevent the waters of the lake from spilling over far down into the invisible tidy white town of Lomnica. The world below we could still see, though so distantly that it appeared to have no connection with ours, for the Freedom Road and all its charming forests and hotels were hidden, and we were looking beyond into the villages and meadows of the plain, nearly five thousand feet below. There the sun still shone, and made small patterns of cloud-shadow and pale green-golden light like embroideries on a quilt; but our valley here had become dark, glossy and ominous with the purple reflection of the cloud-wall moving in upon us. Only the waters of the lake retained light, giving back a burnished image of the brighter eastern sky only faintly filmed with cloud; from here its clarity was lost, and it was a flat, opaque surface of silver.

The first drops of rain fell, a hint only, but if 1 did not know enough of the mountains to accept it instantly, my companions did. Back we went regretfully to the hotel, unhurriedly at first, but an ice-cold rain slanted suddenly down out of the west and roused us to a more respectful haste before we were half-way down the slope. Even with the sun shining it was cold and breathless up here, but in rain and shadow it was degrees colder at once, and by the time we ran across the level and dived into the doorway we were shivering.

There were many stairs to climb to the restaurant, which was our natural refuge, but when we reached it we found it cosy and warm, and settled down gratefully to coffee—"not from coffee", but none the less acceptable, since it was at least boiling hot. Outside the windows on the airward side there was now nothing but one immense whiteness; on the landward side the shadowy greyness of rocks lingered for a while hazed with the steady, veiling rain, and then withdrew from us, and here also there was nothing, only a void of white. Our walking was over, for the mist stayed almost until the departure time of the last car, and then deigned to clear enough to show us marvellous wet, glistening prospects on the way down.

By the time we arrived below, and made for our little train back to Tatranska Polianka and supper, the rain had stopped; in the far-away plain I believe they had had none. I had no idea as yet how capriciously these mountains of ours could veil and unveil themselves from the world, how many rains, how many changing winds, and how much innocent brief sunshine they could pack into one day.

17

The Delectable Mountains

Home life, if one may use that term of a hotel room, was strangely dreamlike in Tatranska Polianka. When we woke up in the morning we had only to lean a little out of bed and look through the window, and there against the picture-postcard sky, at this hour almost invariably gentian-blue, were the brilliant black and white peaks elegantly disposed to make the most graceful picture possible. If we had looked through all the bedroom windows in all the hotels along the Freedom Road we could not possibly have found a lovelier view.

To come down to a factor of more earthy importance, food was a fantasy here; no one wanted coupons for it, though legally they were recently bound to share the rationing system of the rest of the country, and rightly so. We ate, and were never asked for anything. In the confectioners' shops there were sweet cakes, ice-cream in plenty, and even "slehacka", sweetened whipped cream, delicious with the wild wood strawberries which children brought down out of the forests and sold by the roadside. Tormented by the ticking minutes, which reminded me constantly how brief ten days can be, I sometimes resented the time we spent chasing to the shop to buy these delicacies.

The whole of the Freedom Road and its long, gracious, wandering town had something of a dream about it, as does every place which exists chiefly to entertain visitors. Skipping along the slopes here, high above the ordinary

world of farm and pasture, it maintained its hold on reality
only by the thread of the road down to the plain. Another
reality, and a grim one, existed within the white, many-
windowed walls of the vast tuberculosis sanatoria, but
from outside one could hardly realise it because they looked
so like luxury hotels. These white palaces among the black
pines were many and beautiful, and housed patients from
all over the republic and beyond, for the Tatras can offer
similar excellent conditions to those in the Alps.

Sometimes the whole party met again, and had the
coach at its disposal. We went up in this way to the
western end of the road, at Strbske Pleso, and from there
walked to Popradske Pleso, along a wonderful path slung
for most of its length half-way up a hillside above river and
forest. "Pleso" is the special word for these mountain
lakes, of which there are dozens scattered about among
the valleys of Tatry.

The road climbs steadily to Strbske Pleso, circling inward
at the end to form a broad open terrace, from which you
can look down full into the plain without hindrance, and
see clearly, on such a morning as we had, the pattern of
wide fields, level and still and hedgeless, and the occasional
towns strung along them at even intervals, compact as
flowers. From this terrace we turned inward into the
valley where the lake lies, broad and tranquil, edged with
white villas and hotels and scented forests, the land beyond
it rising in slopes of diminishing woodland to a complexity
of snow-peaks in the distance.

Here the party broke up and set off on its various chosen
walks; but when we took the path for Popradske Pleso we
found that most of our companions were doing the same,
for the way is famous. This lake, too, lies among forests,
deep in a crater almost surrounded by precipitous cliffs,
sheltered from most winds, and greenly still. But what
matters is the way by which one reaches it; by diverse

beginnings, over shoulders of woodland, through copses, over small streams, the path climbs to a high level on one slope of a deep, wide valley, a sharp, tumbled descent of rock and scree and trees dropping on the right hand to the stony river in the depths, a sharper ascent on the left going up to invisible peaks. Across the valley dark rising slopes of forest, and the nearer broken mountainsides dwindling from pines through scrub to pale turf; and beyond them again the snow-peaks, frigidly wonderful, at every turn of the path changing their alignment, and presenting new granite profiles.

We had set an unnecessary pace to this height, and began to realise that time was no particular object, and that we were on a lee slope, with incomparable basking places and an ideal sun full on us. We had breakfasted early, and brought out with us the second breakfast as sandwiches, and now we chose an open face of rock full of comfortable shelves, and settled down for a time to sunbathe and eat our provisions. The only thing we had not, and began to think we needed, was something to drink; and when one of the older men of the party came along at a more leisurely pace, and leaning on a hefty stick, Honza politely requested from the top shelf:

"Would you mind striking the rock, please?"

The gentleman obliged with a straight face, but nothing happened.

"Too bad!" said Honza, subsiding in disappointment. "Evidently you're not Moses."

Along the path, however, when we moved on, we found a small spring, with a niche made for it in the rock, and drank water colder and more satisfying even than that of Svata Voda.

At the end our path dipped lower, and the symmetrical valley opened out a little into a bowl. We passed through a last belt of forest, and dived down the final sharp descent to emerge on the shore of Popradske Pleso. On this side of it the usual small hotel and restaurant, spreading itself lazily along the waterside, and looking out over it from open verandas; but no other building at all, simply on our shore the rich dark woods folding closely round the water's edge, and on the other side almost perpendicular cliffs beyond the narrowest precarious edge of trees and scree.

The rest of this day we stayed about Strbske Pleso, walking in the woods and basking in the sun. Sudden light rain came on late in the afternoon, a veil of mist shut off the valley world from us, and we were driven into cover; and having begun, it rained for the rest of the evening, which we spent in the hotel, playing rummy, dancing, and doing a great deal of talking while we waited in vain for the opportunity of another walk.

I am told that our week in the Tatras was by no means an exceptionally wet one, but even so it seemed to me that the weather, from this point on, merely shone on us long enough to lure us out without raincoats, in order to pounce on us in sheeting rain and mist as soon as we were well up the mountainside or deep in the woods. We found ourselves, therefore, making many short excursions which ended in dodging from summer-house to summer-house back to the hotel; and we understood why the walls of all the little pavilions in the woods are closely covered with inscriptions in many languages and even more diverse traditions, from the portentous to the facetious. One must do something while waiting for the rain to stop. We added our quota to most of them.

Someone had invented for amusement the legend that Jan was considering the possibilities of an affair with one of the unattached girls; and Jan, for his own purposes, had been pleased to accept the fable, and taken the trouble to give it his own particular polish. Honza broke into verse about it one morning, perversely upon the ceiling of one of the huts, which he reached by antics in which he was aided and abetted by Magda in her St. Bernard puppy mood. The walls were not only too crowded to accommodate the ode, but also too commonplace. While he was in composition a superior person came along the path, gave us a disapproving look, and in the Czech fashion said precisely what she meant.

"There's a saying," she remarked acidly, "that the names of fools are on every street corner."

Honza contorted himself sufficiently to have an equally candid look at her, and replied politely, and with his most gracious smile: "May I add yours, madam?"

If the rain began before we were out of the hotel there was nothing for it but to make ourselves at home either in one of our various rooms or in the lounge, collect what books we had between us, borrow packs of cards from the waiters, and amuse ourselves from meal to meal until the sun came out. I do not mind walking in rain if I am dressed for the part, but Tatra rain is not the kind in which one chooses to walk for long, and there was little point in risking it, since mists usually came in with it, and visibility shrank inward and cut off all the glorious prospects of the peaks. But on most days there were intervals worth waiting for, when the air cleared magically in a moment, and all the wet range steamed in the sunshine with blue and green vapours, and the pale drapings dissolved away to leave the peaks unveiled against the new washed blue of the sky. Then we would grope hurriedly for our coats, and make off before the weather changed again, up the first climbing path, and back by any that turned downhill, since every descending way met the road somewhere.

Mornings were the best time, and if one seized them promptly a whole day's walking could almost be packed in before lunch, so that we could not afterwards complain if rain set in and drove us indoors for the evening.

One day we rose early again, and set off with the coach to the ice caves of Dobsina, south of the Low Tatras. This time we took a picnic lunch with us, not being sure of a good hotel exactly where we should want it. Our road lay south-eastward into the plain, and south again from Poprad into the extreme foothills of the Low Tatras, beyond the water-shed into the fan of rivers which empty south into the Danube.

Arrival at our destination appeared once more to be arrival at nowhere, just a space of meadows and a fountain on one side of the road, leading across to a field brook, one inn just in sight, and on the other side of the road a rising hillside with easy paths climbing it, through copses, and open heathy country. We left the bus here, and began to climb, and the ascent became sharper as we went, to end in a series of zigzags through which the impatient, ducking under the handrails, had trodden a short cut straight to the top. Here there was a pavilion with postcards, as usual, and seats, and round the corner of this building a high fence, a mysterious door in it, glimpses of rocks above the top of the fence, and a gush of air which might have come straight from the Arctic.

Dobsina is a survival from the Ice Age. How it has managed to survive, at this altitude and in this climate, is a question beyond my answering, but there it is, two layers of caverns of solid ice in the middle of this summer country, obstinately refusing to thaw. They say that there are still more caves unexplored beneath, but they are afraid to break through into them in case the air coming in should bring a warm current, and destroy everything. Even where a small chink in the rock lets in a breath of outside air in the upper caverns, it has worn a deep hollow in the wall of ice opposite.

We had to wait a little while for another party to emerge, and feeling that bitter chill emanating from beyond the door in the fence, everyone began to put on any spare coats he had with him, preparing for the worst. The key was in the lock, and Honza let himself in and went prospecting down the dark stairway inside, towards the mouth of the cave. When he came bounding back with chattering teeth, it seemed the obvious thing to lock him in, and tempting to leave him there to explain himself when the guide emerged from the depths; but we let him out as soon as he heard them coming, for, after all, his reputation was ours. Visitors questioned as they came shivering out into the sunlight testified that it was really worth seeing—"but *cold!*"

Again as at Demanova a long descent received us, steps cut in the ice and the stone; and as we went down, the soft lights showed us a great ceiling of glazed greenish light, and curved glassy walls, and wide smooth slopes slithering away on our right hand to a level floor of light and music below. Now everything around us from the floor under our feet to the arched roof overhead was greenish-white ice, only faintly translucent, half-reflecting light, half-absorbing it. Our shadowy mirror images moved on the surface of it, and deeps of frigid, brilliant colour shone out of its heart. Within that which was almost colourless to the first glance the eye could find from different angles the most unexpected subtleties of colour, and in that which was hard and cold and unadaptable the supplest undulations of beauty. They show you the formations which have accidentally copied shapes recognisable from the outside world, sometimes indeed recognisable only by a slight effort of the imagination; the priest at the altar is the most elaborate example. But these don't seem to me to matter at all. What matters, what is most lovely, is the smooth vast planes of delicately curving, chaste, silken greenness which draw your hands to stroke them, and your eyes to caress where you cannot touch. The very length of line of these jade walls, uncomplicated, fluent and serene, soothes like a long melodic line in music.

The music came in this case from a portable gramophone on a single bench under the ice wall, and was a commonplace but pleasant little waltz; and on the levelled part of the floor of this improbable green fairyland, in a railed-off space, several people were skating. Among them were two tiny girls about four years old, dressed alike and obviously twins, who were executing complicated figures with the aplomb of champions.

We lingered for some time to watch and admire them; so did everyone else, for they were charming. Then we went down to the lower layer of caverns, down a long staircase between those narrowing lofty zircon walls full of lambent light, into corridors almost touching our shoulders on either side, where the cold struck inward brilliantly, and from these through secret low archways into round cells of ice. If Demanova is the fantastic fairyland of the Arabian Nights, this is the austere Scandinavian one of Hans Andersen.

Coming back to the outer world, after this brief astonishment, required a small effort of readjustment which Demanova had not demanded. Warmth and colour went over us like a wave as we emerged and broke up into little chattering groups on the way down the sunlit hill. It was here, on one of the short cuts which lopped off the corners, that I saw a large adder drawing himself leisurely out of the grass. We had been about to cross that way, but Honza peremptorily and quite unnecessarily ordered us to go round, and round we went, leaving the withdrawing snake in undisputed possession.

In the meadows below we ate our picnic lunch and washed it down with bad beer at the inn afterwards. Beer is certainly another field in which Slovakia needs to be brought up to the Czech standard.

On the way back to Polianka our plan was to drive round the eastern end of the Tatra crescent to the village of Zdiar, almost on the Polish side of the mountains, which is one of the spots in Slovakia celebrated for having maintained its costumes, dances, songs, and customs intact, largely with the help and for the benefit of the visitor, probably, but certainly to good effect. My friends chattered volubly in Czech, and used the universal word "folklore" rather cynically. The proper time to visit such a place is on Sunday at church time, and preferably a festival Sunday. We arrived on a Thursday, at the awkward in-between hour of tea, when nothing is happening, and in the heavy rain which we had managed to avoid all day. Something, however, came over, even through the rain.

The village wanders alongside the road in scattered cottages and cattle-huts for a long way, a stream on one side keeping pace with it, and feeding the wheel of a small saw-mill in passing. On the other side, behind the houses and the inn, the rounded hillsides go up to the pastures and the shepherds' huts above. The houses are of wood, finely built and well kept, with no gardens around them; and the little cattle-sheds are as compact and sturdy as miniature cottages. Further on, the houses move into a higher terrace overlooking the road, and the church lies back beyond them, with something of the effect of a little square, and opposite is the hotel at which we, on this particular wet Thursday, hoped to find some tea. These cottages, arranged neatly and separately about the hillside, without the softening hedges and fences of gardens to root them into the ground, and with their prettily-dressed windows full of laces and nets and little plants in pots, had a delicate doll's-house gaiety about them which the rainy sky and the wet green pastures and woods could not subdue into solemnity.

The driver, in response to requests, dropped us in the middle of the village, beside the inn, and we agreed to meet at the hotel; for it was then raining only desultorily. But our small party was slow in deciding its moves, and slower in getting off the mark, so that others were well away before we had moved or the coach had passed on; consequently we were in a position to dive back into its shelter when the drizzle without warning became a downpour. Thankfully we settled down to drive on to the hotel in comfort, folklore or no folklore.

"Ought we to pick up the others when we overtake them?" asked the more conscientious among us.

"No," said the less conscientious, very firmly. "They wanted to walk; let 'em walk!"

Perhaps we were indulging the worst side of our natures, but admittedly it was funny when we passed them at top speed, and funnier still when they finally reached the hotel and tea, to find us already seated at our ease drinking some incredible concoction which went by that name. It was certainly "not from tea". Voices at the veranda and an indignant rustle of raincoats warned us.

"Look out!" said Zdenek. "They are coming!" And: "O-oh!" said Honza in awe, "they have fighting faces!"

We got off scot-free, however, for it was the driver they attacked, and when they had asserted themselves they proved to be really very little concerned about their shabby usage. All they wanted was the argument, and some tea; we could have told them, by that time, that they were not likely to get the latter. Jana, unable to drink the stuff, had asked for mineral water, but this proved to be even more peculiar, a faintly clouded, amber liquid with a taste and odour which defied identification. However, we cut our losses; there was nothing else for it.

There were to be some dances at the hotel that evening, but we could stay only long enough to watch, from the verandas, the first of the local inhabitants coming hurrying down through the rain from the little houses, pipers among them, tall, lean men in cream-coloured felt trousers slit at the ankle and embroidered in diamond shapes up the thighs, with white shirts rich with needlework about the breasts, and sheepskin jackets, and round black hats with their narrow brims turned up all round and stuck with short white plumes.

"All folklore!" said Jan cynically; but we do not have to go abroad to find those local customs which are retained in being by the tourist trade. Zdiar is on the Polish side of the Tatra comb, and a flavour of the Polish mountaineer modifies the dress and bearing of the people. They have local dances which provide a famous spectacle, and no doubt the bear dance and the stamping dance were performed at the hotel that night; but we did not stay to see them.

As things turned out, we need not have hurried away, for we were to pick up one member of the party in the village, and though we waited half an hour for him, and even sent out scouts towards the hill cottages where he was privately reported to be negotiating a deal in butter—how accurately I don't know, it seemed indiscreet to make too many enquiries—he did not appear. While we waited for our messengers to return the rain stopped, and the whole party dispersed into the surrounding country, Honza into the saw-mill, several more people hopefully butterwards, and more than one into the inn. It seemed to be the accepted thing that Slovakia, though now ostensibly under the same rationing regulations as the Czech lands, still had very much better supplies of most foods, and was continuing to dispose of the surplus at whatever prices it could get. A friend in Slovakia was a valuable asset to any Praguer. The deals seemed to be small affairs for the most part, of a pound or so of butter and a few eggs, and altogether one heard considerably more than one saw of the black market.

Honza came drifting back from the little neat cattle-sheds on the grass terrace by the road, and called Magda and me to look inside one, and like fools we took him at his face value, and went. The end wall retreated well under the deep timber eaves, and left an open space within the inverted V of the roof; the door hasped outside, with a staple and long wooden peg, but we didn't notice that in time. We walked guilelessly into a clean straw floor and a rich smell, and Honza, possibly with vengeful memories of the locked door at Dobsina, dropped the peg into the staple and walked away whistling. Not that an active sixteen-year-old Girl Guide found much difficulty in shinning over the top of the wall and dropping on the outer side; but we thereupon wasted our advantage by going gently back as if nothing had happened, instead of waiting out of sight. He *might* have manifested some uneasiness if we had failed to return to the bus; I advance the possibility rather dubiously, but it is just a possibility.

Our friend who had the appointment about the butter did not return, and finally we received an apologetic message that he was staying overnight, and would return to Polianka in the morning. We grumbled, as coach parties do when one person upsets the schedule, but his was the greater inconvenience; so we went back to supper, and left him to look after his own transport.

The last two days of our stay were fitfully rainy from morning to night, and largely remarkable for the number of times we got wet; yet the time passed very quickly, and on Sunday morning we began the return journey to Prague, laden with collections of dried mushrooms, none of them Honza's and mine. I never had luck with mushrooms. We took the same road home for the first part of our drive, by the Vah valley and the Little Fatras, threading the hills by the same melodramatic pass with the two guardian castles. The mountains we left in rain, and that wonderful drive almost the length of the comb showed us only a shifting, sullen and capricious vista of whirling clouds and half-veiled iron-grey peaks, remote and dark, though by noon, when we were almost in Zilina again, the sun came out warmly.

From Zilina we took a rather more southerly course than in coming, by upland roads through the Javornik hills, and so towards evening through Zlin, and on to its attendant town—now a fellow-district of the greater town of Gott-waldov—of Otrokovice, where we stayed that night at the Community House hotel.

Neither of us had actually stayed in a Bat'a hotel before, and we were interested to see what sort of accommodation we should find. Magda and I and another girl found our-selves sharing a self-contained suite, which consisted of a large bed-sitting-room, two built-in wardrobes like small rooms, and a fine bathroom fitted with every gadget a bathroom could possibly have. Honza, coming to see why we took so long to get ready for a walk, was deeply impressed, and inspected everything inquisitively.

The Bat'a hotels reverse the usual procedure for houses wishing to provide reasonably priced service, by giving their customers more comfort privately, and less gilt and mirrors publicly, or so at least I thought. The general effect of the public rooms was spacious, clean, bright, but spare rather than lavish; but the service was good, and the rooms had all the important things, comfortable beds, luxurious baths, telephones, central heating and good ventilation. But the corridors and the great round landings from which they shot off, star-fashion, on each floor, were just clean, bare and useful, not decorative; which seems sensible enough, since one uses them merely to get to some other place.

"Your corridor," said Honza thoughtfully, as we went along to look at the room he was sharing with Jan, "is rather like a hospital corridor. Now ours, as you see, is more like a prison corridor." Which was true enough if one may judge from pictures, for neither of us, happily, has any nearer acquaintance with prisons, at any rate yet.

Next day we passed through Kromeriz and so on to Brno, stopping again at Slavkov to walk the length of a field, climb a hillock, and look at the iron map model of the battle of Austerlitz. I was back on familiar ground. I think it was after we had left Brno that I fell asleep, as I inevitably did after several hours of the coach in motion, and awoke very abruptly to the sound of solemn music, and the sense of stillness. We were pulled up at the side of the road in a Moravian village, and our driver was sitting with his cap in his hand, for a funeral was passing by.

It was the village band which had awakened me. They were playing as a funeral march a slow waltz, very simple and strongly marked, with all their sonorous brass at full voice; playing it with all their hearts, not more accurately than most small village bands usually play, but with such integrity that it had grandeur. The small cortège was led by an acolyte with a cross, and the robed priest followed him, then came the coffin upon a horse carriage, plumed and covered with flowers, and after it the mourners in deep black, everyone walking. The rolling music carried them past us, and we drove slowly on, but the picture lingered with extraordinary vividness, and for days I had the tune in my mind.

A funeral custom which I had seen both in Bohemia and Moravia, and which interested me very much, was the quite usual convention of treating the burial of a young boy as if it had been his wedding. His friends and contemporaries would follow the coffin in light, gay dress, the girls like bridesmaids, often children in their festival frocks, with baskets of flowers, and bright ribbons in their hair. Sometimes his schoolfellows would wear sports clothes, if he had been interested in athletics. They brought the gracious indication of his brief past, and the bridal promise of which he had been robbed, and though my mind feels that they should have been unbearably poignant, my senses found the effect curiously reassuring.

We had dinner at Jihlava, on the border of Bohemia, and here Honza, who always ordered beer for me as a matter of course, and drank mineral water himself, startled me by ordering two beers.

"What can be the matter with you?" I asked. "Here you've avoided the stuff for ten days, and now suddenly you decide to drink it."

"But of course!" he said. "We are almost in Bohemia again."

The run home from here was only a leisurely business of a few hours, north-westward to Prague by way of Caslav, where Jan Zizka died, and Kolin. Just before reaching this latter town we saw, away on our left upon a hill, the three pinnacles of the loveliest piece of Gothic in the country, the cathedral of St. Barbara at Kutna Hora, another of the things which exceeds the guide-book. Those three pointed roofs, a gesture of exasperation to finish quickly a jewel of whose fitting completion men despaired, please and satisfy me by their strangeness, and I would not change them for the most elaborate spires ever devised to crown a church. I do not know what is the correct or even the orthodox view of them from the architectural standpoint, but for my part I hope no one ever tries to improve on them, for I am sure it cannot be done.

By tea-time we were in Prague, and disembarking at the Powder Tower with many farewells, to disperse to our several suburbs and sleep off Slovakia.

18

A Hajovna at Lany

My brother was to arrive by air on Sunday, and I went to Dobris for two quiet days, returning on Friday night. The Burians were just going away for their summer holiday, and we should have the flat to ourselves for the time left to us, which had dwindled now to the length of his fortnight's stay, for we proposed to travel back together. We proposed, but the Czech archery team, which had booked almost all the seats in the plane by which he was to return, disposed, and in the event I had to book my place in a later plane. My stay had been too long for a return ticket to cover it.

On Saturday Honza's parents took out the lorry and made a trip to a dairy near Lany, and afterwards on to a forester's cottage on the presidential estates there, where lived an elderly couple, relatives of the family. I was invited to accompany them, and we took with us also two more friends, a gardener and his son, who would help to load the lorry, for we intended to bring back a load of leaf mould and manure which Mr. Vesely wanted for the planting of the trees in the new garden. They rode behind, and we three in the cab. Honza was out on his own ploys, and probably in the water somewhere, for not even the injury to his eardrum, which I gather can dangerously upset one's equilibrium in swimming, could keep him ashore.

Where the direct road to Lany turns off from the main

road to the spas of the north-west there is a very perilous corner, strictly controlled because of its bad record of accidents; and here we went right instead of left to reach the dairy, which was a national enterprise, not very large but a flourishing concern, standing beside the pond in a quiet village. The director had expanded the business by adding a poultry farm with many incubators, almost all its equipment being home-made. Some of the employees lived in flats over one end of the dairy buildings, and there was a large garden with plentiful raspberry canes, just then at the end of their harvest. While Mr. Vesely and his friends went to talk business with the director, Mrs. Vesela and I were invited to help ourselves from the canes, since the raspberries which remained were at their ripest, and would soon be dropping; we needed no second bidding.

There was a hitch, however, for the director was not there. He was attending, we were told, a wedding in the village, and though he had certainly intended to come away from the festivities in time for this appointment, he had not yet shown up. We waited a while, and went through the incubators in the meantime, where tiers of fluffy heads picked busily through their wires after grain and water from the glass troughs, far too preoccupied to trouble about us. We stroked and scratched them, and they went on feeding and took no notice of our courtesies. We liked best the ones with dark brown heads and backs against the bright primrose yellow of their breasts and faces. "Chocolate-coated," said Mrs. Vesela. But when we had seen everything, and gone back gratefully to the fresh air after this stifling warmth, still the director had not come.

"We'll go and find him," said Mrs. Vesela, and we set off into the village in search of the house where the wedding was being celebrated. Near the church, they told us, and the car was sure to be standing outside, so we should know it by the ribbons and myrtle. We found it easily enough, and asked if the director was there. He was, and came to greet us with many apologies; he had not forgotten the appointment, but merely let time slip by too fast, reluctant to leave the party. He asked us to wait only a minute for him, and he would come; in the meantime, would we not sit in the car, and he would drive us back. We would, and with pleasure, among the ribbons and flowers and hair-fine fronds of fern fallen from the bridal bouquets; and presently came not only the director himself, but a smiling young girl with a plateful of small sweet cakes from the feast, of which we were urged to take two or three each, and eat them as we went. We returned our felicitations to the young couple, and were driven away in state, with small sprigs of myrtle in our lapels, tied with little bows of white ribbon, the badges of the wedding guests.

Buying ducklings did not take long after that. We were fed with more raspberries, and took away with us a large perforated box of fledglings and some other small gifts; and while the men were arranging all this, we two made friends with the tenant of one of the flats, and ended the visit on the landing, in an arduous English conversation with the young manager, a boy still in his twenties. He had studied the English language entirely on his own for a year or so, in the hope of going to America to study dairying methods there for a period; but now he found that he was not welcomed, and there seemed little prospect of the visit taking place in the near future. I think he was pleased to try his accomplishment at last on an English person, and certainly he had reason to be proud of his progress, for though he mispronounced some of the more unexpected and illogical sounds—and no wonder!—he could make himself understood, and follow the speech of other people if they made a few concessions in the way of slow and accurate diction, and his vocabulary was surprisingly large.

I am encouraged to believe that learning from the book can be effective after all.

From here we drove on at length, after many farewells all round, to the main road again, and off to the left, where the little cemetery of Lany lay very quiet and still today, not a soul beside the grave. We went in for a moment to look at it once more, at leisure this time, with no storm of emotion about it to distort or illuminate; just a square green enclosure with the wall behind it, draped with trophies and shaded with trees. A few people were tending the graves of their own kin, just as in any other country cemetery; the air was sunny and warm and still, and very tranquil. This was Lany as one imagines it.

The presidential park here is a whole forest, and the road we took to reach our hajovna was a shady forest ride, where once President Masaryk used to take exercise on that same Hector who shares his portrait in the village school. These are mixed woods, mainly deciduous trees, full of beautiful pathways which run surprisingly up and down like the corridors in a house built on several levels, and our road ran in a long curve encircling the rim, a fringe of trees on one hand and the whole rolling blue woodland on the other. Presently we turned into the depths by a cart-road, and came gradually downhill to the cottage, which stood solid and squat and long in a clearing, single-storeyed, with many encrustations of pig-sty and poultry-house and cattle-shed built on to it at both ends and the back, and three stone steps going up to the front door.

Across the clearing from it was the large garden and orchard, enclosed in a pale fence, and near the gate stood a tall pump for water. How two elderly people could do a forester's work, and look after so many animals and so much ground into the bargain, remains for me a mystery. Obviously they gave the greater part of their time to it, but they had not sunk themselves into it to the exclusion of other interests, for they were very much alive, informed, and able to maintain an intelligent part in conversation on any subject of the day. I borrow Honza's opinion here to reinforce my own, since my conversation with them was naturally a restricted business for other reasons.

Mrs. Slavickova had a very beautiful setter dog, who came to meet us with much noise, and brought her out to the doorway to see who was disturbing him. We found her in unexpected distress, for her husband had been taken ill with what afterwards proved to be meningitis, and removed to hospital at Kladno only a few days previously. Afterwards I heard from Mrs. Vesela that he made a fair recovery, in spite of his age and the serious condition into which he had fallen; but at this time his wife was naturally inclined to fear, and we could not honestly encourage her to hope very much. Meantime, she was alone here, with all the thriving population of animals to look after, and to crown all she had had a cow in calf, and had delivered the infant single-handed. This was the fourth day of its life, and already it was a beautiful, mild-faced, sturdy brown and white thing half as tall as its mother.

The men took the lorry off down the slope to the manure-heap, and fetched forks from the shed, and set to work to load their cargo. Mrs. Vesela turned to in the cottage, and began to make order among the little things Mrs. Slavickova had had no time to tackle; and I was given a free rein to investigate all the intriguing lean-to's and sheds which propped up the house walls, and make the acquaintance of their inhabitants.

I never saw a more various family. At one end of the house was the large cow-shed, where the mother and her baby, with two other cows, shared the main space, and just within the door a small separate stall was partitioned off, which belonged to a large, dignified nanny-goat named

Bek. I have never before enjoyed close acquaintance with a goat, though I have occasionally exchanged civilities with them in passing, as among the allotments in Troja. Bek surprised me in many ways. She answered to her name as courteously as any dog, but with more condescension; you had only to put your head in at the door and call: "Bek!" and she would emerge from her stall with a gravely enquiring expression, and push her lips, which were of silk, into the palm of your hand. She had only a warm, faint smell, was clean tawny and white to look at, plump, straight-backed and sleek, and she had a gentle expression and inquisitive eyes. I liked her, and she appeared to derive satisfaction from the fact, for of course she was well aware of it, as animals always are.

The calf would let itself be caressed, too, though its mother from the straw gave rumbling warnings that she was not inclined to permit too many liberties. One of the other cows was about to calve, it appeared, and I thought at first: "Poor Mrs. Slavickova, however will she manage?" But it was quite obvious in reality that she would manage very well, and though she had certainly to work extremely hard, it was perhaps better than having time on her hands to feel lonely, or worry continually about her husband.

At the other end of the cottage there were poultry-sheds, and at the back of it a little yard with all kinds of pens opening from it, many of them hitched on to the wall of the house itself. In one there were half-grown pigs, and in another a large indignant drake, as big as a turkey, of some black and white species unknown to me, with red wattles round his eyes; he was not exactly handsome in appearance or nature, and had had to be shut up because he attacked the young ducklings, but he could be released now because they were growing big enough to hold their own, and he shuffled about the yard muttering to himself and swearing at every living thing which got in his way.

This space he shared with hens, chickens, ducks, and guinea-fowl, and an occasional turkey. There was a whole wall of rabbit hutches, in which the enormous buck had a flat to himself. The population was varied and wonderful, and apart from casual skirmishes between the setter and the black cat, remarkably peaceful.

Not far from the hajovna was a two-storeyed wooden hut with a veranda all round at the level of the upper floor, the property of the president. Some students were living in it at the moment, and the windows were draped with strings of their drying mushrooms. We went up to the veranda, and on the distant side it looked out over a wonderful blue panorama of rolling woodland, a lovely and peaceful place. Here President Benes and his wife used to like to come, said Mrs. Slavickova, and the setter was a firm admirer of Mrs. Benesova, and enjoyed her friendship from his puppyhood.

Our return journey was by a different route, through a little, winding river valley where a great many holiday chalets had been built; but the deep curves of the banks folded them into surprising privacy, and the little colony was attractive. We drove home very steadily, because we had the gardener and his son perforce still riding behind with the cargo, which was shored up with planks to give them a windward corner. I do not know how the three men had managed to load it and remain so clean. Three days later Honza fetched the remaining load, and signally failed to emerge in such good condition.

My brother was with us by then; we met him at Ruzyne on the Sunday afternoon, installed him at the flat, and spent the whole evening blissfully wandering over Hradcany and the Little Town, reviving his memories of last year. Glorious hot weather had settled in again, and the prospect of another evening trip to Lany pleased us very much. On Monday we had walked over Troja Island, crossing by the chain ferry, and had inspected the dry, raw garden into which the trees were to go. On Tuesday evening we went back to fetch the remainder of the mould and manure which was to help bed the trees into this baked ground.

This time Honza drove, and had my brother and myself with him in the cab, and Mr. Sipek up behind as lieutenant. Mr. Sipek was a grey-haired, rubicund, beery neighbour who occasionally obliged with odd jobs in his spare time. He had a nose like the Good Soldier Schweik, and a blue peaked cap of naval cut, and looked as if he belonged to the merchant service. He sat negligently on the side of the lorry throughout the drive, and several times Honza nearly spilled him overboard at sharp corners, so that we were continually looking back to see if he was still there, and he was continually shaking his finger wrathfully at Honza through the rear window. However, we all arrived intact, and drove in through the lofty old trees to the house, to be met by the setter leaping about us in ecstatic circles of glee, and the turkey-cock erecting his tail with a rustle and creak like the opening of an enormous fan.

Mrs. Slavickova was busy in the garden, and when we had greeted her, Honza and Mr. Sipek lost no time in coasting down to the compost-heap and going to work with their forks, leaving us to amuse ourselves, for I, having been here already, could act as guide without worrying anyone else. Another calf had arrived two days previously, the duplicate of the first one. We went to the cow-shed to admire them, and found Bek disconsolately wandering loose, since the two infants were in temporary possession of her stall. She looked very aggrieved about it, and welcomed sympathy, all the more, perhaps, because she was jealous of the notice the calves were getting.

When we had seen all the animals, and thrown sticks for the setter until he tired of the game and went off after his friendly foe the cat, we elected to try and find some mushrooms for Mrs. Vesela. I knew two kinds past mistake, the cottage-loaf "houby" and the broad brown ones with spores like golden sponge; the former, we were told, grew in the direction of Dr. Benes' hut, and the latter nearer the road. We went first to the hut, and promptly began to find there the wrong kind. Not one "houba" did we see the whole evening, but the sponge mushrooms came to hand readily, both here and in the levels along the road, where they were supposed to grow; so we concentrated on these, and managed to collect a respectable quantity by the time the lorry was loaded. We borrowed a knife and a large paper bag from the cottage for the job, and kept within earshot of the engine, in case they should be waiting for us. But the first time we heard it, and turned back to investigate, it turned out that Honza had got himself well bogged in a hole, and was bullying the engine furiously in order to induce it to lift him out again. It took planks to effect a rescue, but he did it at length.

It seemed to us that in Czechoslovakia there was no such gulf between the townsman and the countryman as can often be found in England. You could take any apparently typical young Praguer, like Honza or Jaroslav, and find that he had firm roots somewhere in the soil and a very close knowledge of country matters. The link not only exists, but is close and strong. We discovered during the war how completely ignorant many town-born English people could be of the most elementary facts of country life. Jaroslav and his family would go off during the summer holidays to help with the harvest on his brother's farm in Sumava. Honza, when he talked about his childhood, often trotted out incidental anecdotes about the hop-fields, and his uncle's draught oxen. Shop-gazing in the streets of Prague, or forking manure and casually shepherding animals here, he fitted into the picture equally securely.

They finished the job at last, and went and washed under the pump; and Honza, thirsty after so much hard work, fetched a tumbler from the house and drank quantities of cold water. Mr. Sipek watched with deep interest, and finally asked for some himself, whereupon Honza rinsed the glass and filled it for him. He drank it reflectively and remarked what a funny taste it had.

It was nearly dusk when we embarked again, laden with the bag of mushrooms, and some parcels to deliver to Mrs. Slavickova's daughter on the way back. Mr. Sipek had made himself a cosy front corner behind us, and appeared to be quite happy. Before we could go home we had to unload again at Troja, sweep out the lorry, and put it to bed; Honza offered to drop us at home on the way into town, but it was a lovely night, and we felt no urge to go early to sleep, so declined to be dropped, and saw the commission completed.

Mrs. Slavickova's daughter was married and had a lovely baby girl, and they lived at an inn in a village several miles away from Lany. The house had a shop-window, and presented no immediate appearance of an inn, except a lit bar and cheerful voices which rather invited investigation. Honza pulled up there, grabbed his parcels, and besought us to wait for him; he would be only a moment. And so indeed he was, though my brother remarked when he returned that there would just have been time for Mr. Sipek to fit in a quick one if he had seized the opportunity promptly enough.

"That's why I was anxious to be so quick," admitted Honza, grinning, "because he does not know it is an inn, and if he had had time to realise it we should have lost him, and I don't know when we should have got home."

By the time we were in sight of Hvezda it was growing dark, and the street lights began to come out wonderfully along the broad road into Prague. We drove to Troja by the Barricades Bridge, which was built up again as in May 1945 with transport, barrels, carts and paving stones, for the nationalised film industry was busy making a film about the Prague rising. The night was starry, warm, and beautiful, though odorous where we passed. We bumped along the half-made road to the house with what was, for Honza, unwonted care, a concession to our passenger behind, and they forked out the load into the soil-heap excavated from the levelling of the garden, and swept out the lorry meticulously with a twig broom before we took it gently back to Holesovice and put it to bed, somewhat after midnight.

After which, I suspect, Honza spent a busy half-hour at least removing the traces from his own person, for when we met again next day he sounded really awed by the memory of his own state.

"But I was so dirty!" he said; and upon our refusing to be impressed by this simple result of so dirty a task: "But *all over!*"

19

GOLDEN PRAGUE

To show Prague to someone else is to rediscover it for oneself. With only fourteen days left to cover as much as possible of the city and the country, and the most dazzling weather of the summer favouring us, we were seldom indoors now, but always out wandering over Letna, through the Old Town, in and out of the small secret squares of the Little Town, along the lofty bricked fortress walls of Vysehrad. Between longer trips we sunned ourselves on the embankments of the Vltava, and searched out all the churches we had not already seen, and followed up all the paths of Stromovka; and between churches and galleries, which naturally everyone goes to see, we ran round with Honza and the lorry, delivering goods and despatching them in back alleys and goods yards which I take it very few visitors see.

In one morning we covered almost the whole of Prague in half a dozen calls, racing madly against the time in which Mr. Vesely had provocatively stated he could do the round. Our last call was on Pankrac, within sight of the walls of Prague's prison, where so many political prisoners died during the occupation. We had two shops to find in the same long street, and while Honza delivered at the first we went nosing ahead to find the second, only to discover that it had a notice in the window, to the effect that it was closed down while the proprietor and his staff went on a brigade. One frequently saw this in shops at this period, for the harvest was beginning, and everyone was expected to put in a week or so of such duty, sooner or later. However, Honza prospected round the rear premises, and found someone who was commissioned to receive deliveries, so we returned in triumph with all our errands done. My part consisted mainly of hoisting the tailboard of the lorry and fastening it after the cases had been lifted down, a self-imposed task in the course of which I contrived to pinch my fingers a couple of times. We did not, even with this invaluable help, break any records over the round.

"And I would like," said Honza, injured, "to see my father do it in two and a half hours!"

Worse, when it came to checking the bills with the money, we found we were ten crowns short, and Mr. Vesely had to be the person to run them to earth. We were not remarkable successes as delivery men, but we liked the job, because it took us into such unexpected places, the working places of the city as opposed to the picture-postcard corners.

On certain days Mrs. Vesela had an elderly woman in to help her in the flat, and then there was great scrubbing and polishing and piling up of furniture, and Mr. Vesely hurriedly took refuge below in the shop or the office, and Honza fled into town on any pretext which offered, and carried us with him. On one occasion, when we were coming home rather early in the afternoon after some expedition, he suddenly threw up his hand in despair, and exclaimed: "It's Friday!" This was early in my stay, and I asked innocently: "What about it?" He gave me a look of awful significance, and said darkly: "You don't know yet what does it mean—Friday and Mrs. Capkova!"

It was not always Friday, though, and there had been an intensive session on this delivery morning of ours, with the result that at dinner we found the flat mirror-bright, and the electric clock, a small cream-coloured, glassless disc on the wall, wildly out in its statement of the time. The family argued about it in Czech, and "Jezis Marie!" swore Mrs. Vesela, being teased visibly but not yet intelligibly by her menfolk.

"My mother has washed the clock's face," explained Honza, laughing, "and now it loses hours. And look, she has made the figure five crooked."

She had indeed, it leaned drunkenly backwards. He went to straighten it, and it promptly fell off the face altogether, and was lost among the cushions of the couch underneath. In a minor panic of giggles, and pursued by abuse and threatened violence from his mother, he hunted for it in vain for a few minutes, tipping off cushions right and left, and having recaptured it, stuck it back into position on the dial, where certainly to my surprise, and I think to his also, it remained. The clock recovered from its attack of indigestion in due course, and kept time dutifully as before; but while its indisposition lasted Mrs. Vesela was not allowed to forget her responsibility.

The Sokol Slet had faded into Prague's memory now, and the chief topic of current interest was the fourteenth Olympiad in London, which everyone was discussing and reading up eagerly. Great hopes were set on the Czechoslovak teams and athletes competing; justifiably, as the event proved. This day everyone was thinking and talking about Zatopek's chances in the ten thousand metres, which was to be run in the afternoon; it was not regarded as so perfectly his distance as the five thousand, but the general opinion was that he meant to make an all-out bid for it, and it was taken for granted that his heart was big enough for any effort.

We went this evening to see Jean Cocteau's film of *Beauty and the Beast*, and arrived back in our own street in Holesovice just as the radio in the inn across the way was broadcasting the latest Olympic results. Honza lingered in the doorway to listen, and came skipping away radiant, to report that Zatopek had won the ten thousand in a new Olympic record, breaking the old one by over eleven seconds. On which happy note we went contentedly to bed, as pleased as if we, too, had had proprietary rights in the victory.

On Saturday afternoon my brother and I went boating on the Vltava with Jaroslav, and afterwards walked over Manes Bridge in the cooling evening to St. Thomas' brewery, where is one of the beer-garden restaurants, complete with trees and miniature orchestra, for which in England we have no parallel. We had supper here, and sat the evening out at leisure over home-brewed black beer, watching the people of the Little Town come out for their Saturday fling. U Fleku, in the New Town, is more picturesquely Gothic, and also dirtier, and has been brewing a similar black beer since the Middle Ages; but St. Thomas' garden, while enclosed in a high wall, is less shut in by buildings, and feeds you well for a modest sum, and on this occasion offered us in the way of music everything from "Sedlak, Sedlak," to "Finnegan's Rainbow", played by four instrumentalists who contrived by whole-hearted gusto to sound like considerably more. English weather, perhaps, could hardly be relied upon to co-operate, or we might do worse than try the effect of such beer-restaurants on our own social life.

By this time I could act as guide through most of Prague without any trouble, even including some obscure short cuts not invariably known to the foreigner. We would set out sometimes without Honza, not knowing where we were going, not greatly caring, since the whole of the town was at our disposal. Over Letna, down the "Mouse-hole" into the Little Town, and then, changing our minds because the profile of Hradcany from this view was so lovely, uphill again by the Old Castle Steps, which bring you into the enclosed world of the castle quarter by a back door. You emerge in a small open space on the bastion, with a round watch-platform built out to look over the city, and before you an archway swallowing up the narrow cobbled street, and usually a very bored soldier on guard there.

Once through this gate you are within the confines of the castle, a small town of its own, with houses, churches, shops and taverns, including Mr. Broucek's "Vikarka". The royal residence, in fact, is mixed up with all kinds of modest dwellings, and the President's apartments are on a high-road which can never be closed, as if the courtyards of Buckingham Palace were an immemorial right of way. Here again in miniature is Prague's genius for assimilation, where Romanesque St. George's, the many periods of the castle itself, the jubilant Gothic of St. Vitus, the new formal rampart gardens of President Masaryk's Yugoslav architect, and the cramped sixteenth-century cottages of Golden Lane, all assemble into a tranquil unity, as if they had been thought out all at one time to create precisely this effect.

The narrow, steep little street climbs towards the court-yards, passing on the right the gateway which leads to the Black Tower, and beyond to the squat round outer tower of the Daliborka, which overhangs the Stag's Ditch on the outer side of the walls. Dalibor is supposed to have been the first prisoner confined here in the unpleasant dungeons below ground. Smetana makes him a hero who struck a blow against tyranny in the early days of Czech history, by killing the Burgrave who had murdered his harmless musician friend as a disturber of the peace. Music can be a dangerously subversive influence, so perhaps I do wrong in calling the violinist harmless. Going down into the dark inward of this crouching tower, partially rebuilt since the eighteenth century, and therefore in its heyday even more displeasing than it appears now, one's imagination fails at the Milada part of the story. Nothing gentle and charitable could survive entry here into so bleak, dusty and adamant a captivity.

Just beyond the gate to the towers, steps move upward from the street, and bring you round a blind corner into Golden Lane, where Rudolf II used to house his goldsmiths in the sixteenth century, all in a row in the most minute houses possible. These are the only living-rooms I know where there is literally not room to swing a cat, where you can stretch out your arms and touch all four walls from the centre, and no furniture can be used but a bench or so affixed to the wall for table or chair, and cupboards flattened into the woodwork. There are cellars underneath, entered through trapdoors which you cross in entering the cottage, and which sometimes give suggestively under your feet and make you skip forward in haste. The upstairs rooms I never saw; but how people can live in such exquisite discomfort nowadays, indeed how they could ever do so, and why it should have been considered necessary to make them attempt it, I cannot imagine. Certainly there would be very little scrubbing and cleaning to do, but I can think of no other advantage. Perhaps Rudolf had a perverted sense of humour; being a king, he was in a position to indulge it if he had. Now the inhabitants lean out from their doorways and invite you in, to buy post-cards, look out from rear windows on the wooded moat of the Stag's Ditch, and repay the experience with twenty crowns or so. After business hours one is tempted to believe they shut up shop and go home to relax in some other cottage with more space, but I fear they don't, for there was washing hanging out sometimes in the alley, and little dogs sunned themselves on the doorstones as if they knew no other home.

Beyond again, and you arrive in Parler Square, named after the second architect of the cathedral, with the choir facing you across a cobbled space, lofty lacework of stone soaring above the peaked roofs of its chapels into many flying buttresses. The narrow street running round the cathedral to the right contains the Vikarka tavern; if, instead, you keep to the left, you enter through a still narrower space, between the cathedral and the oldest part of the castle, into the wide flagged courtyard, inmost of the three, with the presidential apartments on your left hand.

We walked on through the three courts, and down the castle ramp, under the enormous bulk of the Schwarzenberg Palace, into Neruda Street and the warm, intimate corners of the Little Town, the quiet, retired places like Grand Prior's Square, and the green length of the garden end of Kampa, where in the cool of evening many young couples, many sedate families, had come out to walk under the trees. The sun had left the willows along the waterside, and the Devil's River with all its mill-wheels was a richly coloured gloom under the tiers of little balconies. But like other kind, green, watery places, Kampa on a summer evening was plagued with gnats, which bit like devils. We left the waterside early, and walked over the Legions' Bridge to the National Theatre, where we paused to reflect how near we were to U Fleku, and accordingly wandered there to sit in the garden over the usual black beer, with the jumble of decorated Gothic walls in their hoods of low, ridge-tiled roof leaning inward at us, and the first lights coming out among the trees.

There was always much teasing when my explorations of the various beers of Prague leaked out at home, and it was a convention by now that I was the drunkard of the Vesely household. On one occasion I had a learned conversation with Mr. Vesely and Uncle Jan, an acknowledged expert, on the subject; it was soon after my return from Zlin, and I had happened to mention Jarosov. They looked sadly at each other, shook their heads, and pronounced: "It isn't beer!"

"But Pilsener is?" I suggested, sticking to certainties.

They acknowledged weightily that it was. I mentioned several others, but each was met by their thoughtful exchange of glances, and the damning judgment: "It isn't beer!"

"What about Budejovice?" I asked.

Their eyes, meeting solemnly again, brightened. They nodded decidedly: "That's beer!"

This would appear to be the novice's complete guide to Czech brewing, for I could find no other of which they expressed wholehearted approval.

One of our last visits in Prague was one of the loveliest. Often I had walked through the courtyard of the Premonstratensian monastery at Strahov, under the westward end of the Hunger Wall; another of those islands of quietness, half tree-shade and half sunlight, which abound everywhere in the city, only just aside from the main streets. Beautiful gates and fences of wrought iron are here, and within them gracious spaces of grass between dark-cream walls, and warm red roofs, and little bulbous spires. You go to Loreto, small and demure under the monstrous shadow of the Cernin Palace, to hear chimes like dropping honey, and see a king's ransom—or a pope's, perhaps—in monstrances, patens, vestments and jewels, gold, diamonds, incredible pearls, smith's work to take your breath away. But you go to Strahov to see books.

I had been in the libraries of the Clementinum with Helena, and duly admired not only the hall full of astronomical clocks, so precious that no one dares to try to find out if they still work, but also the biggest stove in Prague, almost ceiling-high in the vast lofty reading-room which was once the refectory; now we went with Honza to see the equally famous libraries of Strahov, so old that a fire

here in the thirteenth century destroyed what was already
a renowned collection.

They say there are a hundred and twenty thousand books
here; but they break you in gently by way of an intro-
ductory hall full of cases of curios as well as books, where
there is a strange treasure in the shape of a collection of
wooden books, or boxes in the shape of books, illustrating
the lives of trees. Each is made from the wood of its own
tree, and opens to show you its own history, leaf and
flower and fruit and seed, segments of growth, the bark,
all that can be put together into two small compartments
to show the beauty and complexity of nature, and the
loving patience of man in the days when he had leisure
to do things well, and had not yet been swept away into
the passionate necessity to get them done, or even half-
done, at the crazy tempo of the race between life and
death. Indeed, everything in Strahov bears witness to that
time, when a man could expend his whole life and wear
out his eyes on one illuminated missal of inconceivable
delicacy and perfection, and think his wealth well spent.
Chinese slave-girls used to go blind in a few years of work
upon the incredibly fine embroideries they produced for
their masters; I wonder how many monks lost their sight
over these minute scripts and hair-fine drawings now
reposing under glass in the theological hall.

They show you here bibles innumerable, some in as
many as twelve different languages, from the Middle Ages
and earlier, beautiful manuscript music of the thirteenth
and fourteenth centuries, missals large as table-tops, with
illuminated capitals of gold, and colours as fresh as if they
had been laid in yesterday; early printed books, including
one of the first printed Cæsars, fragments of Wycliff's
tracts, maps of the world, and of parts of the world which
passed for the whole in the uncomplicated days when
Europe was blissfully ignorant of a second hemisphere.

I*

They show you, too, the evidences of an intolerance and censorship of opinion which perpetually cries out now on other censorships and other partialities; at either end of the theological hall, high out of reach in locked cages, are the church prisoners, the books proscribed by the Index, the thoughts which may not be thought. The church loves enlightenment, and the search for knowledge is the way to God; but the locks have not come off the doors yet.

They will tell you that this hall is the most beautiful baroque room in Prague; I can hardly claim to have seen them all, but I cannot imagine a lovelier. It has not the black marble corkscrew pillars which support the gallery in the Clementinum's main hall, nor the fierce complications of that ceiling; and for me it gains in wanting them. It has no gallery; its ceiling is a shallow arch, divided into regular ovals and shields by frames of heavily encrusted plastering, and full of painted scenes and figures as agitated as most paintings of the period; yet the result is a singleness and a calm which baroque does not often achieve. The walls are all books and windows, and globes and lecterns, bearing the most massive old musical volumes, stand along the centre of the room. There is nothing more, and nothing more is needed.

The philosophical hall is beautiful, too; its ceiling one great painting, its walls, from the floor to the feet of the painted philosophers above, all books, warm brown wood, and gilding. It is double the height of the theological hall, and has a gallery running all round it. Here is a wonderful desk which really makes provision for keeping several authorities at once in consultation; a narrow table for the writer to work on, at either end a wheel, and fixed between these several bookshelves, swung to adjust themselves to the movement when the wheels are revolved. You can draw down to the level of your table the shelf on which is opened the first book you want to consult, and when you have done with it, a mere flick of your fingers spins the shelves round to bring to hand the next one. Six or seven philosophers at once you may keep at your beck and call without rising from your chair; now we need only an infallible apparatus for remembering beforehand exactly what authorities we are going to want, and it may then be worth putting this ingenious arrangement into less exclusive production.

Last of all we came, of course, to the visitors' book, and the unexpected company of Horatio, Lord Nelson of the Nile, Duke of Bronte, who came here in 1800 with Sir William and Lady Hamilton. His signature is large, firm and clear, as uncompromising as his nature. The book falls open naturally at his page, from which I conclude that it is really the treasure of the collection, and not shown merely to his fellow-countrymen. Even a Communist state, in a frantic hurry with social schemes and welfare arrangements, need not change this attitude of pride in him; for our greatest sailor was also the greatest reformer of sea-going conditions in the history of the fleet, and the most persistent and pugnacious friend of the lower deck who ever walked the quarter-deck.

It was two years after the Nile when he came here, a man broken in health and spirits, sickened with an inactive life of inglorious squabbles and small diplomacy, having seen the desired command of the Mediterranean given to Keith over his head and worn out his half-blind and left-handed body in the tedium of blockading Malta. The Hamiltons had been recalled from the court of Naples, and Nelson in sickness and despair had asked leave to go home; they travelled together across Europe by way of Trieste and Vienna, and so came here.

Spite and adoration in equal measure had followed this "little man, without any dignity" across Austria, as they followed him all the way to Yarmouth Roads, where he landed in November. The spite came from the Mrs. Elliotts and Mrs. St. Georges of court and diplomatic circles; the adoration from the people, wherever he passed by. I like to think that Prague understood Nelson as it had understood Mozart, and satisfied his tired and nauseated spirit with its beauty and gracious friendliness after the usual share of envy, hatred and malice which the great inherit. The absurdity and the splendour of his love were alike at their height; magnificently and ridiculously oblivious of husbands, wives, and the world's titterings, he and his Emma made their triumphal progress across Europe with eyes only for each other, reputations, careers, countries, mere wrack in the sea of their passion. They passed through here, and signed their names; the old man, too, whose complacent part in the triangle has never been satisfactorily explored in all the millions of words written about them. And they left a breath of strangeness and speculation behind them, provocative in this setting. Nelson was not a bookish man; why did he come to Strahov? Was it the dilettante Sir William who wanted to see the famous library? Or had Emma made enquiry of what the cultivated lady ought to visit while in Prague?

From Strahov, as from any other high place in this city of hills, the towers of Prague assemble into a picture which cannot easily be forgotten. See it in the sunlight, and you can understand the name "Golden Prague". The air is bright, pale, glossy as corn-fields, the green copper cupolas, the Indian red bulbous spires, the rosy ridge-tiles and dark cream walls, all film their colours over with a glimmering of gold, and the river is a changing thread of blue and silver stringing together bridges like pearls. It is impossible to write about Prague without growing lyrical; the impressionist paintings of Antonin Slavicek in the modern gallery have the quality of spontaneous song, and even the cold-hearted camera, turned upon this sonnet in stone, seems to show signs of imagination, and to do more, much more, than reproduce.

Prague is an accidental work of art. From the rotundas of the tenth century to the modern villas of Baba, it has been built up in as minute detail as a reef of coral, every generation adding and adapting in absorbed accordance with its own needs; and yet there grows out of the heart of Europe and their unconscious dust a great bright rose of a city, as single as if God and no other had used all those centuries to bring it to bloom.

20

Up the Vltava

On Sunday we went all three to Stara Boleslav, to see the Smolik family.

Jitka had said she would meet the bus, but our arrival was a few minutes ahead of schedule, and we encountered her half-way along the road, hair flying, head down, biking madly towards her appointment. She greeted us warmly, and led us back to a house already full of people. Ana and Antonie were missing, it is true, being away just then at their school camp somewhere in the mountains; but to supply their place there was Jitka's brother and his wife and infant daughter, and another baby into the bargain, borrowed from some other relative, besides two present friends, a doctor and his wife, and one absent one who would be back after lunch. We made quite a large circle, and commandeered all the chairs and hassocks available as we sat and talked out the first volubility of meeting over plums and biscuits.

Venousek presently appeared, attired in a pair of dungaree trousers braced over his small shoulders, with the legs turned up two or three times over his sandals because they were a trifle long for him, and even without complications of that kind his gait was erratic. He let himself in, a feat for which he was just tall enough, and shot across the room to the dish of biscuits without pause to locate it. It dawned upon him that he had a large family to feed, and he began to distribute the biscuits in his usual impartial manner, all

258

round the circle. It took him a long time, but no one could accuse Venousek of lack of perseverance; and having completed the round, he assumed it was time to start at the beginning again. Plums or biscuits, he was not particular, and neither, he felt, should we be; but as some of the plums were ripe, and his grasp as determined as his nature, biscuits proved more popular. Betweenwhiles he would begin work on one or the other for himself, but was as likely as not to hand his half-demolished biscuit to the nearest person in an ecstasy of generosity; then one accepted them in the spirit in which they were offered, and gravely ate them.

"How is it," I asked, "that Venousek can walk this time? When I was last here he knew only how to run."

"Ah, we have found out how to slow him down," said Jitka, and smilingly produced the means, a small-boy-size polished walking-stick, with a head like a mountaineer's axe, and carved designs on it, such as you see for sale in many holiday centres. Obviously when one has such a stick, one must walk at a pace to fit in with its use.

Venousek found company stimulating, and since he still talked very little, expressed the fact by continuous motion. His rolled-up dungaree legs began to come down and trip him, and Honza pursued him across the floor to roll them up again, but it was like trying to hold an eel; every time the infant revolved out of his hands, turned rapidly about, and fell over in any direction which happened to offer a clear way. This floorward manœuvre he executed as blithely as if he had no bones, and recovered the upright position with the same aplomb; and all the while his light, bright eyes observed us steadily, and his face was all gravity. Venousek's silence rendered him inscrutable; I am not sure that that is not the reason why he was in no hurry to learn to talk.

The doctor and his wife were staying at the hotel at

Houstka, the little spa which lies among the woods only
five minutes drive from the square. Presently we drove
round with Petr to have a look at the place while Jitka
prepared dinner. At Houstka you can dine, drink, play
tennis, ride, bathe, or even drink the spring waters; and
all Stara Boleslav makes occasional use of it as a social
centre. A short drive curves in among many trees from the
lane, passing by a garden restaurant, and brings you to a
sweep of gravel before the terraces of the large white hotel.
We had no sooner stopped the car and got out than Petr
was met by a pleasant young man of Jewish aspect, who
advanced from the doorway and asked if we were delegates
to the conference. We regretted that we were not, and
asked for enlightenment, for until now we had had no idea
that a conference was taking place here. It proved to be a
world conference of Jewish students, and now that we were
on the alert, we could see the evidences of occupation
everywhere. Great numbers of dark young people, in
various stages of undress, were to be encountered among
the gardens; very lively, very quick in exchanges of speech,
very vivacious, many with books and papers tucked under
their arms. Israel was new in those days, and only half
acknowledged; Britain glared resolutely in the opposite
direction for six months more, and continued to assert that she
saw no signal. But here the blue and white flag of the new
state was draped from the first-floor balcony, brave and
new in the sun, with the star of David in the centre. It was
the first time I had seen it flown anywhere, and it had a
clean, hopeful and joyous look, curiously moving.

The doctor had a lecture to deliver somewhere next day,
and emerged from the hotel with a furrowed brow, and
clutching many papers, for he had yet to prepare all his
notes for the occasion. He sat at a little distance from us,
in the grass beside the tennis-courts, and went to work,
while we watched the play and discussed what we should

do with the rest of the day and the one week we had left. Petr said he had enough petrol to drive us somewhere, and could take one day off, at any rate, and we debated what would be best to do with it. The main omissions seemed to be the whole area of south Bohemia, with the Hussite town of Tabor, the border forests and hills of Sumava, and one place which for very different reasons from beauty or historical fame we none the less wished fervently to see, the Little Fortress and town of Terezin, in the north-west, the most infamous ghetto and political concentration camp in CSR during the occupation. To choose was difficult, but to offer Sumava one day seemed an insult, and besides, one ought to go to Terezin. We voted for this painful visit after much hesitation, and Petr promised to come and collect us on Tuesday morning early. When we went back to dinner, and told Jitka what had been arranged, she agreed upon condition that some day she should show us Sumava at more leisure.

The Smolik household lived up to its reputation brilliantly. We sat down seven to dinner, the truant friend arrived half-way through, and three more people appeared by the time we had reached coffee. We expanded our circle and the conversation accordingly, ranging over the whole field of Czechoslovak industry, nationalised and private, and from that to industrial conditions in general, from the industrial revolution to the present day. By mid-afternoon, when we had adjourned to the roof-terrace and deck-chairs in the sun, we had progressed to politics and religion, and only the determination of half the party to go bathing in the Labe finally broke the thread. We went instead to show my brother over the cathedrals, arranging to meet for supper at Houstka; for he was still armed with the kind of ration card they issue on entry into the country, where one ticket can be used to cover a complete meal. Three dinners and three suppers—they are of the same value and therefore interchangeable—meant that six of us could eat out, and no providing to do.

We made the usual round of St. Vaclav's cathedral, and dawdled along to Houstka already very late, to find everyone else assembled.

"The cooking here is very good," said Petr, "but one is expected to come here for religious reasons, and therefore not to be in any hurry."

"Nor to have any appetite," said Jitka.

He agreed. "Visitors to shrines are supposed to have minds above food, and therefore the helpings are inclined to be very small. Really we should take the precaution of writing labels for our backs before we come: "I am *not* a pilgrim!" "

We ate an excellent supper with one eye on the time, for the last bus was due out in a distressingly short time; and our farewells were made ungracefully with less than five minutes to spare.

"Never mind," said Petr, "if we are too late to catch it at the square we can chase it into Brandys."

Petr's little car had recently been in dock, and was none too sure of itself now, but it raised a terrifying turn of speed along the lane and into the street. The square was empty, and we drove on without pause over the Labe bridge and up through the hair-raising narrow blind turn into the streets of Brandys, under the walls of the castle. We caught the bus exactly as Petr had prophesied, tumbling out in the square of Brandys to join the end of a long queue, and wedge ourselves into the last few inches of space; but the great thing was to be aboard at all. We pulled away and left Petr waving and grinning in the middle of the square.

This was the beginning of our last week, and naturally we were anxious to contact as many of our friends as possible. We spent Monday morning with Dr. Novák, who was in Prague only for the week-end; just time for a walk in

Stromovka and some coffee, and then we accompanied him into town, and parted from him on Wenceslas Square.

Mr. Vesely was in Troja that evening, and the rest of us ended our day, as was quite usual when we were home early, with a leisurely walk over Letna. A young man with a large bag of tools was doing some job below in the shop, and it was quite unintentionally that we forgot all about him, and went off blithely to enjoy the dusk and the lights of Prague, leaving him firmly locked in. We were sitting under a wall baked from the long hours of sunlight, and admiring the last of the roses in the beds before us, when Mrs. Vesela suddenly shrieked: "Jezis Marie!" leaped to her feet, and set off back at a furious pace. We perforce rushed after, demanding explanations, but almost before any came Honza had also remembered, emitted an even louder shriek, and stretched out his seven-leagued stride to leave us all behind.

The worst of it was the thought that Mr. Vesely might be back before us, and find the poor prisoner trying to break out; in which case our incompetence when his back was turned would be fair game for leg-pulling all the rest of the week.

"The poor boy has to go quite a long way out of Prague," explained Mrs. Vesela, conscience-stricken, "and I don't know if there will be a bus now to take him home."

But the disaster was not so great. Mr. Vesely was not yet home when we got there, and the prisoner was released and went off in good humour, and with time left to catch a bus. Relieved of the fear of being found out, we did the natural thing, and told Mr. Vesely, when he arrived, the joke we had been so anxious he should not discover for himself. He said nothing we did could surprise him any longer.

We took care to be ready and waiting in good time on Tuesday morning, and were sitting with folded raincoats ready to hand, and the mesh bag stuffed with bread and butter and chocolate, and three hard-boiled eggs, when the telephone rang. Petr was already late, and immediately we jumped to correct conclusions. Honza came back with a resigned face, and reported:

"He can't come. Auto caput!" The uneasy brakes, it seemed, had given up the struggle. "He will come on Thursday instead, if he can get it put right. But in the meantime, we are all ready, and now we have no plans. So what shall we do?"

There was no lack of things to do, then or ever; it was rather a matter of selection. But the recoil from the plans which had already been made left us at a loss for the moment, and it was Mrs. Vesela who arranged everything. Here was what looked like being another glorious day, hot and cloudless, and for once she was not desperately needed in the shop; we would all four set out and take a boat up the river from Palacky Bridge, where the bright, clean little Vltava steamer services begin, and somewhere we would laze away the hottest of the day in the water. This met with Honza's full approval, since some of the best bathing places in the town itself, those at Podoli, where the river enters still clear and pleasant, were closed at this time owing to an alarm of infantile paralysis, of which the suburb had produced several cases. The more central enclosures he never liked, and marvelled that his mother could occasionally bring herself to bathe at Stvanice. How far should we go by boat? That could be settled when we got to the quay, but we ought to go quickly, to have the whole day. And should we need food, then, after all? Possibly not, but there it was, packed and ready, and we might as well take it. We collected our bathing costumes, stuffed everything into the amazing bag, and set out.

Palacky Bridge is the first bridge as the Vltava enters Prague, except for the iron railway bridge which crosses

it just within view, at Vyšehrad. There was some disagree-
ment between Honza and his mother about the best way
to use our day. She wished to book right to the point where
the boats turned, at Stechovice, about three hours upstream; Honza, on the contrary, thought we should do
better to take tickets for some midway spot, and not spend
so long afloat. We were neutral, seeing virtue in either
solution; and Mrs. Vesela won. We booked all the way to
Stechovice.

Already the steamer was full of people, and most seats
were occupied; however, we found places by the rail,
sharing a seat with a beautiful small boy, about five years
old, dark as a gypsy, and a girl who looked like his sister
of fourteen or fifteen, but proved to be his mother. They
were out for the day, too, and laden with a capacious bag
from which came sandwiches, fruit, and a large thermos
flask of tea, not to mention its lower layers of bathing
costumes, and towels, and further provisions for the return
journey. More people continued to crowd aboard, and
when all the deck seats were occupied, folding stools
appeared in the clear spaces to accommodate the latecomers.
The bright white decks, already warm from the sun, disappeared under a tide of coloured cotton frocks, tanned
bare legs, brilliant headscarves, large sun-hats, dark glasses
and canvas beach-bags of more colours than Joseph's coat.
Before we had even hoisted our gangway the usual traffic
in soft drinks and hot sausages had begun, and from many
of the beach-bags were emerging hefty sandwiches for
distribution among hungry families. Like Napoleon's
army, the Czech family marches on its stomach.

We left at last in a creditable flurry of nautical noises,
ropes and woodwork creaking, sirens blaring, engines
thrumming. Sea or no sea, Vltava sailors have the authentic
rolling gait, and the teak faces, and the cheerful far-
pitched voices proper to seamen everywhere, from the

Mersey to the Volga; the same boots, too, and the same jerseys, and the same knotty dark-brown forearms emerging curved and ready from rolled sleeves. The angle at which the peaked cap is worn may vary a little from country to country, but it would need a mathematical eye to detect it. From the moment that we moved off upstream the little boy, who was bosom friends with Mrs. Vesela by this time, could not keep still, but was always off to observe what the sailors were up to forward, or standing up on the seat to hang overboard, anchored by the nearest arm, or edging round a corner of the rail to where only a chain protected the passage down to the water.

His mother called him back from here, and he made the inevitable innocent reply: "Why?" not at all belligerently, but with the genuine bewilderment of one who had never heard of danger. Honza, who was nearest, kept a large hand somewhere on him whenever he strayed too near to this fascinating place; and he was the most accommodating of children, and bore with the stupidities of grown-up solicitude with perfect politeness and good-nature.

It was holiday time already, and mothers and daughters, girl friends, sweethearts, visitors from abroad, whole hopeful families, had come out tripping for the day in search of coolness, water and country air. An unmistakable American, middle-aged, prosperous and patient of face, immaculate in a silk shirt, light-grey flannels, a cream-coloured Stetson and a Dali tie, sat opposite to us, nursing an elaborate camera, and beaming at everyone who moved about the crowded decks. There were many Americans in Prague still, of whom he was, I think, fairly typical. Their cumulative effect was infinitely more pleasing than that made on me by American troops in Liverpool during the war; but John Brophy said beforehand in "City of Departures" all that I could say on that subject.

We creamed our way augustly up the first stretches of the Vltava, passing under the iron bridge; and beyond it, on the left, rose the high brick ramparts and hanging gardens of Vysehrad, the tall twin spires of the church shot through with glimpses of blue sky, and the foaming green of trees about them; Libuse's Vysehrad, the legendary cradle of Prague, with the Slavin, the cemetery of the great ones, the musicians, the artists, the writers, poised magnificently on the topmost terrace. The great rock on which the fortress was based comes full down into the river at one point, fragments of castellated wall careering down its dark faces; and the road and the tram-lines here dive through a tunnel to continue their journey south. You can stand on a small terrace viewpoint above, and look across at the whole sweep of country beyond the river, where the Prague Skoda works spreads its many buildings in a long, orderly procession towards the cliff of Barrandov; or down sharply below you to where the harbourage of the Prague Yacht Club opens aside from the main stream of the river. Often the various racing eights of the town are training on this stretch of water, and there are many lighters and trains of barges to watch, the whole traffic of a capital city.

Vltava has many long, narrow islands; the main flow runs between two of them here, though the one is not properly an island, being joined to the left bank at its extreme end by a causeway. Beyond here were the closed bathing places of Podoli, and beyond again, on the opposite bank, the cliffs of Barrandov, with the road beneath them squeezed close to the river, and the terraces of the restaurant perched on top; and a little inland and out of sight, the studios of the nationalised film industry of CSR.

Upstream from here the passage becomes increasingly difficult for boating, and to take a canoe up is extremely hard work, to judge by the half-clad young men we saw doggedly towing their empty craft from the bank. The elongated islands continue to divide the stream, and there are some stony shallows, so that the steamers must sometimes slacken speed and pick their way. Once or twice we came to low bridges which would not let our smoke-stack pass, and then two sailors came along, and with a nice judgment and some signalling to and from the man at the wheel, wound it down by a pulley so that it folded in two, and on emerging promptly wound it up again, greatly to the delight of our small boy.

The country opened up around us in rolling riverside meadows and farms and villages, with charming little Vltava ports of white hotels and hopeful shops sitting about the frequent jetties, the sun hot upon their red roofs. Beyond them the gently lifting fields went up to little hills, with an occasional small feathery peak like the cone of Zbraslav, crowned after the imaginative Czech fashion with an infant castle or a spired church. We tacked from side to side of the stream, from pier to pier, and here the calling places were many. Beyond Zbraslav we were in strange country to me, and I was waiting to see the dam at Vrane, and the locks, and the lake above, of which Honza had talked sometimes.

"When you row along it," he said, "it seems endless. I suppose it is not really so great, but even in the steamer you will see how long we take to cross it."

The line of locks rose level and dark before us across the river, we steamed in almost silently between high concrete walls, and from the deep shadows and sudden striking coolness below rose rapidly into sunlight again, looking along the ridges of steel and silver water as the forward gates opened, and we slid out into the lake. The power station sits along the dam like a miniature fortress, looking out over the lower levels, but above it is a great sheet of still, burnished water, with abrupt wooded banks, and no more reminders here of factories, or transport, or electric power and its thousand uses; only the daylight, and the lake, and the hills about it. The slopes grow steeper, the woods on one side withdraw, and there are faces of sheer rock steel-grey among the green, and perched in airy places the week-end huts and villas begin to appear.

The passage of the lake is long, but its width dwindles at last, though the same sudden hills, foaming with trees and broken with rocks, continue to enclose it. There is lovely scenery here, all the way up beyond Davle to where the Sazava flows into the Vltava, entering gracious and large between its own enfolding forests, the dark green of the trees warmed with many red roofs and creamy walls of villas, and the shallows of the confluence gay with bathers. At this point we were nearing the end of the journey, and reflected comfortably that we should arrive at Stechovice just in nice time for dinner.

We came about under the bridge, and drew in to the jetty, and everyone gathered up his children, his wife and his baggage, and prepared to go ashore. The steamers go no higher, for beyond here are St. John's Rapids, and navigation is impossible.

We made straight for the largest and most imposing restaurant, exactly as everyone else was doing; but for some reason it looked less large, less accommodating, than it had done from the boat, and dwindled even further when we saw some of our fellow travellers already coming out of it and making off up the town. However, we went in to make sure, in case they had merely taken fright at finding it full. No luck! There was no more food to offer us, with the best will in the world. We began to have premonitions as we hurried to the next one, and the next, and so on along the river frontage and away by a side-street towards the hills, trying café after café and finding no hope of dinner. As we had been rather late in the procession to leave the boat we were continually meeting some other passengers emerging where we were only arriving, and then their rueful grins broadened at us, and they lifted their shoulders, and off we all went again in the fruitless search for food. We exhausted that part of town, and turned back to continue along the riverside road; and in making one enquiry which the others had by-passed we let them get ahead of us, and lost them. There was the road ahead, empty; they could not well have gone right out of sight, and therefore somewhere they had either found a haven, or given up the struggle and gone down to the river.

"There's one more restaurant," said Honza, "they must be in there."

The particular party which we had been following had already dwindled to about half a dozen, and we ran them to earth in the last remaining café, and for a moment, when they raised an ironical cheer on our entry, cherished a fond illusion that they had actually found someone who was prepared to feed us. Nothing of the kind, it seemed. They had simply given up hope, and since the landlord had offered drinks, at any rate, they had sat down here to eat what remained in the beach-bags, and determined to make a quick bid for sausages or whatever could be bought on the boat going back. At least we should be spared the dangers of bathing on a full stomach.

We had three hard-boiled eggs, a proportionate ration of bread and butter, a slab of chocolate, and some plums, between four people, which in the case of the eggs presented a nice mathematical problem. However, the company was lively enough to make us forget that we were still a little hungry.

Afterwards we joined forces with two of the party, a mother and daughter from Prague, and went across the stretch of turf and pebble to the river banks. Vltava was fairly narrow and fast here, deeply scoring the rock face opposite to us; and on our side there was a stony beach as wide as the water, and then the rolling slope of grass, and no discreet cover at all, though few people minded that. We merely split forces for the few minutes it took us to undress, and Mrs. Vesela and I came back to find Honza already picking his way gingerly through the stones to the water. He was the only swimmer among us, for Mrs. Vesela comforted me very much by being one of the few Czechs I have ever met who never learned the art; but on such a day we both liked to laze about in the water. My brother preferred to lie in the sun, where we joined him after we had played long enough in the stony shallows. It was not an ideal bathing place, and reinforced Honza's argument that we should have done better by booking to some midway spot instead of coming so far; but there was water, and there was sun, and I would not have missed that boat-trip. I am only sorry that we never made the long cruise in the opposite direction, downstream to Melnik; but it took only a third of the time to get there by bus, and time had value, too.

Here at Stechovice, as we saw when we had dressed again and walked back a little of the way towards the jetty, there was a small shipyard for river vessels. We had passed it in our quest for food and paid it no attention, but we were able to stop and stare this time. Some large timber boats were in building, their graceful hollow ribs making complicated patterns against the blonde grass and the grey rock face beyond the water.

On the other side of the valley, beyond the town, the slope of the hills carried what looked like another Hunger Wall, careering down from the plateau which levelled along the skyline. Here, said Honza, there was a water channel to take off the pressure from a large lake which lay there out of our sight, and provided with this fall a ready supply of electric power. He explained the operation of this system with great care, because I had once distinguished myself by marvelling that the water-power station at Brandys made no smoke, a gaffe which I was never thereafter allowed to forget; hence it was necessary, in technical matters, to come down to monosyllables when instructing me.

We had to leave by a boat somewhat after five o'clock, for even downstream the journey was about three hours; and as soon as we were aboard again Honza dived below and bought quantities of hot sausages and rye bread, with disastrous effects to the family's meat rations for the month, since even such etceteras as sausages are on coupons. This perhaps accounts for the fact that they are only very distantly related to what we know as sausages in England, and would not, I feel, desire to claim even that relationship. We ate them in our fingers, peeling off the skin, for these were the fat kind, and drank black beer to wash them down; and it was very noticeable how quiet we grew as soon as we had eaten enough. We had been in fresh air since eight o'clock in the morning, and required only satisfaction within to become exceedingly sleepy. Half-way across the lake, passing by the week-end castles and hermitages once more, I believe I slept a little; by the time we reached the dam and went down into cool gloom in the lock I had revived, and again grew interested in people.

Nearing Prague on this homeward run, we began to pick up fewer trippers like ourselves, and more of a rather different kind of passenger, townspeople who had come out in the warm evening to shake off the heat and dust of a day's work, foreign visitors, business men making use of the steamer service on occasions not wholly of pleasure, boys who had come so far up-river after school to be able to bathe in uncrowded waters. Everyone was a little sleepy and quiet and relaxed from soaking in river and sunlight. Even Prague, seen from the quay at Palacky Bridge when we came finally to rest there, had a drowsy sound at this hour in the evening, though the restaurant quarter would just be thinking of waking up.

We went home contentedly to make tea, eat our supper, and hang out our bathing costumes to dry.

21

Terezin and the Little Volcano

Petr, arriving on Thursday morning to take us to Terezin, brought a car-load of country people whom he had picked up on the way into Prague to the markets. We looked out of the window, and saw him decanting them on the corner. No telephone call this morning; everything was going according to schedule, and we had the net bag again full of provisions, and were ready and waiting.

Our way out of Prague lay north this time, across the river from our suburb by the Barricades Bridge, as if we were going to Troja, but turning right instead of left on the other side. We went gently uphill, along a busy road with trams, until we came to a hair-pin bend which swung left and began to climb more steeply. Here, as we turned with it, Honza suddenly said:

"This is the corner where Heydrich was killed. The men who did it waited for his car here, and fired at him as it came round, and afterwards escaped on bicycles into the town."

So this terrible gesture was made in our own suburb, or on the very doorstep; I had not realised that until then. Unhappily the dedicated people did not escape far. I had already seen the place where they died, murdered or self-murdered when it was clear they could survive only to endanger others—I never found a Czech who was willing to judge by which of these two means they left life. In the crypt of the Russian Orthodox church of Saints Cyril and

Methodius, just off Charles Square, they were run to earth, and for some time defended themselves, as the scarred stone slit of window on the street bears witness; but once found they could do nothing but die at last, and even that could not be done in time to save the priests of this church from dying with them, Bishop Gorazd and every lesser priest of the faith with him. Perhaps no one really knows how many people died for that one infamous life snatched at and captured at the foot of Red Army Avenue. Nor was everyone, I found, prepared to say that the gesture justified itself. Economically it was obviously a loss; imponderably it flamed through the captive country as a promise of the end of tyrants, but the Czechs do not judge emotionally, and their steady resistance was not dependent upon any romantic stimulus, but continued durable, self-sufficient and unvarying, and quite probably was only shocked and hampered by the impact of Heydrich's death and the terrible reprisals which followed it.

They are not, you see, a romantic people. They have not the kind of vision which can make facts invisible; and the facts of this grand gesture, unspeakably heroic though it was, were that Franck was substituted for Heydrich, that Lidice was wiped out, that the Russian clergy were murdered, and many others after them, and that there was such a tightening-up of restrictions and surveillance that the work of the underground became very much more difficult. Something in the imagination nevertheless resists the belief that the act was altogether wasted; it may be true that man must have a torch to see by sometimes, even if some of his own kind must burn to provide the light.

We climbed into Kobylisy, on to the high open country looking away towards the military airfield, and took the Melnik road, but left it fairly soon, where the main motor road to the north-west separates from it. It was an uncertain morning, pleasant and sunny one moment, sulky and moist the next, and we drove through some astonishingly local rains, a few minutes in the centre of a brisk shower, then again rolling along a bone-dry road on which no drop had yet fallen. There were no large towns on our way, we travelled among plateau country of farms and villages, grain and crop country, paling now towards harvest, for August had begun.

It was raining when we arrived at Terezin. Level country still, and a little bare, but with hills in the distance, for we had our faces towards the Ore Mountains; and along the fields before us on the right rose a regular dyke, walls of brick slanting up to a broad turf walk on the crest, and brick surfaces and chimneys breaking out here and there, not unlike some of the buried forts around English shores, from the days when we waited for Napoleon.

"We are here," said Petr.

"But I thought there was a town," I said.

"There is, beyond. But this is the Little Fortress." He drove past the corner of the squat, half-camouflaged wall, and along the side of a great space of graves, which filled the triangle between the road, the front of the fortress, and the avenue of trees which led to the gateway. At the stone cairn which stands where the road and the avenue meet he stopped the car, and we looked through the driving rain across the national cemetery.

The dead lie very close at Terezin; they have to, for there are about twenty-six thousand of them; and they can afford to, for most of them are ashes. The little plots lie down together in neat ranks, straight beaten paths between them, as accurate as a drill by guardsmen. There are some individual monuments, but most have identical little white crosses, to which have been added, where living relatives remained to bring them, the usual little trophies of vases for flowers, and framed photographs of the dead. In the middle of the plot is a tall wooden cross with a crown of thorns, and a white stone cenotaph; and in the middle of one group, but not segregated from the rest, a standard with the star of David, for many Jews are here.

The town of Terezin was a national ghetto during the occupation, into which were packed all the Jews who were suspect or disliked but not yet in political trouble. In a way they were luckier than most prisoners, since appalling though their overcrowded conditions there were, at least they were allowed to live as a community, to some extent managing their own affairs, so that what they could not cure for one another they could at least alleviate by the common kindnesses which most people can produce in such circumstances—to the great hope of man. I believe they did show here a curious and admirable solidarity in their shared hell; for it was a hell, when these advantages over actual concentration camp conditions have all been taken into account. They could not move from the town; they were made to undertake forced labour in the arms factories of the Nazis in the district, in conditions which rendered their lives as expendable as those of any front-line troops; they were subject at any moment to the caprices or necessities of the Germans, so that a visit from the International Red Cross—as far as I know there was only one, and the preparations for it do not bear contemplation—meant the sudden deportation of thousands of them to the gas-chambers of Osviecim; even at "normal" times, with "normal" deaths, the crematorium burned two hundred and fifty bodies a day; they lived packed like animals, and on insufficient food. On the credit side they could, with luck, remain together; they did not spend all their time under the eyes of Germans or even native guards; they were allowed to organise whatever social alleviations and amusements were possible, provided they did every-

K

thing themselves, and had even cinemas, dances, games, of their own making.

That was Terezin town. You will have some idea, then, what the real concentration camps were like when I record that Honza could explain all this to us with grave consideration, and sum it up by saying very seriously:

"Really they had it very easy here. It was not a bad place; they were lucky ones who came here."

But no one says that of the Little Fortress.

Maria Theresa had these strong-points built, and the town is named after her, but I believe the fortress was never in use for the purpose for which it was made. The Nazis used it to contain political prisoners; many of the lucky Jews from the town found their way here for slight cause, and were lucky no longer, even by those standards. Few, I think, ever came out of it alive, for even at the liberation, when the Red Army reached it in their drive west, they found that typhus was there before them. They broadcast immediately for volunteer doctors and nurses to tackle the epidemic, and my friend Dr. Novák answered the appeal, and took charge of the medical group at the fort while the whole process of treatment and evacuation went on. He would probably have gone in any case, but he had his own reason for wishing it. His younger brother was a political prisoner there, and after many weeks without news he jumped at the chance of going to look for him, typhus or no typhus. The younger Novák had been a judge; but he had been dead of typhus for almost a month when the doctor reached Terezin.

When the rain stopped, we went into the fortress.

The outer wall proved very wide, so that the gateway was nearer to being a tunnel. From a guardroom door on the left a police officer put out his head, and invited us to go right through at once into the courts, as a party was at this moment being shown round. The police take care of the showing of this place, and visitors are not asked for money. There are no tickets, no entrance fee; on a table in the gateway is a wooden bowl, into which you may put money if you wish and if you do it will go towards a permanent memorial which is not yet beyond the stage of being planned. But no one makes the horrible mistake of treating Terezin like any other show place. People come in here very quietly, with apprehensive eyes, walking a little more softly than usual; and the police guides have nothing of the professional manner, nor has habit reduced their recital to patter. I do not think it ever will.

Inside the gateway of the Little Fortress the prospect was at first much more pleasing than outside it, for there is a miniature square in the first court, with strips of grass, and trees, and on either side, behind railings and hedges, house-blocks with gardens. But the impression is only momentary, for already you can see ahead of you a gross change to closed courts like stable-yards, whitewashed walls, narrow doors and barred windows. The pleasant private quarters belonged to the Nazi commandant, his family, and the German guards who served under him; you must move on to see Terezin as the prisoners saw it.

We passed by the first side-courts in order to join the party ahead of us, who had walked through the length of the fortress into the fourth court. We entered it by a squat square doorway through another twelve-foot wall of brick and earth, with a small watch-tower from which guards could cover every possible way of escape. The court was rectangular in shape, but built up into a platform at the far end, and shallowly pointed into the brick ramparts, which were high enough and smooth enough to make even the attempt at escape difficult. The long sides were composed of two low whitewashed blocks of cells, with almost flat roofs, and chimneys of a few inches only. In the centre of the court our small party stood grouped about a middle-aged policeman, who was explaining some of the things which had happened here, before he showed them the interiors of the cells. His delivery was patient, grave and factual, without comment.

It was obvious that the place had been cleaned up out of all resemblance to its war-time state; even so it was dingy, chill and unspeakably dispiriting, and some of the stains were coming through the fresh whitewash. The cells, when we entered, smelled viciously of chloride of lime. The rest one imagined. On the right, single cells, windowless, with a crude wooden sleeping-bench, and a bucket latrine in one corner; the size you would expect a single cell to be, in a place not designed for comfort of any kind, but in this space were confined more frequently between twenty and thirty people.

"But how?" we asked incredulously. "How could they possibly get in?"

"They must have stood, all the time; there is no other possibility."

On the left, a row of communal cells, each with a small barred window on either side of the door; these were meant for about forty people, and held, regularly, between two and three hundred.

On the platform at the end of the court two more mass cells opened, and where the rampart walls met at an obtuse angle the bricks were spattered with holes chipped out by bullets, for here four people were shot as a warning against attempts at escape. Two who actually did get away, and were recaptured and brought back, were saved for a worse death. The policeman showed us the place where they were stoned to death, desultorily over a period of three days. Here, too, in these end cells, at the last gasp of the liberation, the most resolute and embittered prisoners made a gallows with the intention of hanging the commandant in this very spot where he had caused others to die. But the authorities, Russian or Czech or both, insisted on the processes of law, and delivered him safely to a later hanging after a full and fair trial.

One thing here was not ugly. In the concrete platform was a little grave-shaped patch of soil and flowers; one of the nurses who answered the appeal for volunteers to fight typhus took the disease herself, and remained in Terezin, where she at least had come of her own free and compassionate will.

From this court we turned back, leaving it by the same way, and went aside into a smaller yard, where in less squalor and more privacy, but still in quarters one would sanction rather for cattle or horses than for humankind, were kept the more important prisoners; for the curious fact is that, though being a cousin of the Czech President could not save you from death, it could ensure you privileges for so long as it was convenient to keep you alive. Even among the prisoners there was class distinction, though none of their making. At least one relative of President Benes was confined here. Beyond again, drawing nearer to the entrance gate, is the yard which held the guard offices, the barbers' and tailors' quarters, the reception office, and an office for the commandant, so that he might lose no time in inspecting newcomers; his personal record was bad in every way, and it seems to be a simple fact that to use his hands upon men who could not retaliate or defend themselves gave him pleasure.

An arched gateway at the end of this court leads through into further barred cells of the prison, and over it is written in German the deceptive legend: "Work leads to freedom". There is a large solitary cell here where the commandant himself was imprisoned before he was taken away. He had been in the habit of keeping several men in it, with no furniture of any kind, and no sanitary arrangements; but for him a camp-bed was put in, and a chemical latrine,

K*

and at least a minimum of human decencies, and it remains as when he was the tenant. In another small room are kept now some of the many small cardboard boxes of unidentified human ashes left behind here; more of them are beyond a curve of the dry green moat, in what was once the mortuary, where bodies lay awaiting removal to the crematorium. An inscription in Czech over the doorway dedicates this shrine "To those who died to bring us freedom!"

This curve of the moat system provides a small bridge, for which the German commandant had a novel use. He had not a free hand with all his prisoners so far as life and death were concerned, though he could do much as he liked with them short of death; but he seems to have had *carte blanche* in the case of the Jewish prisoners. When his problems with regard to overcrowding passed even his powers of compression he relieved the situation by staging here Horatian combats, arming numbers of Jews with pickaxes, shovels, crowbars, and setting them to fight one another, with the assurance that those who survived should be set free to return to their people in the town. He did not even forget to notify their wives and families, and they were invited here to see their husbands batter one another to death on a bridge which led only one way. They reached the town, sure enough, but their destination there was the heavy oiled trolleys of the crematorium.

They show you here, close beside the bridge, another place, a whitewashed, mottled stone cavern from the walls of which plaster has broken away in gouts in suggestive places. There are low arches and thick brick pillars among which you move as in a catacomb, and in the centre, in the clearest space, an iron ring is fixed in the ceiling and iron staples in the floor, with an upright iron spike, smoothed and blunted by undefined use, in the middle. The walls about it are much discoloured, only partially with damp, though the place is clammy, too. In the uneven floor there are deep, stained channels, which drain off into the moat. Within living memory they have been filled with blood. What went on here proceeded so far beyond the possibility of extracting any answer to any question that one can only assume it was elaborated for fun; even the defence of orders from above therefore disappears.

The commandant of Terezin had two daughters, young girls in their teens. They seem not to have minded the life here in the fortress, except that there was little to do; and they asked for a swimming-pool to be cut for them within the walls, so that they could bathe when they liked. Labour, after all, was no problem, father had any amount of it at command. The policeman led us away to the rear of the German living quarters, and showed us the pool which was made for them, empty now, its concrete stained and dirty, but of a respectable size and depth. It was dug out by a squad of young students who were prisoners here. Their tools for the job were simple; each boy had already a pair of hands, and nothing more was considered to be necessary. So equipped, they provided the amenity which Terezin had lacked, and here the sisters used to bathe almost daily, and sunbathe afterwards on top of the grassy ramparts.

This is what I can never understand. It is not perhaps so difficult to imagine the stages by which a more or less normal German youth could be induced to accept the Nazi view of his own and other races, and the expendable character of human life; but the subjugation of the individual judgment and the sense of responsibility, the apprenticeship to bestiality, the gradual breaking in of the senses by participation in cruelty, cannot explain the women, or only those few of them who actually served as wardens in the camps. These two girls lived an ordinary domestic life, and had never themselves been broken in to the sacred service; their mother, so long as she lived, for I believe that she died here, shared their bland, interested and detached attitude, while having no more connection than they with the internal administration of the fortress. All three of them contemplated the appalling misery of the prisoners without apparent aversion or pity, merely concerned with making their own life as comfortable as possible in these not exactly ideal conditions. It did not discommode them to have to swim in a pool which had been dug by the bare hands of Czech boys, and when there was no other entertainment they were not averse to watching the daily executions from the overhanging ramparts. The policeman pointed out one particular vantage-point which they frequently occupied on such occasions. How can one account for such women? The harpies of Ravensbruck are less difficult to understand than these wives and mothers and daughters who took no part in the cruelties, yet saw them at close quarters and found no fault with them; who probably could not personally have ill-used a puppy which belonged to them, but felt no repulsion from seeing men shot and hanged by dozens at the hands of their husbands and fathers.

There is an open space just beyond the pool, and another squat, arched gateway pierced through another twelve-foot wall. Here the condemned were marshalled and led away to the place of execution, through the Gate of Death, downhill towards the flat marshes, then to the right through another wall, into an enclosed place under the ramparts. Here is a bank of earth piled up tightly against the wall, where prisoners were stationed to be shot; a great cross of silver birch stands there now, with wreaths laid before it on the ground. On the left is the gallows, a mere post and cross-bar joined to the brickwork, with two or three wooden steps mounting to it. Each of the condemned was forced to hang the man before him. When the Russians came, they found the remains of six hundred people buried in mass graves near this spot, for the supply of fuel had given out, and they could not be burned. They were all exhumed, and buried in the cemetery outside the fortress.

Everyone was very silent. The policeman tugged off his cap in front of the cross, and asked us for a moment of stillness, though already the hush was absolute. We had children with us, bored but obedient. Their mothers drew them close against their skirts, and held their hands tightly; the children thought it was done to keep them quiet, and bore it patiently.

"Thank you, ladies and gentlemen!" said the policeman, and led us back to outer air, to the cleanness and sweetness of the graves, where relatives have brought flowers, and the little lights wait ready for All Souls' Day.

We walked back to the car very slowly, separating along the little paths among the graves, pausing to look at portraits and names. There are old men there, and boys of fourteen, some remembered by laughing photographs from before the bad time; Jews and Catholics and Protestants; men and women together, it is all one. They come from all parts of the republic, and visitors from their own regions have left them many small trophies, like the Chod axe driven by the haft into the soil, with the promise on the blade: "Domazlice remembers!"

From this place we went to the crematorium, by curious ways among more brick fortifications, which turn this whole stretch of country into a maze. Small boards kept us on the right way when we were in doubt, and brought us at last on to an open waste of fields, mostly poor, vacant pasture, and in the midst of this expanse was a low white building, the main body of it having a row of squat windows high up in the walls, two ventilators on the crest of the roof, and a short brick chimney on either side, no higher than the chimneys of an ordinary house. Two square lean-to wings, with gently sloping roofs, were joined one to either side, and had normal windows. A row of sad little half-grown poplars was spaced along the road before it. There was nothing horrific about the appearance of the place; it looked like a small factory.

A little hunchbacked man in his shirt-sleeves watched us climb out of the car, and came to speak with us. Yes, we could go in, of course. No other visitors were here at the moment, and so we were able to linger and talk as we went. We followed him in through one of the side doors into the main body of the building. From door to door a wide path extended along the centre of the room, climbing five steps to cross the central section, which was built high between the cremation ovens. Of these there were four, two on either side; and from each, at the end of the room, iron rails ran out to carry the corpse-trolley. He showed us how these worked, running easily by a balance of weights, so that he could draw out the long shelf readily, an iron carriage ballasted with bricks, with a broad rail built up to breast-height at the end, to give convenient leverage for thrusting it back into the oven with its cargo. Sometimes, he said, three or even four bodies were piled on top of one another to keep pace with the work, and the four ovens were worked for as long as they would stand it, until they were almost red-hot, and only one rested at a time. He told us, but I have forgotten the amount, how much oil was required to encourage fire to consume even one human body; it was incredibly high, and even so the more durable bones have to be raked out afterwards and broken up. It seems it is almost impossible to destroy even so much of a man as his body, much less any more obstinate part of him.

The white walls went up blankly to the row of windows high above, but from every window the great sagging brown stains of damp ran down almost to the floor. The temperature here must have been appalling when all four ovens were going. It was the Jews themselves, of course, who had to do this work, and in the medical rooms at this end of the building, where the dissecting tables are still kept in position, and the shelves still have many of their jars intact, Jewish doctors had to work on the bodies of their own people under the supervision of German scientists. There is one room here which used to be the mortuary, and is now quite empty, and freshly painted; eventually it will be a memorial chapel for the dead. At the other end of the main room there are more small rooms, where are preserved a few of the numbered cardboard boxes which contain the ashes of victims, and a curious plaster erection which looks like a clumsy branched candle-stick. We asked about this, as it seemed to have no possible use, and with the aid of a photograph the guide showed us for what purpose it was made.

In 1944 the International Red Cross, after considerable agitation, was allowed to send a mission of inspection here, though I think they were not permitted to enter or even approach the Little Fortress, which was past cleaning up sufficiently to pass muster. What this permission meant in effect was the death warrant of thousands of Jews, who were promptly weeded out and despatched to the gas chambers of Osviecim, in order to bring the measure of overcrowding down to credibility. There was some hurried tidying up of the crematorium, too, to make it respectable; to disguise the death-rate twenty-six thousand boxes of ashes were carted away and thrown into the river Ohre; and to prove that the Germans had a proper respect for death itself an incredibly bogus-looking tomb was erected on a brick site, with this demented cross between a candelabrum and a stringless harp perched on the top of it, and no body nor fragment of a body either within it or under it. Its function was to look pious, which it must have done about as successfully as Hitler, in his equestrian portraits, attempted to look like Joan of Arc.

Now the very fact that such drastic alterations were necessary before even this "easy" concentration camp, this "really very good" place dared be visited, shows once again how unthinkable were conditions in the others.

Most of the flat ground here, close beside the building, was seen on a closer approach to be an area of mass graves, neatly shaped into rectangular plots, but marked by no stones nor monuments of any kind. A single symbolical plot of flowers on the river bank marks the spot where the thousands of urns were emptied.

It had been a sobering morning, but one I would not have missed for a great deal.

"What did you think of it?" we asked one another, as we went back to the car.

"I do not know what I expected," said Honza, furrowing his brow, "but nothing like that. Something smoky, perhaps, great high chimney stacks, but nothing at all like that."

We agreed; outside, it is not even ugly. But at this time we did not talk about it any more; in this particular I was acquiring Honza's habit of digesting first and formulating afterwards.

We drove away by another road, and found our way without difficulty into the town of Litomerice, not far away. It has a beautiful big square, with some arcades, and fine step-gabled buildings grouped about it, not to mention several large hotels. We parked the car, and went to examine all the bills of fare, thereupon choosing the most substantial. It was a long time since we had eaten, and we were hungry. My brother and I, choosing by title, ate something called Spanish bird, which was neither Spanish nor any part of a bird. Petr chose fish, and we feared it must be for lack of coupons, since fish is free; but when we offered some it turned out that he had every intention of following it up with beef. Honza selected some lengthy name I did not know, and was served with a wonderful dish of about seven compartments, a whole tray in itself, the centre compartment containing meat, the outer ones small portions of various vegetables in a dazzling array of colours. The addition of a side-plate of dumplings to this feast seemed a superfluity of riches. We were genuinely gay, perhaps on the rebound from abnormality.

"What shall we do now?" asked Petr. "We have all afternoon."

Not knowing the ground, we were willing to be taken wherever they thought best, and between them they decided that we should drive on towards the border, into the land of the little "Middle Mountains", which parallel the line of the frontier Ore Mountains with their miniature feathered peaks, abrupt and graceful and dainty, toy mountains with the profiles of real ones. They came with the volcanic outbreaks which accompanied the breaking up of the earth's crust, and their highest peak, the Mile-sovka, is about 2,700 feet high, a comfortable afternoon's walk.

We drove on, accordingly, after dinner, and climbed into the charming little range among pretty, compact villages. The little volcano went up to a neat point, almost entirely covered with trees, and perched on the top of it, in the approved fashion of Bohemia, was a small building with a tower, battlemented with red crests. It did not look like a castle this time; we hazarded that it was either a restaurant, or a chapel marking some holy place where a saint had seen visions; for these, as well as castles, are frequent on Czech hilltops.

"Well, we shall climb and see," said Petr, and looked for somewhere to park the car, since we seemed to be drawing

K**

as near to the slope as we could go. We left it at last drawn in to the edge of the road before an inn, where a path moved uphill towards the rising woodlands. As we were setting off, a woman came out of the inn, and suggested that the car would not be very safe unattended. She hinted that for a consideration she would keep a friendly eye on it for us. Petr opined cheerfully that it would be perfectly all right whether she did or not.

"Very well!" she said darkly, "but don't blame me. The people round here are awful thieves. Don't say you weren't warned if you come back and find half your fittings gone."

"Don't believe it!" said Honza blithely, and we left the car to its fate without a qualm.

"Perhaps it's a protection racket," we suggested slyly. "Maybe everything portable *will* vanish, since you didn't pay up—vanish into the inn!"

"Then we shall try strong-arm methods to recover them," said Petr, refusing to be intimidated.

We climbed, and soon were in the woods, winding and zigzagging by a steady path under the trees. The morning had been sprinkled with fitful rain, but the afternoon became sunny and gloriously hot. Up the first and gentlest slope we found some wild raspberry canes, and went aside to strip them; in the middle of which operation Honza gently pointed out that I was standing in an anthill. This proved to be true enough, and had caused great agitation among the ants, who were rushing out of the ground and making off at frantic speed with their salvaged young, looking like grains of wheat as they were carried away. I stepped back to the path, and shook the strays from my ankles, and I hope the alarm of atomic warfare, or whatever had been sounded below-ground, was recognised for a false rumour, and the poor little evacuees soon recalled to their home. The damage on the surface did not appear to be great, but I am no lightweight, and there may have been extensive reconstruction work needed underground.

Our path branched, and a blue blaze kept us on the right way. On the higher reaches of the hill the way spiralled upward, still among trees, but crossed occasionally by naked drifts of stones, which had cleared a passage before them to the valley by the quickest route. A last twist brought us to the summit, a clearing neatly small, just accommodating the turreted building on the highest spot, and a single-storeyed restaurant of the casual country kind under its shadow, with space for a few outhouses, and scratching ground for chickens round about the little garden. A wall surrounded the tower and the kitchen garden. We walked all round it, climbed on the wall on the further side, and finally observed a small notice on the inner gate, stating positively that there was: "No admittance." Promptly we desired to enter.

"I shall go and make enquiries," announced Petr simply, and did so by the nearest way, which was over the wall. He disappeared into the open doorway, and came back in a few minutes to beckon us in.

"It is permitted. It is free!"

"I shall go twice!" said Honza with satisfaction, and slid his long legs over the wall.

The place proved to be a small observatory and meteorological station belonging to the University of Prague. We climbed up the tower by a spiral staircase, between whitewashed walls on which visitors from many lands had scribbled their greetings in many languages. It would be a pity ever to whitewash over that wall again, for some precious historical documents would be defaced in the process. For instance, it is recorded that Julius Cæsar came here in 1946. There is also a pathetic inscription left by some young lady from Prague, who felt herself to be the only girl in the world without love, and expressed her inability to understand this, since she found herself reasonably endowed with charms and virtues. "If anyone wants my love, let him come and look for it here:" and she appended her address. I wonder if anyone has ever accepted the challenge? I can imagine it having an effect, for the lady had a turn of phrase which argues a sense of humour as well as a grievance, and if the charms come up to specification a man might easily do worse.

On top we emerged upon the roof, a little turret and masts mounting still higher over us. We leaned on the red crests and looked out over north-western Bohemia to the borders, where the mountains climbed fold on fold, and down to the rich woods and meadows below us, where the village of Milesov was tucked close under the lee of its patron mountain. All round the crenellated walls ran lightning-conductors, for this is a volcanic area, and remembers some notable damage from thunderstorms. On the stairs hung a photograph taken from a neighbouring town on one occasion when half its power was blown out by lightning, showing the moment of the strike, and the little peak of Milesovka on the skyline peacefully absorbing at the same time a flash as intense as that which struck the town.

We came down at length, leaving by the gate instead of over the wall, as we had entered, and went to hunt for coffee in the little restaurant, and to eat the rest of our provisions. The coffee was not from coffee, but it was not bad. There were postcards, and according to a hand-lettered notice, a savage dog, of which we must beware; but of him we saw no more than this possibly libellous description. We wrote some postcards, and left them here to be despatched, and then made our way down the hill more easily and rapidly than we had climbed it. The car was still there, complete even to its horn.

"Now that we're so near," said Petr, "we may as well go on and have a look at Teplice Sanov."

We were perfectly willing; full as the day had already been, it was almost the last we had left, and could hardly be overfilled. So we drove on, and creeping back to the main road, turned left and headed again for the mountains, and within an hour we were in Teplice.

Another spa, and an old one, too, for Roman coins have been found here, and jewellery said to be of Celtic origin; yet the town produces an effect quite unlike that of any other spa I know, and reminds you constantly that it is also a mining town and an industrial centre. There are the handsome gardens, the usual spa architecture of white colonnades and terraces and wedding-cake hotels, and domed bath pavilions, and summer-houses in the parks, all adequate and true to pattern; but there are also the eminently businesslike shopping streets, the warehouses, wharves and yards, never far to seek, and outside the central area of gardens the whole appearance of the streets of modest, sensible houses suggests an industrial population.

The marriage appears to be quite a happy one, for neither partner looks at all out of countenance. But for some reason, when we arrived at an awkward hour too late for tea and too early for supper, at the end of the afternoon sunlight but too soon for the lights and liveliness of the evening, it had not a very happy look. We stopped, naturally, among the gardens, where many of the people we saw must have been visitors taking cures; and I suppose that if one is ill to begin with one need not be expected to be particularly gay; moreover, most of these patients were elderly, which is understandable, since Teplice treats, among other things, rheumatism and all its attendant ills, and some other ailments of old age; but this was one town where we saw very few smiles. Honza and Petr noticed the same thing; indeed, we worked out between us a theory that a safe test to distinguish the permanent resident from the visitor was to smile at your guinea-pig, and if he smiled back he was almost certainly a resident.

Perhaps our first view was a little jaundiced, for we walked round for some time looking for the ice-cream and coupon-free cakes which Petr had assured us were often to be had in the border spas; and when they failed to materialise we expressed a very poor opinion of Teplice Sanov. But our attitude changed when we found a terrace restaurant which was open, had ample space for us, and could offer both the delicacies we desired. The gardens grew rapidly greener, the flowers brighter, the people less forbidding, as we ate our way through many sticky cakes and mounds of ice-cream which I swear contained milk.

"Very nice town!" said Petr, beaming benevolently over the strollers in the park below us. "Lovely gardens! Look at that water—marvellous!"

One thing which we particularly noticed was the type of person who was here for treatment. There may have been a few foreign guests, but if so they were not in evidence; almost all of these middle-aged people were clearly workers, had the hands, the faces, the clothes, the gait, the slightly helpless look in these holiday surroundings, of people well acquainted with labour and worry, and uneasy strangers to leisure. Now I am unable to assess the precise importance of this, for I do not know how new it is. I had seen Karlovy Vary only in exceptional circumstances, an empty town; and Marianske Lazne on a previous visit had certainly shown a very different type of patron, elegant, expensive, and cosmopolitan, but in 1947, not 1948. I do not know if Teplice always catered for workers in need of spa treatment, or whether this controlled use of the facilities is new and general; possibly, as an industrial town itself, it may always have led the way in this field. I can only testify that most of its patients in August 1948 appeared to be workers.

On our way back through the town we stopped to look at the square, with its two churches sitting cheek by jowl, and its tall plague column. The pastor of one of these churches had provided interesting reading matter in the notices pinned out on its doors, which included some lively and caustic reviews of the films to be shown at the various town cinemas during the coming week. These were evidently a regular feature, and their matter was admirably unexpected, for they were not treated merely on their moral tone; he gave brief notes on story, acting, quality of direction, and general category into which they seemed to him to fall, including the infantile. "Good up to the mental age of twelve."

We were about fifty-five or sixty miles from Prague, and very close to the border, only the Ore Mountains intervening. It was early in the evening when we started the journey back, and therefore when we passed the cemetery at Terezin the light was just at that transitional pearl-greyness which dims every colour, but makes everything which is white seem still whiter. All the small uniform crosses were like low, steady flames, the cenotaph a taller flame in the centre. I should like to pass by it in darkness when all the lamps are lit on the graves.

It was dark when we reached Prague, and from much fresh air we were already half asleep. Petr had still the remaining drive home to Stara Boleslav, and therefore dropped us on the corner, where we parted from him with many thanks, and promises to meet again "the next time".

So ended the fullest day I spent in Czechoslovakia, and the strangest.

For an English person, used, though unconsciously, to the unique feeling of security due to living on an island, a circumstance which irons out extremes in other things beside climate, it requires an enormous mental effort to relate Terezin in any way to the twentieth century, or to humanity as we know it. Therefore we fail to make full allowance for a different viewpoint in those who do not share our insular advantages, and who are continually forced to fit into their world and their plans for the future considerations which we can ignore. The Czechs seem very like us, we say—and indeed I believe they are—why do they not think as we do? The answer is on the map. They simply cannot afford to. Neither, of course, can we, but we have not awakened to that fact even yet; for we are moving into an era in which, the atlas notwithstanding, there will be no islands.

CSR suffers under the disadvantage of the least tenable position in Europe, not even barring the Low Countries; she is not simply the most westerly of the Slav countries, but a peninsula of the Slavs jutting well out into the Germanic lands. I use the terms of the past and the immediate present, because we have not yet escaped from their kind of world, and therefore must speak its language to be understood. She looks back on a history of unending troubles, wars and wrongs, all because she made the mistake of being the very antithesis of an island, the core and crossroads of a continent. In her world Terezins have never been far out of mind, never far back in memory.

We, then, who have been the lucky ones, owe it to her, and to others who share her problems, to try to fit into our imagination this factor which they know from bitter experience. It is not enough; it will not equip us to understand; all it can do is compel us at least to *try* to understand. It sounds and it is little, but it is better than nothing; and to have seen Terezin, even cleaned and disinfected, is a step on the way. Who could come back from there and have the arrogance to ask: "Why are they so insistent that we should fulfil our programme of denazification in Western Germany to the letter? What do they fear in our plans for Ruhr industry?" It does not follow that one would always agree with their views; but I have seen little disposition on our part as yet even to listen, much less to attempt understanding.

Sympathy could alleviate all our differences, between nations as between men; but it requires a changed world to cure, a world in which the terminology of races and frontiers, of tariffs and customs, has ceased to have any meaning, a world far beyond the sovereign state or the far more dangerous regional grouping which is no more than the sovereign state made a little larger and more cocky, and if anything even more sanctimoniously given to "chosen people" theories. A really united nations; a really single world. That is the only answer to all the political problems, all the political fears and fancies, of CSR.

Or, for that matter, of humanity.

22

The Last Days

My brother was to leave on Saturday afternoon, and I had to follow him on Monday. Friday evening was pledged to Helena and Karel, and in the afternoon we had some last shopping to do in town; but in the morning we managed to fit in a visit which I had been promising myself for some time, to the Masaryk Homes for Old People, at Krc, just on the outskirts of Prague. Some time ago we had got as far as making enquiries, and been told cheerfully to turn up whenever we liked, though preferably during the morning; no further notice was necessary. Accordingly we jolted out of Prague by tram and bus, and dropped off at the gates, and walked in.

I was interested in any experiment in the accommodation of old people because I had some local acquaintance with the old Guardians' Committees in Britain, which were just at this time ending their mottled but well-meaning existence, and I knew a little of the difficulties of trying to make a home out of institutional buildings a hundred years old, which absorb the energies and ideas of even the most devoted staff as blotting-paper soaks up ink. I do not suggest we were all either as energetic or as devoted as we might have been, but I do know that these buildings, impossible to cure no matter how much one spent on them, impossible to vacate until conditions permitted an alternative, damped all enthusiasm at a glance, and made one aware of the uselessness of effort. Now the Masaryk Homes, though on the enormous scale which is deprecated nowadays, was finished as lately as 1934, and has always been considered as a model of its kind, so at least it could furnish a standard for the large institution so long as building on a sufficient scale for full accommodation in cottage homes remains an aim for the future; which will be some years yet, I am afraid.

I had already talked about current ideas on the subject with one or two people, and found that when Krc was mentioned they were inclined to say: "Yes, it is good; but I doubt if that is really the answer." So do we all. Their minds, like ours, were lingering fondly on the ideal cottage home; but it will have to be built for the job, if it is to be ideal, and it will have to be built in such numbers as we cannot immediately contemplate. The great thing is to make a start. In the meantime, the best we can do in the way of large homes to cover the expansion period will not be any too good; so we went to pick up tips at the Masaryk Homes.

Buses drop you at the gates, which are large, sweeping back from the main road, and equipped with seats where the tenants can sit in the sun and watch the world go by. The place is a village in itself, of twenty or more large, flat-roofed, three-or-four-storey blocks, spaced out about three main avenues, with flower-beds, covered colonnades, and on the first central building through the gate, a clock-tower. It looks and is modern, and it could be said that it even looks institutional, if one accepts the best sense of that word. Woods extend behind the site, the main road crosses before it, and beyond the road are open meadows, and a turning off into a village; it has town on one side, readily accessible but not intrusive, and country on the other.

We walked into the office at the gate, explained that we were English and interested, and asked if we could see the place. We were at once taken through to the doctor's office in the main administrative building, where we found two other English ladies just on the point of setting out on a similar tour; so when we had all introduced ourselves we set off in a body, going first to the hospital blocks.

The Germans had been in possession here, and left their traces in the dull grey paint which covered some of the walls, but many had already been repainted in their original light cream, and rid themselves of the suggestion of a military hospital. All would soon be restored, said the young doctor happily. The striped pyjamas and red dressing-gowns in which convalescents were strolling about the colonnades were also condemned, and in use only until everything could be replaced. His tone in referring to many aspects of the colony was unnecessarily deprecating, I thought, but: "This is still not good enough!" is always a healthy attitude.

The enormous advantage of modern buildings shows up everywhere. A great part of the wall-space of these blocks is occupied by windows, many of them full-length, with small balconies outside, almost all with flower-boxes. Inside there are modern floors, lifts, lofty ceilings, ample light, all the invaluable fruits of new and intelligent building. I remarked enviously how lucky he was to have such conditions in which to work, and he objected with perfect seriousness that in some ways these buildings were quite out of date, being as much as twenty years old. Those of which I was thinking were nearer a hundred and twenty.

This attitude comes naturally to the Czechs, and here again history and geography enter the picture. We, on our island, have suffered the drawbacks of too much security, just as we have enjoyed the benefits; the steadiness of our development, the continuity of our institutions, has overburdened us with the old and outworn, from traditions to workhouses and schools unchanged from the days of

Dickens. The Czechs, on the other hand, after the long twilight of suppression, emerged in 1918 with a great burst of creative energy and an almost clear field for it to work on, and they built madly and joyously at all the things they needed and had lacked. I think it is true to say that you can go into almost any Czech village, look round you for the finest and most up-to-date building you can see, and conclude with safety that you are looking at the school. Their standard in these matters, therefore, is not ours. To the doctor, twenty years in a functional building constituted at least middle age.

Inside, the most notable thing was the lightness of the colours, creams and pale golds and greens, cheerful and sunny to look at, receptive to the rich light which was everywhere admitted and made welcome. This held good everywhere, in hospital blocks and house accommodation alike. What the doctor chiefly disliked about the wards was their size, accommodating from eight to twelve beds. This, he held, was by no means good enough, and he was jubilant because they were all to be altered, made into small rooms for only four people. In the first block this work had not yet been begun, but in the second and third it was in full swing, and going forward at great speed.

"All will be completed within the year," said the doctor with satisfaction.

We remarked that this looked like a formidable undertaking, and asked if he really thought it could be made good.

"Yes, certainly! We have already been guaranteed the labour and the material necessary to complete it in the time." He was quite definite about this, and made it clear also that he was being encouraged to develop the laboratory. He had a theory that his job was not merely to alleviate the ills of the old in this place, but so far as possible to prevent them; and he wanted to take on a great deal of research into what have usually been considered the inevitable accompaniments of old age.

It was in the house blocks, however, that we were most interested. He took us first to the one which he held to be least satisfactory, and the burden of his tale as he led us into it was again: "This is not good enough, but for the moment we have to make do with it." The rooms had the same plenteous windows and gay light colours, but what offended him about them was that they did not satisfy his ideas of privacy, or provide the sense of individual ownership which he thought necessary. The sleeping accommodation was in wards; that was the worst offence. The dining-room had long tables instead of small ones for pairs and foursomes, and the bathrooms, though blamelessly bright and cheerful and clean, seemed to him too perilously near to deserving whatever is the Czech equivalent of the term "ablution block". Everything good of its kind, even the china, which we saw laid out for lunch, and which had nothing institutional about it; but everything, he thought, fitted into the wrong framework. So much for the worst, and now for the best.

The second block was very different. The dining-room was still shared by all, but it had little tables spaced about as in a hotel, and instead of the wards there were small bed-sitting-rooms for two people, where husband and wife, or two old friends, could live together, and put up their names on the door, and receive visitors as proudly as in any flat in Prague. He tapped on some of the doors, and asked if we might look inside; and we were welcomed everywhere, so much so that neighbours, discovering our presence next-door, would lie in wait for us as we came out, and invite us into their own small home.

The rooms were compact, with some cupboard and bookshelf space, and beautifully varied, for only the limited space determined what possessions the tenants might bring in with them, and they had all their own photographs, pictures, hand-worked cushions or pillow covers, books, small ornaments, and many of them their own bedspreads, wireless sets, and larger things. These single rooms can be real miniature homes when furnished with one's own possessions. Possession in the personal sense, of such intimate things as letters, photographs, books, and the means of enjoying music, is almost half of living, and I should think that to be deprived of these on entry into a home in old age can be the greater part of death.

Later on, according to the doctor, it is hoped to provide facilities even for individual housekeeping, so that old couples who are still capable of doing their own shopping and cooking, and wish to look after themselves, can choose what they like, cook it as they like, and dine privately. In such a colony they will presumably always be a minority, however, and as yet the arrangements do not make provision for them.

The Homes have their own cinema, and their own chapel, which by sensible agreement does duty for all denominations. There are no visiting hours; relatives and friends may come and go as they wish, and so may the inhabitants, except those who are under medical care, of course, the sick and the small proportion of the usual sad and permanent deficiency cases. The city library provides a branch for readers, and city transport is laid on at the gates. The staff have an attractive day-nursery for their children, a good nurses' home, and a degree of freedom less often found in English hospitals, I think, to judge by the number of young nurses I saw wearing ankle socks instead of stockings in this hot weather, and the cheerful, bright informality of their exchanges with doctors and with one another. Indeed, I do not think the Czechs take naturally to the forming of hierarchies in any profession, but prefer a more resilient and adaptable relationship between the varying levels of duty and proficiency. A young woman doctor working in the day-nursery wore grey slacks under her white gown. A bunch of orderlies skylarking harmlessly in the middle of kitchen duties did not, as I had expected, skid self-consciously away out of sight when we approached at the noisiest moment, but met the doctor's eye with confiding grins, and though they quietened down, did so without suddenness or embarrassment, and without looking in the least impudent or foolish, which I regard as a very unusual and healthy reaction. Indeed, relationships here among all concerned seemed to be easy, energetic and happy.

The Homes are the property of the City of Prague, and admission to them is granted by the governing committee. The criterion is need, not merely monetary need, for it is possible to come in here and pay for your accommodation if you have money, or to come without means of any kind, and have it paid for you. The old have other needs, chiefly for companionship and friends, which money itself cannot supply. So there come to Krc not only the destitute, but men and women of the professions, left alone in old age, occasional ex-officers, lawyers, judges.

"And you would be surprised, perhaps," said the doctor, "to hear that some romances begin here among the old people. Marriages in our chapel are not by any means unknown."

It seems to me that the problem of old age has moved at any rate a stage towards solution where cheap retirement has been made so dignified that all sorts and conditions of men are willing to share it, and so optimistic that many of those who would once have been considered to be waiting for death are contemplating embarking upon a new life. No doubt much remains to be done, and for many years yet we shall still have to shake our heads and say, like the doctor: "It isn't good enough!" But at least we have moved forward a few steps.

It was about noon when we boarded the bus again and left for town. The afternoon we spent doing our last shopping, and in the evening had supper in Dejvice with Helena and Karel. They were surprised to hear that I was not travelling with my brother, but perforce staying over until Monday, for no cancellation had occurred on Saturday's plane.

"Then why don't you and Honza come over and see us in Podebrady on Sunday?" said Helena. "We have a flat there, and shall be staying over the week-end. There's a good bathing place there, on the Labe."

"Would you like to?" asked Honza, brightening at the mention of water.

There was nothing I could have liked better for my own last day. Better to be visiting some new place and old friends than sombrely contemplating departure in Prague. So it was arranged, and Helena made Honza memorise the address, so that we could find our way to their flat on arrival.

We spent the evening, as we always did here, talking hard until nearly midnight, and crept home by a late tram at last, half asleep.

The next day my brother went home. There was ample time to pack in the morning, and even time for a last walk in Stromovka, before the early dinner which Mrs. Vesela had prepared. Then Honza and I went with him to the air terminal, but the entire Czechoslovak archery team was just setting out for London to compete in the international tournament, and there were no seats left in the bus when all the passengers were aboard. We had to take leave of him there, instead of at the airport. In two days I should be following him by precisely the same processes.

When the bus had left we walked back to Holesovice. After a sunny morning the day became very sultry, which I found unusual in CSR, even in the city. Mr. Vesely was in Troja, but Mrs. Vesela and Honza and I had an early tea, and then took a tram out to Zizkov, and walked up to the Resistance Memorial, the vast white ship which never sails from its station on top of the hill. The effort to climb the rising paths became almost too great; there was no air to breathe. Someone had storms, for later in the evening, when we were walking home, the atmosphere had lightened somewhat, and there was a small breeze; but in Prague there was no rain, not even a shower.

We separated early that night, and I went off to wrestle with the coke-fired geyser in the bathroom for the last time; but as I had only to heat enough water for myself on this occasion the room did not have time to raise a temperature like one of the antechambers of Dante's Inferno. The radio in one of the flats below was playing: "How are things in Glockamorra?" which was all the rage, and sounded appreciably better in Czech, so much so that at first I had failed to recognise it. I had heard the morning chorus of carpet-beaters for almost the last time, and for the last time Mrs. Vesela's little alarm-clock was ticking on the table beside me, to remind me to get up in time for the early bus.

On our way to Slovakia we had already passed through Podebrady, with only a glimpse of the spa side of it under many trees, before we were out again upon the main road. Now we alighted in the square, under an equestrian statue of the town's most famous son, the Hussite King George of Podebrady, probably the best-loved ruler the Czechs ever had. They elected him, which may or may not be the reason for his quality, for I can imagine elected kings who would be equally complete failures. George, however, was decidedly a success, as soldier, ruler, and—though in this centuries ahead of his time—as internationalist; for he was the first statesman to submit to the powers of Europe a plan for a union of consent, which should provide for the settlement of all disputes peacefully, by mutual agreement. That was in the fifteenth century. He was apparently as intelligent domestically as he was in this matter, and altogether something of a phenomenon, though the world was not ready for him. In his portraits he is easily recognised, a big man, rather stout, with luxuriant hair and a brigand's moustache.

We had Helena's address, but no notion of where the street lay; so we waited beside one of the springs in the square until someone who looked like a native came along to draw water. Inevitably, in spite of all appearances, she was a stranger; but before we had time to involve ourselves in more enquiries we had found a map of the town sensibly displayed upon a house-wall, and by that easily traced our way through the park, and one short street beyond.

Podebrady, like most Czech spas, is two towns; the old town, rooted deep in history with the gabled houses about the king's statue in the square, and the castle with its courtyard and its thick round tower in the meadows beside the Labe; and the white floral colonnaded city of pavilions and baths and parks, exquisitely kept, full of lily pools, and flowery clocks, and turf as smug as velvet, where the heart sufferers saunter and sit away their days between treatments at the Winter Baths or the Cardiological Institute. It is an old town, but a new spa, and a very beautiful one. We walked all through Masaryk Park, marvelling at the labour which must have been spent on raising the gardens to such a peak of perfection; and almost at the end of our green and blossomy walk we met Karel coming to meet us.

"Helena sent me out to fetch you," he said. "Come along and have a look at our little flat, and then we can go straight to the bathing place."

The flat had actually been let, but they retained one

room in it for these occasional visits, and passed cramped but pleasant week-ends sharing this limited space with the whole of their piled-up furniture. When we arrived, Helena was cutting generous sandwiches on the safe assumption that we should already be hungry. She had her beach-bag packed ready for the river, and was dressed for the glorious day which was just coming to flower. We had started early, and the sun was still only slanting across the trees in the park, and had not reached the Labe shore, but soon it would be very hot. We ate our snack, abandoned everything leavable, my raincoat among the rest, and set out at a leisurely pace through the town.

We were early and alone at the bathing place, for it was still cool and shady, and not for another half-hour did the sunshine reach this bank of the river. Pleasant meadows lay along the other side of the water, and on our side a wide pathway followed the bank through woodlands, with this enclosure of fine sand and hollow square of dressing cabins cosily installed in a curve of it. We took our time about undressing, and then sat along the stone edge of the embankment, and trailed our toes until such time as the sun should advance to meet us. For me there was a little enclosure with the children, unobtrusively railed off for non-swimmers; and there I should probably be the only bather above eight years old, for most Czechs compensate themselves for being born landsmen by apprenticing themselves early to fish.

The sun came, creeping up out of the silver and green water and across the yellow sand, and fingering us gratefully as its range grew. More people arrived, and more cabin doors opened upon elegant bathing costumes. Off went my three companions at last, one by one down the stone steps and into the water, where they struck out blithely for the opposite bank. As for me, I went and lay in the sandy shallows of the children's enclosure, where the sun warmed right through to the pebbles, and I could bask without burning. The beach was large, but before dinner it was full to capacity, and some of the earliest arrivals among the girls had reached their second costumes. When Helena and Karel and Honza came ashore for a rest we all sat along the edge of the embankment and kicked up fountains of water as we dried in the sun; and it was while we were sitting here, watching the swimmers, and the occasional small boats which passed us heading up-stream, that I began to hear voices calling in English. I remarked on the phenomenon, and Karel explained:

"There is a conference being held in the castle, and I think there are quite a lot of English people there."

"What kind of conference?" I asked.

"Something about pre-school and early school education. They are UNESCO delegates who are meeting, I believe."

Once we knew this, we could begin to pick them out, even in the water; I do not know whether I was still identifiable as English at a hundred yards, but I discovered that they were, though I still do not know by what sign. At first, when we began this exercise, we found only the young people, boys and girls in their teens, rowing about in small boats. Then there was a more portentous rustling and crashing among the bushes and reeds which screened the boat-houses upstream from us, and there emerged a fantastic boat-load of serious people, six paddling native-canoe fashion, except that these six were paddling in all directions. They were of both sexes, and indiscriminate ages, by Czech standards rather overdressed for such a day and such an occupation, even to coolie straw hats, and they dipped their paddles with majestic gravity and in slow time, setting their individual courses with the authority of people accustomed to knowing their own minds; and the boat, compromising with a serenity which I only wish the world could copy, staggered away upstream with the

deliberation and dignity of a drunken matron, followed
by many admiring glances from the beach. One of my
most endearing memories of the summer of 1948 is of the
boating of UNESCO.

"Look!" said Honza, when we were all lying half-asleep
in the sand, somewhat later. "They are coming back!"
And so they were, in the same austere fashion, with equal
determination and equal uncertainty. Everyone watched
respectfully as the boat wobbled into harbour; no one
commented, except for the faint, awed smiles, half amusement, half wonder to see them still afloat. Yet I think no
boat would have the heart to sink under so grave, reverend
and confiding a crew.

I had lain in the sun for a long time, and was just beginning to realise, too late, that I should suffer for it. However,
we dressed, and went in search of dinner at one of the spa
restaurants in the park, and afterwards decided to go
upriver through the woods to where a small tributary
joined the Labe, for the bathing place here in the town, said
Helena, was solid with people in the afternoon, and quite
uninhabitable. There were boats plying, but we arrived
between their times, and the pathway was shaded, though
the heat by now was intense; so we walked. Most of the
way we were close to the river bank, but the last stretch
took us a little away from it, and deep among the trees,
where the midges were biting as if evening had already
come. At the confluence there was a restaurant, and a
ferry taking swimmers across either to the tongue of turf
between the rivers, or to the far bank of Labe, whichever
they pleased. But here Labe was for swimmers only, and
I could venture only into the tributary, which was already
populous; and of both the edges were reedy, and without an
inch of beach. However, we crossed to the point between
the waters, and undressed in the woods; whereupon it
appeared beyond question that I was burned crimson in

painful places. Honza's eyebrows shot up almost into his hair when he saw the expanse of burn; but by this time it was taken for granted in the Vesely family that I had not sense enough to come in out of the sun, and he wasted only a resigned shrug and a shake of the head upon me, forbearing to throw away words.

"We shall bathe with you first in the little river," said Helena, "and afterwards we will swim a while in the Labe."

We had hardly observed that the sky had clouded over, but before we had been ten minutes in the water it began to rain. Since we had left our clothes on the bank we had to scramble ashore and dive with them into the shelter of the trees, where we dressed, instinctively, I think, for how else can one explain it? Bathing costumes already wet would seem the ideal wear for showers, yet we scuttled out of them and into our clothes as if life depended on it, and plunged down to the ferry again, and over to the restaurant, where we found an indoor table until the storm blew over.

Before we had drunk our tea the sun was out again, but shining in a stormy manner which warned us that it would not last long. We debated whether to walk back or wait the greater part of an hour for the boat, and run the risk of being crowded out of a place aboard. Besides, the boat would leave us only twenty minutes or so before the departure time of our last bus back to Prague, and my coat was at the flat which had formed our temporary base. However, Karel thought we should have time to retrieve it, and if we began to walk there was certainly a risk that we should arrive half-drowned.

"And if we wait for the boat," I said, to make up Honza's mind for him, "you could bathe again, now, while it is fine."

He agreed, brightening, that he could, and slipped away to take advantage of the brief sunshine, and presently we saw him take to the water again. The weather let him

alone for a quarter of an hour or so, and then down came
the rain for a second time, and resignedly he came in and
rejoined us indoors, satisfied at least with the sense of having
snatched a brief enjoyment out of the interval. This
settled it; we should have to go back by water.

The boat, when it came, took everyone aboard, on the
same principle as Czech buses, and offered us at any rate
standing room under a rainproof awning; and indeed we
who stood were luckier than those who had seats along
the sides, for they got all the drips. Labe is very lovely
from the water, with level banks of meadow and soft woodland, gentle country here and without hills; but we saw
it for most of the trip through a slanting downpour of
thunder rain. The awning sagged over our heads so heavily
that we began to fear it would burst, and someone cautiously
poked it upward, with the frightful result that a sudden
waterfall descended upon the unfortunates seated along the
side. No one ventured to do this again, though it presented
tempting possibilities.

On this day, however, our luck was in, for by the time
we went ashore at Podebrady, just within sight of the castle,
the storm had again passed, and all the woods and silver
birches along the river walks, and the turf, were looking
newly washed and innocently placid in the evening sun.
We crossed to the path which passes under the walls of
the castle, under the thick, short tower capped with a roof
like a steel helmet, and the high faces of masonry shored
with brick buttresses, and so came out into the square. One
bus was already in, and loaded, twenty minutes ahead of
time; but people who were waiting there told us comfortably that there would be a second one to take the overflow, and in that one we should, with luck, get seats.
Karel and Honza shot away to the flat to fetch my coat,
while Helena and I drank mineral water at the nearest
inn, keeping a ready eye cocked for the incoming bus,

and even more anxiously for the return of the two men.

The bus came, so we staked claims in it, and in good time the couriers returned. This was my farewell to Karel and Helena for this year, though Honza was already invited to join them again here the following week-end. They stood waving us away until the bus turned out of the square, and we lost sight of them.

We drove back to the city in the scarlet glow of a wonderful but ominous sunset, talking gently together in the sleepy stages of content which follow in the dusk of a particularly happy day. Half-way home the bus filled to capacity, as usual, and Honza gave his seat to a plump middle-aged lady with a large basket of ripe plums, for whom perforce, but with goodwill, for I felt friendly towards everybody, I nursed half the load upon my burned and angry knees. When we reached Florence it was growing dark, and we walked home over Stvanice in the first shy lights of the town, drowsy and satiated with sun and water and fresh air, to describe our day to the family over a late supper.

Next day I packed, not without difficulty, for one acquires many odds and ends during three months. The morning went away very quickly in the last little tasks which always crop up; and before I realised it I was being summoned to dinner, declining beer, and being overruled by Mr. Vesely, who reminded me that it was the last chance. Honza in any case had already taken the jug and gone to fetch it. Leave-taking could be only brief, as indeed it always should be; then we were hurrying away to board a tram for the Powder Tower, and waving feverishly to his parents from the corner for a moment before we dived out of sight. There is never anything to say at the last moment, though many things come to mind afterwards; luckily it is only an illusion that it is the last moment, for the first thing one does on reaching home is to write letters to the people one has just left behind.

Honza came to Ruzyne with me, for this time the air-line bus was not full. One or two Americans were going home via London; a young English student was returning from a visit connected, probably, with Union business. That appeared to be all. Later we found that we were also taking on at the airport a party of Russians from Berlin, who were coming to London on business; and on their account we had to wait for the Berlin plane, which was badly delayed, and made us very late in taking off.

Honza and I shook hands and separated at the barrier of the Customs; he had cast a recognising and speculative eye on a car outside, and opined that with luck he could get a lift back home, and there was certainly no point in his waiting for the take-off, since it was expected to be very late. One needs a formula for farewells. I thought of little Marie at Cheb last year, waving the train out tear-fully with a scream of: "Cheerio, and Bob's your flip-ping uncle!" Honza grinned, and hoped that if we came down we would please not do it, so, crash, on land, but so, plop! in the sea. "It's softer!" Someone called me from the passport control office, and we loosed hands regretfully, and the door closed on his valedictory smile.

There was a tedious wait, but the Berlin plane came at last, and our twelve fellow-travellers had their papers checked, and joined us on the tarmac, and in ten minutes more we were in motion, the steel ribbon of the runway unrolling under us. I sat forward of the wing, for I like to watch the ground turning below in a complicated pattern of woods and fields. From there you can believe how really beautiful, productive and generous it is.

The white buildings of Ruzyne, the hedges and distant cottages, heeled and swayed and fell away from us. We were in the air suddenly and smoothly, and embarked upon a calm journey; and that richness of green below, dropping, drifting like a leaf, coloured with white houses and red dots of roof, striped with crops, was the coast of Bohemia, on which my ship had barely touched. Just long enough, perhaps, to note and remember one or two landmarks, to take bearings by a headland here and there, to know how the currents set, and to be able to find my way back into port there when good weather should bring me again into those parts.

Soon, I hope, for I want to explore the interior.

COMMON READER EDITIONS

As booksellers since 1986, we have been stocking the pages of our monthly catalogue, A COMMON READER, with "Books for Readers with Imagination." Now as publishers, the same motto guides our work. Simply put, the titles we issue as COMMON READER EDITIONS are volumes of uncommon merit which we have enjoyed, and which we think other imaginative readers will enjoy as well. While our selections are as personal as the act of reading itself, what's common to our enterprise is the sense of shared experience a good book brings to solitary readers. We invite you to sample the wide range of COMMON READER EDITIONS, and welcome your comments.

www.commonreader.com